Abolishing Boundaries

SUNY series in Chinese Philosophy and Culture

Roger T. Ames, editor

Abolishing Boundaries

Global Utopias in the Formation of
Modern Chinese Political Thought, 1880–1940

PETER ZARROW

Published by State University of New York Press, Albany

For information, contact State University of New York Press, Albany, NY
www.sunypress.edu

Library of Congress Cataloging-in-Publication Data

Names: Zarrow, Peter Gue, author.
Title: Abolishing boundaries : global utopias in the formation of modern
    Chinese political thought, 1880–1940 / Peter Zarrow.
Description: Albany : State University of New York, 2021. | Series: SUNY
    series in Chinese philosophy and culture | Includes bibliographical
    references and index.
Identifiers: LCCN 2020039949 (print) | LCCN 2020039950 (ebook) | ISBN
    9781438482835 (hardcover : alk. paper) | ISBN 9781438482842 (ebook)
Subjects: LCSH: Political science—China—Philosophy—History—19th
    century. | Political science—China—Philosophy—History—20th century. |
    Utopias—Philosophy. | Kang, Youwei, 1858–1927. | Cai, Yuanpei,
    1868–1940. | Chen, Duxiu, 1879–1942. | Hu, Shi, 1891–1962.
Classification: LCC JA84.C6 Z37 2021 (print) | LCC JA84.C6 (ebook) | DDC
    320.0951/09041—dc23
LC record available at https://lccn.loc.gov/2020039949
LC ebook record available at https://lccn.loc.gov/2020039950

10 9 8 7 6 5 4 3 2 1

*To Shan-chih, for all the support over all the years,
and for all the years*

Contents

Preface

Much scholarship on modern China rightly focuses on the rise of nationalism, state-building, and statism over the course of the late nineteenth century and through the twentieth century. Nationalism spoke then, and often still speaks now, to the needs of liberation from oppression. Still, the "exclusionism" of nationalism is not just potentially destructive, but inherently so. Nationalism is premised on the existence of nationals, and therefore the existence of aliens who lack the qualifications to be deemed nationals. Defined in ethnic, linguistic, racial, religious, or some other ultimately arbitrary (though always useful) distinction between "us" and "them," national groups must be exclusionary or they are nothing. Modern Chinese thinkers have almost all been nationalists, for reasons that are more than understandable. Without nationalism, China would not have survived. It goes without saying, I believe, that the demise of China would have been an incalculable loss to the world. Scholarship on modern Chinese thought has rightly focused on intellectuals who devoted their lives to changing China so that it would survive. Yet many of these same people also sought to change the world. The world is richer for them.

I understand "statism" to constitute an ideology that overlaps with nationalism. It proclaims that nationals are citizens: members of the political community with rights and duties (however amorphous), but that ultimately the needs of the state (self-defined as the general community) trump those of the citizen. All citizens have the duty to be willing to die (and kill) for the defense (or interests) of the state. Nationalism cannot exist without the state. States, conceived as the general category of political organization ranging from city-states to kingdoms and empires, do not necessarily need nations, though the modern form of the state is of course intertwined with the nation. Modern statism, of which fascism is the paradigmatic example, depends on ramping up nationalist sentiment.

Since much of modern warfare and genocide have been justified on the basis of nationalism, antinationalist movements have naturally arisen. Human rights movements are dedicated at least in part to tempering nationalistic excesses. Scholars have also asked whether certain nonsovereign state forms can temper nationalism. See: United Nations, European Union, to some extent international economic organizations, and, again, the human rights movement. After the ravages of twentieth-century nationalism it is understandable that a certain nostalgia for empire has emerged. Supposedly, early modern empires such as the Ottoman, Qing, and Austro-Hungarian adopted a kind of pluralistic tolerance for the various national populations under their control, or at least some of those nations, even granting them a degree of self-governance. This very rose-tinted view, however, conveniently forgets the violent systems of oppression at the heart of the state formations of empires.

Modern nationalism, with its notion of the equality of citizens whether or not sovereignty allegedly derives from the people, arose in reaction against empires and their monarchies. In this process, in its innumerable variations across time and space, the link beween nation and sovereign state was forged. A person's national identity defined a new subjectivity. Various national identities were rooted in historical narratives and origin stories: King Arthur, the sun goddess Amaterasu, the founding fathers, the Third Rome, the Yellow Emperor. These narratives determined who belonged and who was outsider. Yet as intellectuals and political leaders forged these historical narratives, counternarratives also emerged. It is these counternarratives—imagined alternatives to the dominant stories of our modern subjectivities—that we call utopias.

Such is a very simplified premise of this book. This book, however, is not actually about modern Chinese utopianism as a discrete "ism" or as a movement. Rather, it is about fractured and partial utopian counternarratives and how four particular Chinese intellectuals made use of their glimpses of utopia to construct theories of the path that the Chinese people should take to build a better future. This book is constructed on a series of case studies to show how, in various fashions, orthodox narratives of nation-building mixed with counternarratives based on universal principles to shape Chinese ideas about modernity.

I use the Hanyu pinyin romanization system for Chinese terms and names, except for the customary (non-Mandarin) spelling of Sun Yat-sen and Chiang Kai-shek. Chinese and Japanese names are given surname first, except in citations of persons writing in English.

Acknowledgments

This book, which involved my writing about topics outside of my research specialization, is indebted to many people who gave me guidance and correction. None of them, of course, should be held responsible for my opinions, much less remaining errors and omissions. This book has benefited from discussions with Marianne Bastid, Pablo Blitstein, Anne Cheng, Joshua Fogel, Thomas Fröhlich, Béatrice L'Haridon, Max Ke-wu Huang (黃克武), Joan Judge, Joyce C. H. Liu (劉紀蕙), Liu Qing (刘擎), Mark McConaghy, Alexus McLeod Achim Mittag, Axel Schneider, Sarah Schneewind, Rudolph Wagner, Xu Jilin (许纪霖), and Wen Yu (于文). I am grateful to Yan Geng (耿焱) for first suggesting that I might be interested in taking a look at Cai Yuanpei. I am grateful to Thomas M. Alexander and Gu Hongliang (顾红亮) for helping me understand Dewey and Dewey in China; to Selena Orly and Pan Kuang-che (潘光哲) for helping me understand Hu Shi; and to John Troyer for helping me understand Cai's understanding of Kant. Also, three anonymous press readers forced me to sharpen my arguments.

The list above unfortunately leaves out many of the people who gave me useful suggestions and challenges as I presented earlier versions of what went into this book at conferences and talks at Academia Sinica; the University of Erlangen-Nuremberg; Tel Aviv University; the Northeast [U.S.] Conference on Chinese Thought; the Association of Asian Studies annual conference; the Critical China Studies Reading Group, York University–University of Toronto; the Karl Jaspers Center, University of Heidelberg; the Fairbank Center, Harvard University; Harvard-Yenching Institute; the Si-mian Institute for Advanced Studies in Humanities, East China Normal University; the Neo-Confucian Seminar, Columbia University; the University of Connecticut Political Theory Workshop; and the Seminar on Intellectual History of China, Collège de France.

Ways to Conceptualize Utopianism

An Introduction

The new society of the new era that is our ideal is honest, progressive, positive, free, equal, creative, beautiful, good, and peaceful, and it is marked by loving mutual aid, joyful labor, and benefits for the whole society. We hope everything that is hypocritical, conservative, passive, restrictive, privileged, conventional, ugly, and detestable, and is marked by war, conflict, inertia, depression, and benefits for the few will gradually shrink and disappear.

    We youth of the new society naturally respect labor, but labor should match the individual's talents and interests, and become free, joyful, artistic, and beautiful. A sacred thing should not be made into a requirement for sheer survival. . . . Although we do not hold a superstitious faith that politics is omnipotent, we acknowledge that politics is an important form of our common life, and we believe true democracy certainly means that political power is distributed among the whole people.

—*New Youth*, 1919

All in all, utopianism did not survive the twentieth century in good shape. The great slaughters and prison-houses of the twentieth century are associated with the utopian promises of Stalinism and Maoism to make omelets by breaking eggs. Even fascists promised a utopia of sorts, at least for the obedient and racially pure. As soon as the Berlin Wall was torn down, certain forward-looking writers promised a utopia of capitalism and liberal democracy, even the end of history: a promise that in fact was already beginning to look illusory by the end of the century. It is also worth noting that from the second half of the twentieth century and at an accelerating pace through the first decades of the twenty-first century, dystopias began to vastly outnumber utopias in novels, films, and TV shows.[1] Nonetheless, utopian thinking has hardly disappeared, and plans to radically reform existing conditions are ubiquitous. Indeed, it is hard to find people who entirely lack at least some kind of utopian dream—a peaceful world without war, or a prosperous world without poverty, a spiritual world devoted to the true faith, or a democratic world based on the principle of equality—even if they cannot envision how this world might come into existence. Defenders of utopianism note that it provides a salutary critique of the status quo. Utopias denaturalize existing conditions that might otherwise simply be taken for granted. They show that this world is not necessarily the only possible world. And at times of crisis, utopianism provides emotional escape and even an approximately practical guide to action. It is hard to imagine historical progress without at least some people holding up a utopian vision of what progress can attain.

The twentieth century cannot be understood outside of the utopianism of intellectual elites and popular movements. It has proved difficult to gain historical perspective of this phenomenon. On the one hand, the social sciences in general and Marxism in particular both proclaimed their scientific nature and thus denied their own utopian nature. This tends to make aspects of utopianism invisible. On the other hand, the glib practice of drawing a straight line from the utopianisms of the century to its disasters tends to equate ideology with utopianism and proclaims its dangerous omnipresence. We are all moderns now, perhaps, and live in a world of scientific progress, which is to say rationality. Religious and transcendent experiences are bracketed off. The rational, however, is blind to its own elements of utopianism. Cornelius Castoriadis:

> The modern world presents itself, on the surface, as that which has pushed, and tends to push, rationalization to its limit, and because of this, it allows itself to despise—or to consider with respectful curiosity—the bizarre customs, inventions and imaginary representations of previous societies. Paradoxically, however, despite or rather due to this extreme "rationaliza-

tion," the life of the modern world is just as dependent on the imaginary as any archaic or historical culture.[2]

Granted that the utopian is difficult to pin down, we can determine its appeals, effects, and limits through historical analysis. In the case of China, utopianism was a major theme in early-twentieth-century thought from the late Qing period through the Communist Revolution and, arguably, even the ideology of the postrevolutionary state capitalism of our own age. The period from about 1900 into the 1920s might be called China's moment of "peak utopianism." This period was marked by enormous social, cultural, economic, and political change and ferment. The Qing dynasty was overthrown in 1911. In the wake of the political chaos that ensued, the "New Culture movement" emerged—a kind of cultural self-critique and a more systematic exploration of the notions of democracy, science, and equality than had been possible in the late Qing period.[3] In 1919 the "May Fourth" protests brought thousands into the streets and led to the embryonic political organizations that were to take over the country in just over a few decades.

The ways in which utopianism fueled a range of ideology-making during this period form the core of this book. Utopian thinking in a variety of ideological spheres—particularly anarchism, socialism, and liberalism—shaped the formation of those "isms." Utopian thinking continued through the 1930s and informed Maoism. This book thus concludes with a brief comment on the hegemonic form utopianism took in the Maoist period from the 1950s and the counterutopianism of the Dengist period to today. In the 1980s, the catastrophes of Maoism as well as the implosion of Marxism-in-practice left many in China in a distinctly anti-utopian mood. However, some of the orthodoxies of the post-Maoist period, such as the promise of "socialism with Chinese characteristics" and the glorification of economic development, suggest that certain strands in contemporary Chinese thought are better conceived as counterutopian than anti-utopianism; that is, utopianism that denies its own utopian nature. True, utopianism no longer forms the core of Chinese political mentality, which is marked equally by grim determination and by cynicism. Still, the twinned visions of prosperity for the Chinese people (xiaokang) and "wealth and power" for the Chinese state—the chief goal of state-building since the nineteenth century—have after a century been encapsulated in official slogan of "the China dream."

However, official political discourse such as the Chinese dream is highly nationalistic and thus does not meet the definition of utopianism as I understand it for the purposes of this book. Utopianism in the sense I use it here is an optimistic form of egalitarian and cosmopolitan humanism. It is a product of the Enlightenment and modernity. By "humanism" I simply mean an abiding concern with the well-being of humankind as a whole: a sense that all individuals matter and possess dignity and agency.[4] By describing the humanism of modern Chinese thinkers as "cosmopolitan" I do not merely mean to heighten their humanism but also to highlight their engagement with the world: their search for universal truths in a newly interconnected world. At the same time, the Chinese thinkers considered in this book remained deeply commited to the regeneration of China. Indeed, they helped create modern Chinese nationalism. A certain tension arises between cosmopolitan engagement with the world and commitment to nationalism. Yet as Joachim Kurtz notes, "At the same time, this engagement, in line with global trends, became enmeshed with a decidedly nationalist agenda."[5] Utopian thinkers could reconcile these tensions by looking toward a future where the mutual enmity of nations gave way to a moral world order. Cosmopolitanism thus involved both engagement in the present and a vision of a borderless future.

I also take "utopianism" to refer to a secular belief in the perfectibility (or near-perfectibility) of the world based on respect for human dignity and communitas. I acknowledge that there is much that is arbitrary about this definition.[6] Utopianism in this sense is not concerned firstly with individuals: it is a social vision. Furthermore, the utopian social vision is not mere belief that things can get better but a leap of faith that all the evils of this world can be abolished. Utopianism is thus distinguished from ordinary optimism or, for that matter, mere reformism by its conviction that the ideal future is not only achievable but is close to inevitable and pretty much around the corner. Optimism is an attitude; reformism is a project; utopianism is a faith or a vision.

The following pages will focus on a great deal of this kind of utopianism—visions of the future. But utopianism is also here and now. Terms such as *vision*, *future*, and *faith* make utopianism sound like a fiction (which it is). However, utopianism can also be seen as immanent in the individual and society. Individuals who engage in utopia-making (as fictions) are already practicing utopianism (within themselves). This is so, not merely in the sense that in some psychological, imaginative mode of experience they are living in utopia, but in the sense that they participate in an ongoing tradition of utopianism. Societies are already utopian in the sense they already possess the seeds of utopia in various forms of nonexploitative and voluntary association. Whether this utopian potential can be fully realized in the revolutionary transformation of society is another question.[7]

Utopianism

"Utopianism" is variously regarded as ancient and universal, or, more precisely dated to a particular time and place: Renaissance Europe. It is possible to regard the "utopian propensity" as well-nigh universal.[8] There are various ways to classify utopian thinking. It is possible to project utopias into the past, the future, or the present elsewhere, or some combination of those temporal-spatial alternatives. Plato's Atlantis was distant from Athens in both place and time. Religious visions of Heaven may be contemporaneous as well as potential future states, and may even (less commonly) be regarded as here rather than some kind of there. And poets and philosophers played with utopias every so often. But it was with the Renaissance that utopianism became just that: an "ism"—a way of thinking about society systematically, even scientifically. This modern utopianism rested on the assumption that society could be reconstructed on rational grounds.[9] More's *Utopia* had its playful and probably self-satiric side, and we cannot know how seriously More himself ever took his own exploration of communism. But it inaugurated a form of literary expression that soon migrated into political treatises. Thus "utopianism" refers both to a literary genre and to a style of political thought associated with Rousseau, Marx, and other revolutionaries and reformers.

Definitions of "utopia" are numerous and various. They often begin with the ambiguity of More's Latin pun on ou-topia (no place) versus eu-topia (good place), which establishes the paradoxical nature of the concept. And of course your utopia may be my dystopia.[10] It is fun but less important that utopias have often predicted later developments both general, such as steps toward gender equality, polyamory, the elimination of slavery, and the like, and specific, such as the newspaper, public garbage collection, the telephone, the flush toilet, and the like. More importantly, utopias highlight the limits of our social imagination. They denaturalize conscious and unconscious assumptions. To imagine alternatives to the existing state of affairs, allegedly founded on cosmic laws or the image of God or some other higher force, is to engage in utopianism.

If utopianism is a universal predilection, it is more noticeable at certain times. Roughly speaking, there have been two great periods of utopian writing in the West: the sixteenth century beginning with Thomas More's *Utopia*, and the nineteenth century of Bellamy, Morris, and Wells, as well as Rousseau, Saint-Simon, Fourier, Proudhon, Owen, and Marx. (The "Sixties" might count as a third period, though a briefer one sandwiched between Marcuse and LeGuin.) Rich fictional accounts and finely argued political theory often appeared roughly at the same time. Arguably, this was true for China at the end of the Qing dynasty; however, as the twentieth century proceeded, political theory retained a strong utopian flavor while literary utopias disappeared.

Relatively little Chinese writing can be labeled full-fledged utopian screeds or "speaking picture" utopias—that is, detailed visions of perfect societies set on distant isles or sometime in the future.[11] Even fewer Chinese writers can be called full-fledged utopians. The *Great Commonweal*, written around 1900 by Kang Youwei, is the single exception to this generalization before the twenty-first century. I discuss Kang's work in the next chapter, but it is worth noting here that Kang himself maintained an extremely ambiguous attitude toward the utopian project. Kang held that his utopian knowledge was so dangerous that most of it could be revealed only to trusted disciples, and only parts of it could be made public until after his death.

Nonetheless, Kang was not the only utopian writer of the last decade of the Qing. This, the first decade of the twentieth century, saw a surge of "political novels," many of which were utopian to one degree or another.[12] If utopian novels had found an enormous readership in the West in the last half of the nineteenth century, offering a critique of Victorian capitalism and industrialization while reflecting an optimism buoyed by economic growth, novels in other parts of the world soon emerged to criticize colonialism and show how oppressed peoples might become citizens of their own countries.[13] Chinese utopian short stories and novels published in the last decade of the Qing included Cai Yuanpei's "New Year's Dream" (*Xinnian meng*, 1904), Wu Jianren's science fiction novel *New Story of the Stone* (*Xin shitou ji*, 1908), as well as Liang Qichao's unfinished novel *The Future of New China* (*Xin Zhongguo weilai ji*, 1902), and many other literary representations of the "new" and of the future.[14] Jules Verne, Edward Bellamy, and Suehiro Tetchō were all known to

Chinese readers. Many aspects of ideal societies, not to mention visions of a strong China, were expressed in late Qing fiction. As Catherine Yeh has shown, the political novel in China taught readers about linear progressive time and about China's place in the larger world. With their protagonists traveling across various continents as they wrestled with solutions to the problems of the present day, novels helped envision a China that "began consciously to join a translingual and transcultural universality of ideas, ideals, conflicts, and controversies."[15]

Strangely, literary utopias disappeared after the fall of the Qing. However, utopian thought flourished. In this book, I focus on political treatises rather than fiction. Fiction retains a certain ambiguity and multilayered-ness (unreliable narrators, for example) that political treatises ideally abjure. The utopian fictions of the Renaissance were set in distant places inspired by the New World. The utopian fictions of the Industrial Revolution were set in the future. Both imagined something that the author presented as a perfect society—or perhaps as satire in some cases and escapism in others. But utopianism is not only a literary genre. Another type of utopian writing is directly political; that is, it takes the form of theorizing. It does not primarily focus on the details of a perfect society but rather constructs an argument about how to perfect society: process as much as state. This type of utopian thought was central to Chinese political writing in the twentieth century.

To return to the utopianism of the earliest years of the twentieth century, some of that explosion can be explained in terms of the institutions of rapidly growing global capitalism. Western imperialism required states to provide administrative regulation domestically precisely to foster the interpenetration of national economies through the exchange of goods. Unlike earlier and non-Western imperialism, this process required relatively large civil and military bureaucracies; of course, it was profoundly unequal and depended on violence. The role of the state in protecting so-called private property, investing in infrastructure and military protection, and maintaining a degree of market stability meant that it was impossible to envision a world composed of autarkies. State-building and the effort to demolish state boundaries thus went hand in hand. The infrastructure of global communication built to link expansive states with their empires—regular shipping lines, railways, and the telegraph—information, ideas, and people began to circulate in unprecedented fashion. While modern literary utopias were a Western export, it was a handful of intellectuals in Asian states that were colonized or threatened with colonization who created the first truly global utopian visions. Edward Bellamy's *Looking Backward* of 1888, for example, acquired a truly global following, as we will see, but the novel's vision of the perfect world of the "industrial army" was limited to America and Europe, and its characters just briefly note that the peoples of Asia and Africa might (or might not) catch up some day.

The Chinese utopian writers of the late Qing, on the contrary, were smashing the boundaries of Western empires. Indeed, they challenged the very power of boundaries. As national boundaries could be transcended, so too the boundaries between colony and metropole, empire and empire, and even self and other, subject and object.[16] Finding new, utopian orientations was one response to a seemingly alien modernity.

"A state of mind is utopian when it is incongruous with the state of reality within which it occurs."[17] The sociologist Karl Mannheim's definition of utopianism provides the key to the textual phenomena that I find widespread in twentieth century Chinese thought. Although Mannheim was interested in utopian social movements—such as those of the Anabaptists, modern bourgeois liberals, the conservative romantics, socialists, and others—his description of the "utopian mentality" as the basis of behavior that would "tend to shatter, either partially or wholly, the order of things prevailing at the time" also serves as a precise depiction of the starting point of an intellectual search for a radically new social order. Or in Mannheim's terms, to "burst the bonds of the existing order."[18] Utopian motifs in Chinese political writing were precisely oppositional in this sense. Furthermore, it was not just the political realities of China that came under attack but the international order as a whole. This oppositional orientation led to creative analyses of liberation and community. Needless to say, this was invariably an orientation toward the future—a temporalized utopianism, in Koselleck's terminology.[19] Such an orientation is simultaneously historically minded, for by reading history properly, we can determine its direction and speed up its course. We know the future by the past.

The various strands of utopian thought in the first decades of the twentieth century in China often opposed one another (as seen in the competing structures of liberalism and Marxism, for example). In a sense, they represented utopianism in form while their content differed.[20] In fact, all utopias, while sharing certain generic features, differ in content, so it is not surprising that Chinese utopian thinking expressed itself in a variety of directly opposed guises. Thus, I argue below that utopian strands of thought were constitutive of distinct ideologies in China, which cannot be understood properly without taking into account their utopian aspects. As well, experiments in utopian living appealed to many in the 1910s and 1920s and beyond.[21] There were communes of youths living apart from mainstream society. There were tightly-knit organizations that remained integrated into school and employment. There was the "new village" movment, which took reform-minded youth into the country-side.[22] Communism but especially anarchism, or anarcho-communism, inspired many such experiments. This is to say that utopianism was by no means always temporalized toward the future but was an ongoing project for the present.

The Utopian Impulse

Central to my study is the notion of the "utopian impulse." Utopian thought is not limited to the writing of full-fledged or "speaking picture" utopias, whether fictional or theoretical. In the cases of some political thinkers, the *utopian impulse* is an integral part of making proposals to shape the future. Utopian impulses are radical visions of change, and so they are not merely optimistic assumptions, but they need not be limited to totalistic schemes or models of a perfect society. Nor are they necessarily associated with revolutionary transformations. Ameliorative reforms may display a utopian impulse if they are part of a larger project designed to lead to a (not necessarily specified) genuinely emancipatory future. If "utopia" generally refers to visions of societies that work on an entirely different basis and set of institutions from our own, the utopian impulse refers to brief glances that reflect but do not explore such visions in detail. The utopian vision is there, just left unmapped.[23] As Frederic Jameson has noted, "It has often been observed that we need to distinguish between the Utopian form and the Utopian wish: between the written text or genre and something like a *Utopian impulse* detectable in daily life and its practices by a specialized hermeneutic or interpretive method."[24] This approach echoes Mannheim's emphasis on "orientation" and the reality of utopia in revolutionary social movements. However, I am using the notion of the "utopian impulse" to describe elements found in certain political texts rather than desires that emerge in the course of daily life. These textual elements do represent desires, and they function as "fantasy mechanisms" that allow the theory in question to operate.

They are not in and of themselves single-shot solutions to all our ills,[25] but they are moments in the texts when complexity is reduced to a formula. They serve as deus ex machina of theorizing.

In my view, it might be best to see in late Qing and Republican intellectuals an unstable mixture of disillusionment and of desire. Disillusionment first with the capacity of traditional cultural resources to meet the demands of modernity, and then disillusionment with capitalist modernity that took the form of imperialism. But also desire for modernity that took the form of joining the world, of cosmopolitanism. Nationalism and cosmopolitanism were perhaps in tension at times, but were not necessarily contradictory views.[26] In this way, utopia became a resource to shape an extreme form of secular progress. Modern Chinese intellectuals simultaneously saw Meiji Japan and the West as models of world progress and as highly flawed and limited societies.

In modern Chinese political thought, the utopian impulse was extremely widespread. To begin to make sense of it, I present four case studies in the following chapters: Kang Youwei (1858–1927), Cai Yuanpei (1868–1940), Chen Duxiu (1879–1942), and Hu Shi (1891–1962). All four men were well-known intellectuals, social critics, and political activists. Their utopianism lies in their cosmopolitanism, aesthetic theory, democratic thought, and scientism. These four thinkers illustrate a range of different kinds of utopian impulses and thus begin to suggest an anatomy of the utopian impulse. In ideological terms, Kang is associated with Confucianism, Cai and Hu with liberalism, and Chen first with liberalism and then Marxism, though these labels obscure more than they reveal. Kang Youwei is the foundational figure of modern Chinese utopianism, but scholars have long wrestled with the question of how the same man could promote reformism—which was cautious and explicitly antirevolutionary—and also believe in a utopian vision that was in effect a revolutionary prognostication. Ultimately, Kang believed that history was leading in a direction that would allow humanity to transcend all the distinctions that separated members from one another, and finally that would allow humanity to transcend itself. He was the first to speak of "abolishing boundaries." The series of political reforms that he proposed in the 1880s and 1890s was simply to be a step on the ladder of historical progress.

Of these four men, only Kang wrote a full-scale utopia of the "speaking picture" type. Cai Yuanpei, however, also wrote a utopian short story. More importantly for my purposes, Cai believed that the transcendence of human difference was possible, though this erasure of the boundaries between people would come about through willed acts learned through education in aesthetic appreciation, rather than through historical inevitability. Cai, though a revolutionary supporter in the years before 1911, is not usually though of as a utopian thinker but best known as a cultural figure, educational leader, and finally as a liberal anticommunist.

Chen Duxiu, radical and Marxist, might seem as obvious a utopian thinker as Kang, but he never outlined what the future perfect world would be like. Rather, he proclaimed that democracy could provide the Chinese people and ultimately all humanity with a kind of tool that they could use to build such a world, the very building of which, though its final shape was unknowable, gave rise to a kind of processual utopia. After Chen's Marxist turn in about 1920, he found in class struggle the means to build a better world and promoted the dictatorship of the proletariat. It is as first a remorseless critic of Confucianism and then a founder of the Chinese Communist Party that Chen is best known. But I believe that Chen's communism was *not* based on a utopian impulse in the sense I use the term here to indicate, among other things, a leap of faith. Neither historical materialism nor the ultimate victory of the proletariat, though "utopian" in a general sense, proved to be core elements of Chen's thought. Rather, by the end of the 1920s, he was already reworking his earlier faith in democracy. Remaining an unorthodox Marxist, Chen found democracy, understood in class terms, to be the true motor of history.

The case of Hu Shi illustrates another kind of processual utopia: if humanity devoted itself to the pursuit of reason and science, in Hu's view, it would be living through an ever-developing utopic landscape. Few observers at the time or since associated Hu with utopianism, because he was a supporter of measured reform through what he called "experimentation" based on his interpretation of Pragmatism. He was highly critical of the radicalism of this day. However, for Hu, the very search for truth through experiment was a kind of utopian experience. His faith lay in the process, which he thought promised infinite improvement. Conceiving that reason and science were based on experimentalism, Hu also justified a commitment to political liberalism or pluralism that was, perhaps in contrast to most Western liberalisms, based on a thoroughgoing optimism.[27]

In sum, the utopian impulse was not precisely the driving force in the thought of Cai, Chen, and Hu, but it was integral to their system building, and as much necessary to their means as to their visions of their ends. Why study the thought of these four men? I do not claim that they are representative of any larger intellectual tides beyond the centrality of the utopian impulse itself. Indeed, I am interested in their differences. Having said that, it is true that they had much in common: all were born almost within a generation of each other, all highly educated, all well known, well published, and well interviewed in their own times. All were male. Cai, Chen, and Hu, at least, were intimate frenemies. But this was a time of extremely rapid change, and so the generational gap between Kang and Cai was already deep; and the gap between Kang and Cai, with their thorough classical educations, on the one hand, and Chen and Hu on the other was even deeper. Generational standing and educational background only explain so much, of course, but it is important to remember that these four men were scarcely cut from the same cloth. It is also true that four completely different thinkers could have been chosen, though Kang Youwei is always going to have a foundational position in any study with reference to Chinese utopianism. Qiu Jin, Sun Yat-sen, Liu Shipei, He-Yin Zhen, Wu Zhihui, Li Dazhao—these are another set of political thinkers and activists whose utopianism is worth examination. Utopianism could also be applied to popular ideologies such as anarchism, Marxism, and various socialisms. However, this book is *not* a study of utopianism as such, but of the utopian impulse. The utopianism of anarchists is obvious (this is not to dismiss anarchism as mere dreaming). My goal is to tease out the utopian strands in thinking that is not obviously "utopian" at first glance.

Broadly defined, a utopian impulse might be found in fascism, which made promises that appealed to some, but offered a vision based on discipline and struggle and explicitly denied universal values and equality.[28] Religious worldviews, especially in the Buddhist revival, and perhaps those thinkers tinged with mysticism such as Liang Shuming, displayed utopian longings. But I am limiting my consideration to egalitarian and cosmopolitan forms of utopianism.

The four case studies used here illustrate how distinct political philosophies, ranging from a modernized form of Confucianism to liberalism and Marxism, all depended on utopian leaps of faith. These four case studies also illustrate some of the fundamental conceptual resources that people found to be of use just as the grounds of politics, society, and even culture were shifting beneath their feet. Kang Youwei and Cai Yuanpei based their utopianism on metaphysics. They used philosophies that spoke to questions of ultimate reality to ground their social thought. In contrast, Chen Duxiu and Hu Shi were secular thinkers. Their utopianism helped ground their political theory, but this was self-contained theory that did not rest on any kind of metaphysical speculation. These four case studies do not exhaust the role that the utopian impulse played in modern Chinese thought, but at least they illustrate some of its scope.

Roots of Utopianism in Modern China

In spite of its ubiquity in modern China, utopianism has gone relatively unnoticed; or, rather, it has been noticed but not explored systematically.[29] Scholarship has, rather, focused on radicalism and revolutionism. A focus on the utopian impulse highlights not only the motive force behind radical understandings of Chinese politics but also some of the features shared by radicals and less extreme political theorists. As well, attention to the utopian impulse highlights the radicalism that was hidden within ostensibly conservative understandings.

The study of Chinese utopianism that is closest to the one I pursue in these pages is Hao Chang's article on what he calls soft utopianism and hard utopianism.[30] Chang begins by noting that the entire traditional sociopolitical and even cosmological order was breaking down by the 1890s, even as an influx of Western thought gave thinkers new tools to reimagine the world. Utopianism was among the concepts that rushed in to fill this vacuum. Chang also uses a case study approach to suggest that hard utopianism was represented by thinkers such as Tan Sitong, Liu Shipei, and Li Dazhao. In Chang's analysis, the distinguishing features of their thought were their belief in the imminence of a utopian world and their revolutionism. Soft utopianism was represented by Kang Youwei and Hu Shi, referring to their gradualist approach and their skepticism of too-rapid change. Nonetheless, Chang does not show how their specific emotional and intellectual reactions to crisis—the impending collapse of the traditional cosmological order as well as the political order—shaped the specific utopian impulses of these thinkers. In the following pages, I will attempt to tease out the specific life conditions that shaped individuals' utopian impulses. As well, I do not believe the hard-soft distinction is the most useful way of sorting out the utopian impulses of Chinese thinkers. For example, however gradualist were Kang and Hu (and possibly Tan), their philosophical premises and ultimate goals shared almost nothing in common. Or if we take the gradualist Hu and the revolutionary Chen Duxiu, although their immediate political proposals had little in common, they shared a set of premises about historical progress utterly alien to those of Kang. And the metaphysics of Cai Yuanpei were sui generis.

Now, given the widespread nature of the utopian impulse in modern China, three sets of questions arise: First, how did it come about?—what needs did it meet?—how did it shape political discourse? This book concentrates on answering this set of questions. I focus on these four case studies as a way into the larger, highly variegated world of Chinese political thought. Second, if the utopian impulse was extremely widespread, where do we *not* find it?—what thinkers were immune to its sweet scent? And third, if the utopian impulse was so widespread, how can we say it is of any importance?—do we not conclude that if (virtually) everyone is a utopian, then no one is?

In answering the second question, we can point to forms of reformism and idealism, as well as conservatism and fascism, that were not utopian in nature. First, the utopian impulse cannot be reduced to idealism, which refers generally to ethical principles without necessarily delineating or assuming a radically better world. No doubt, statements reflecting idealism and what I am calling the utopian impulse overlap to some extent. But holding high ideals generally refers to an individual's responsibilities, while the utopian impulse is an element of a social theory. Second, the utopian impulse is not synonymous with radicalism, since it can inform politically moderate or even conservative views as judged by the standards of the day. Indeed, as suggested above, much of the writing of Kang Youwei himself was not utopian in nature. This was even more true of Hu Shi and Cai Yuanpei. If Kang and to some extent Chen have intuitively seemed utopian to historians, such has seldom been the case with Hu and Cai. Furthermore, with the exception of Kang, these thinkers never regarded themselves as utopian. And third, there are indeed cases of complex thinkers who were largely immune to the utopian impulse. Liang Qichao, notwithstanding his unfinished utopian novel *The Future of New China*, was fundamentally not a utopian thinker. Liang's arguments for reform did not depend on the leaps of faith that mark the utopian impulse. Liang focused on the concrete steps necessary to make China a stronger nation—certainly a worthy ideal, but not quite a utopian vision. Liang's mind simply worked in more modest ways, not tempted by over-rosy pictures of the future. Such also seems to be the case for the lawyer and educator Zhang Shizhao (1881–1973), notwithstanding a youthful flirtation with revolution.[31] Neither Liang nor Zhang was a narrow nationalist, but their lack of faith in the future of a world community drastically narrowed the scope of any utopianism they had felt in their younger days. Furthermore, their styles of thinking might simply, if too simply, be described as particularistic rather than universalistic. This particularistic approach, resistant to the lures of universalism, perhaps explains why a number of historians were immune to utopianism.[32]

In answering the third question—about the significance of what is, nonetheless, a widespread phenomenon—it might seem that the more widespread a phenomenon is, the more important it must be. But it may also seem that this phenomenon cannot tell us what makes each thinker distinct. On the one hand are historical conditions specifically amenable to secular, or at least this-worldly utopianism. On the other are traditions (Chinese and Western) that inspire particular utopian notions. Attempts to understand modern Chinese political thought without a systematic interpretation of its utopian elements remain incomplete.

Kang Youwei's scholarship and his utopian vision were both, in skewed ways, rooted in the great social and intellectual transformations of the eighteenth and nineteenth centuries—both the historical conditions he faced and the intellectual traditions at his disposal.[33] The Taiping Rebellion, which at least briefly created a new dynasty in central China in the 1850s and early 1860s, was a strongly millennial movement shaped by both Christianity and the ancient ritual classics. The Taipings used the *Rituals of Zhou* to delineate a tightly organized, hierarchical but putatively just politico-socioeconomic system. The Taiping movement eventually imploded in the face of determined opposition from the Qing and local gentry—some twenty million people died in the wars, famines, and slaughters before the Taipings were finally exterminated. Their memory inspired revolutionaries in the twentieth century, but their religious orientation, and especially its Christian flavor, found no echo in later generations. The Taiping's use of the *Rituals of Zhou* as a basis for reorganizing the very nature of society, however, was neither unprecedented nor alien. Kang Youwei himself located the message of linear progress that culminates in the *datong* in a chapter of the *Record of the Rituals*, and perhaps his egalitarian but highly patterned vision of a good society owed something to the ancient descriptions of supposedly even more ancient dynasties of yore. In any case, Kang was certainly heir to the evidential studies movement among scholars of the eighteenth century. They devoted enormous energy to dry philological research: dating ancient texts and thereby determining their authenticity (or inauthenticity). But there was a utopian, almost mystical side to the evidential studies movement as well: that is, a belief that getting the ancient texts right might lead to the recreation of the ancient Golden Age. This was not so much a matter of following a recipe as gaining insight—perhaps enlightenment—into a set of ethical norms and cosmological principles on which a good society could be based. Interest in the ancient "sage-kings" and the "Three Dynasties" could be antiquarian, but it was also a search for an ideal polity that some saw as impossible to recover ("utopian," so to speak), some as a standard for criticizing present-day arrangements, and some as a goal for the future.

As Rudolf Wagner has pointed out, late Qing thinkers from the 1860s not only compared the institutions of the Three Dynasties favorably to those of their own day, but they believed the modern West had come close to recreating them.[34] Reformers called for local officials to serve in their home districts and giving commoners a voice in their evaluation, a systematic census and updating maps, poor relief, and so forth. Such calls were based on updating imperial precedents as well as appealing to the supposed spirit of the ancient sage-kings, which was said to be in accord with Western institutions such as newspapers, universal schooling, and elections. It is not that democracy or republicanism became a new source, much less the sole source, of governmental legitimacy until later, but that moral as well as efficient government needed to be based on open communication between ruler and ruled. Such communication had allegedly existed during the ancient Three Dynasties, creating an era of strong community feeling, and vanguard thinkers by the 1880s proposed that parliaments were simply the best way to recapture this past paradise.

If reformers in the late Qing often displayed a utopian impulse, how much more did revolutionaries do so. Many of the early revolutionaries were no less inspired by the golden age of the Three Dynasties than the reformers of the 1860s. In time, revolutionaries such as Sun Yat-sen came to believe that if the Han Chinese simply rid themselves of Manchu rule and declared a republic, then all problems would be solved. More cosmopolitan thinkers were critical of such narrow nationalism. Already by the mid-1890s Tan Sitong had worked out a complex scheme ultimately based on a vision of humaneness (ren) as a cosmic principle. In Tan's view, built on his understanding of science, Christianity, and

Buddhism as well as Confucianism, humanity would eventually achieve loving freedom as boundaries of state, race, nation, and gender eventually collapsed.[35] Groups of anarchists, active into the 1920s, also criticized narrow nationalism, no matter how emancipatory its rhetoric, and promoted a cosmopolitan vision of a human future marked by equality and liberty. One of the few nonfictional utopias of the late Qing was penned by the anarchist Liu Shipei in 1907. "On Equalizing Human Labor" proposed a scheme that would free everyone from the pressures and inequality of employment.[36] Districts of a thousand people would replace today's nations and local governments; everyone would speak a universal language. Children would be raised in residence halls, and at the age of ten they would begin a program of half-work, half-study. Those over fifty would give them nurture and education. Between twenty and fifty, everyone would engage in labor, but because of better machinery and a rational social organization, no one would have to work more than two hours a day.

Utopianism, Chinese Concept of

This book deals with a concept-in-motion, a traveling concept. Utopianism did not merely "move" through different political positions being laid out in modern China, it was a global concept circulating—to name the countries most important to the Chinese—through Japan, the United States, Britain, Russia, and France.[37] This book gives a good deal of attention to Western political thinkers with whom or on whom Chinese intellectuals worked: Edward Bellamy, John Dewey, Immanuel Kant, and Leon Trotsky. From the point of view of Western history, those Western political thinkers may appear a motley group, but the logic of their appearance in a history of China should emerge in the pages below.

No doubt, there were flows of "influence," but it is not my concern in this book to attempt to trace those flows. We can also think of Western and Chinese thinkers as engaged in a kind of conversation—literally in the case of Hu Shi and Dewey and, to a lesser degree, in the case of Chen Duxiu and Trotsky; literally in the case of Cai Yuanpei and certain neo-Kantians; and metaphorically in other cases. Nor, in setting certain Chinese thinkers and certain Western thinkers side by side, am I interested in the question of how accurately the Chinese understood the Westerners (or how well Westerners understood China—I do not evaluate Dewey's or Trotsky's views). Rather, this book highlights the ways two sets of ideas intertwined and echoed one another over and over again. Modern political discourses were global, especially in the case of transformational political discourse. We know more about nationalism, socialism, and anticolonialism than we do of utopianism or the utopian impulse, because utopianism was for the most part hidden in the most particularistic doctrines of emancipation. But they all provided a repertoire of ideas, by no means necessarily originating in the West, that thinkers of the age could use for various purposes.

In focusing on four Chinese men known for their political writings, I start to fill in something of a lacuna in modern Chinese intellectual history. By bringing them into conversation with certain Western thinkers, I contribute to the new field of global intellectual history. To some extent, this book engages in comparative philosophy, but with the proviso that I am not a philosopher and am more interested in the processes of creative adaptation than the implications we might draw today from cross-cultural dialog.[38] A different book could look at these men's "conversations" with thinkers from their own tradition—Kang and Cai were accomplished classical scholars and certainly, as this book will show to a modest degree, concerned with Confucian and Buddhist concepts. Cai explicitly and Kang implicitly sought to create a synthesis of Chinese and Western thought, based precisely on the realization that neither constituted a system that could be essentialized as an indivisible whole. Chen and Hu had also been schooled in the classics, and Hu conducted extensive research on the history of Chinese thought. Much of the historiography of the field has brought out some of the ways their ideas were shaped by tradition. I do not intend to slight the importance of the Chinese past in informing the thought of these men of the turn of the twentieth century, but I do intend to show that, among other features of their thought, they were engaging in conversations with thinkers of the West, past and contemporary alike. They participated in global conversations on such subjects as democracy, race, class struggle, and of course socialism and utopia.

This book is an etic rather than emic study insofar as I am applying a concept not explicitly used by the men I am studying. I hope to convey something of what they were doing in their own terms as well, but the "utopian impulse" offers a perspective on four different political orientations that was not available to the men exploring those orientations. Indeed, the modern term for *utopia* had only existed for a generation and was seldom used. Kang Youwei's *datong* had an ancient pedigree, but the term did not always refer to what was so clear in Kang's case: a recognizable utopia.[39] As noted above, Chinese literature had produced many utopias over the centuries, but there was no general, abstract label for them. "Utopia" was not a category of thought, though as the genre term *utopia* in the West was derived from Thomas More's fictional travelogue, so Chinese could generally refer to "peach blossom springs" and like literary precedents. Be that as it may, there was a vacuum of sorts that the great translator Yan Fu filled with his invention of what became accepted as the modern term for utopia. Strangely, Yan's invention of *wutuobang* came in the late 1890s in his translation of Thomas Huxley's *Evolution and Ethics*. Yan used this term to translate a passing reference to the "garden of Eden." Yan glossed the term as equivalent to the ancient Chinese *Huaxu*, an imaginary country of bliss.[40] Yan Fu used the term *wutuobang* again in his 1901–02 translation of Adam Smith's *Wealth of Nations*. Smith was pointedly comparing the chances of Britain adopting free trade policies to the chances of its becoming Utopia. Yan finally took the opportunity to give a fuller gloss of the term:

> *Utopia* is the name of a book written by the English Prime Minister Thomas More in the tenth year of the Zhengde reign of the Ming Dynasty (1516). It is a fable that describes a democratic system and the flourishing of perfect rule. "Utopia" was the name of an island nation that is said never to have really existed. Therefore, when later people spoke of profound and lofty theories that could not be executed and were hard to reach, everyone called such schemes utopias.[41]

Dictionaries of the early twentieth century tended to give two definitions of *wutuobang*: More's book, and an ideal but imaginary land. The term thus inserted itself into Chinese discourse, and became associated both with a literary genre and with attempts to think through what a radically transformed society would look like. However, there was more to utopianism in China, as elsewhere, than can be discovered by looking for self-avowed utopianism. This book is a study of the utopian impulse, not of *wutuobang*, though the former cannot be understood without the latter.

Insofar as this book contributes to a conceptual history of utopianism, it is a utopianism that largely dared not speak its name. Cai, Chen, Hu, and even Kang did not call themselves utopian thinkers and would have disdained the label. But in their different ways, that is exactly what they were. A concept can be powerful even when it is not named.[42] Perhaps it is even more powerful as a subliminal consciousness: that is, the utopian impulse. The utopian impulse is thus something less dominant than what Karl Mannheim called the "utopian mentality," which emerges "only when the configuration of the utopia at any one time forms not only a vital part of the 'content' of the mentality involved, but when, at least, in its general tendency, it permeates the whole range of that mentality."[43] If the utopian impulse in the thought of the intellectuals studied here did not permeate the whole range of their mentality, nonetheless their thought cannot be properly understood without a full appreciation of its utopian elements.

In his study of late Qing utopian fiction, Lorenzo Andolfatto notes that it emerged only very briefly in what he calls a transitional period in the wake of the 1898 Reform Movement and the 1911 Revolution—"both a discourse of expectations as well as the synthesis of, to some extent, a failure."[44] Granted the disappearance of utopianism as a literary genre, the utopian impulse surfaced in politics in its stead. In a sense, utopianism did not so much disappear as it went underground. Andolfatto suggestively refers to the genre "as a literary by-product of the ideological subtext of history; as a repository of its surplus of imagination and ideas; and as a primary constituent of this unstable ideological ground." I further argue that a faith in universal values was the premise that justified both the sense of failure and the expectations in all their cognitive dissonance. China's subordinate position in the empire—or empires—of the newly emerging system of global capitalism was intolerable. The needs for explanation and for solution were inextricably linked. The iron laws of social Darwinism spoke to all societies, everywhere universally, but they lacked moral standing.

Chinese intellectuals were caught between empires in several senses. First, between the empire established by the Western powers with dominion claimed over the globe on the one hand, and the traditional "all-under-heaven" claims of the Qing on the other. Second, between the Manchu-Qing Empire and the cultural Chinese empire. And third, between a world in the midst of "national imperialism," in Liang Qichao's phrase, and an imaginary world of justice. There is a risk that a study of this sort of makes passionate and argumentative activist-intellectuals sound like second-rate dons nattering over their port. But the background of national trauma to the discussions recorded in the chapters should be kept in mind at all times. So should the active public lives of the four men whose ideas I explore in these pages. It was, after all, anger and terror and desire that inspired utopian thinking.

2

Cosmopolitanism and Equality

Kang Youwei

A world without any distinctions of nation, class, race, gender; a world government made up of decentralized democratic organs—a generally homogenous world though also a world leading ultimately to complete love and liberation from all suffering. Such was Kang Youwei's utopian vision, based on a realistic analysis of present-day conditions and then unfolding through the remorseless logic of history. Kang conceived of himself ultimately as a cosmopolitan patriot.[1]

Kang Youwei is remembered for two distinct failures. The first was the catastrophic collapse of the reform movement of 1898. The second was the utopian vision of the future that Kang himself seemed ambivalent about. Yet Kang's radical political ideals and activism shaped the last years of the Qing dynasty, and his utopia was an inspiration for his followers. Although Kang cloaked himself as a scholar and sage, he was neither; rather, he was a powerful prophet. His leading disciple once termed Kang "China's Martin Luther," meaning that Kang had reconstructed China's central Teaching, Confucianism. That view is historically questionable but captures something of Kang's impact. It is impossible to understand either Kang's political career or his utopianism without taking into account his self-image as a sage, a teacher with a unique understanding of cosmic forces.

Kang's utopian scheme, *Datongshu* ("Book of Datong") is a weighty tome of more than 150,000 characters. *Datong*—"great unity" or "commonality"—was a term found in the *Record of the Rites* (*Liji*) in its chapter on the "Movement of the Rites" ("*Liyun*") where it referred to a perfect social order. The passage described the sadness of Confucius, who lamented that he had missed the age of *Datong*, when the empire belonged to all (*tianxia wei gong*), wealth was shared, people were not concerned with private profit or loved only their own kin, and charity was extended to young and old, widow and widower, and orphans and cripples.[2] Kang read the chapter as a description of the future rather than the past, taking the title of his utopia from the climatic sentence of the "*Liyun*" chapter. I translate Kang's title as *The Great Commonweal*. This term captures Kang's sense of a shared and egalitarian universal political order, redolent of its classical precedent but with infinitely greater detail. Kang was largely concerned with what he described the inevitable evolution of a truly universal and egalitarian political order. *The Great Commonweal* ends with a vision of a kind of mystical breakthrough that has embarrassed most scholars of Kang and that the term *commonweal* cannot capture, but Kang's ultimate vision of a world of flying buddhas must be acknowledged, if we are to understand modern Chinese utopianism. Indeed, Kang's final vision was not incompatible with the scientific spirit of the day nor entirely incompatible with today's posthumanism.

This chapter does not offer a comprehensive overview of the *The Great Commonweal*, which is well discussed in scholarly and popular literature and is available to English readers in an excellent translation.[3] Rather, I highlight the work's theme of the abolition of boundaries and the work's place in a moment of global utopianism. *The Great Commonweal* is China's first comprehensive, detailed or "speaking picture" utopia.[4] Essentially, the work was completed between 1900 and 1902: this is the historical moment it reflects.[5] Kang may have begun entertaining some of the notions and approaches of *The Great Commonwealth* as early as the 1880s, and he spoke of it to his disciples in the 1890s, but he did not put it together until stay in Darjeeling in 1902. By this time he had visited Canada, England, Singapore, and Malaya, as well as Hong Kong, Japan, and of course India, though he continued to tinker with it in ensuing years.[6]

Progress and Reform

Kang's cosmopolitanism and optimism are beyond doubt. At the same time, however, his utopian vision was rooted partly in his despair over the inability of the Qing government to meet the challenges it faced and partly in his existential despair over the condition of humankind. Kang's refusal to publish *The Great Commonweal* in his lifetime suggests that he resisted the radicalism of his own ideas, fearing their potential influence. Thus, Kang consistently opposed revolution. His calls for a parliament in the 1890s were radical in their way, but he had no intention of overthrowing the monarchy.

How can Kang the cautious political activist and Kang the wildly imaginative utopian thinker be reconciled? In a word, he could simultaneously hold conservative, reformist, and radically utopian views because of his belief in linear historical progress. For Kang, utopia was real—even historically determined and inevitable—but in the future. Radical ideas, prematurely introduced to the public, would hinder the step-by-step progress that Kang regarded as a kind of natural law. At the same time, Kang believed that the sage, through a proper understanding of the deep trends of the times, could promote progress but could not leap over the necessary stages of progress. Sagely understanding meant only that progress could be promoted—through leading the people to the next stage, not transcending those trends of the times.

Essentially, Kang postulated that Three Ages (*sanshi*) as foretold or even established by Confucius was a form of gradual evolutionism. Kang was undoubtedly influenced by Western views of progress, but his version of linear history rested on a particular reading of the Classics. Kang claimed that history moved from (1) the age of Chaos, to that of (2) the Lesser Peace, to finally (3) the Great Commonweal. This notion played a key role in clearing the path for Chinese intellectuals to reach a consensus holding that history was linear and progressive. This consensus soon had to take social Darwinism into account, recognizing the possibilities of regression and extinction as well as progress, but its essential optimism was never entirely lost.[7] Kang himself remained relatively immune to the social Darwinism that came to dominate the discourse of progress at the beginning of the twentieth century. Meanwhile, he helped make the classical terms *lesser peace* and *great commonweal* into common parlance in modern Chinese, if in ways largely divorced from his sense of progress.

Kang's vision of the future was rooted in an essentially religious vision of New Text Confucianism. The New Text school was based on a set of the Classics produced during the Han Dynasty (206 BCE–220 CE) in the wake of the Qin Dynasty's attempts to eliminate them. The Old Text versions, in pre-Han scripts, were allegedly discovered in the original residence of Confucius (who lived circa sixth to fifth century BCE). While the two versions and the schools associated with them were not diametrically opposed, the initial success of a New Text school was associated with more prophetic and Confucius-centered interpretations. The Old Text school, however, came to dominate scholarly and official discourse from the late Han period through the eighteenth century.[8] At that time, reformers dismayed by the corruption of Qing politics began to find in the Han dynasty New Text school commentaries new ways to justify reform proposals. They were also able to prove that key passages in the Old Text classics were "forgeries"—that is, written no earlier than the Han dynasty. Basing their theories on New Text commentaries on the classics, reformers by the nineteenth century—still before the coming threats from the West were understood—stressed that Confucius was not merely a "transmitter" of tradition but the "uncrowned king," a visionary prophet who not only personally wrote all the classics but founded new institutions.

As well, the theory of Three Ages was found through the New Text tradition. Kang was not the first to highlight the philological problems of the Old Text classics, nor even to blame them for holding back reform, though in the 1890s he did so in a particularly confrontational way that won him many enemies. Kang's innovation was to separate the Three Ages from its correlation with the "Three Systems" (santong)—the notion that in cyclical fashion every new dynasty adopted a new set of institutions (characterized as red, white, or black). Freed from the theory of Three Systems, Kang's Three Ages soared into the infinite future. And he extended the story of China's progress through the historical ages into the future by freely attributing virtually magical powers to Confucius and with utter confidence in himself as Confucius's high priest (or Martin Luther). Historically, the age of Confucius himself was that of Chaos, and the age of the post-Qin imperial order was the Lesser Peace, and then looking into the future the coming age of democratic development would mark the Great Commonweal. Or, perhaps we were still in the age of Chaos with the Lesser Peace of democratic orders now developing, and the Great Commonweal to arrive eventually. Although Kang was not entirely consistent as to timing, he attributed foreknowledge of the Three Ages to Confucius.

> The sage-king Confucius, who was of godlike perception (shenming), early considered and worried over this [existing

societies' failure to achieve happiness]. He thus established the law of the Three Systems and the Three Ages. That is, after the age of Chaos will arise Increasing Peace and Absolute Peace; and after the age of Lesser Peace will arise the Great Commonweal.[9]

For Kang, this pattern was determined by the nature of the cosmos. However, a question then arises: Can humans really promote or retard the unfolding of history? The British philosopher and social theorist Herbert Spencer (1820–1903), whose writings were influential at the time, strongly believed in the inevitability of progress. He compared the development of societies to the "law of organic process"—that is, "the development of a seed into a tree, or an ovum into an animal, constitute an advance from homogeneity of structure to heterogeneity of structure."[10] Spencer is best known as the primary author of social Darwinism, treating specific societies as organisms and the individuals within them as all engaged in the struggle for survival out of which only a few would flourish—Spencer coined the term "survival of the fittest" to describe what he regarded as a universal natural law. However, the point here is that Spencer's particular view of historical progress was based on the premise that any deliberate attempts to improve society were bound to either be ineffectual or backfire. In later life, at least, Spencer opposed any reforms that smacked of socialism. Basically, Spencer preached classical liberal doctrine in opposing state interference with private economic conduct.[11] As well, he believed that progress could only be gradual, as, again, with the growth of a plant. The course of greater and greater heterogeneity is set.

Kang also believed progress was gradual and—from a cosmopolitan viewpoint—inevitable. Something of Spencerism was available to Kang through Japanese translations, missionary writings, and the recent essays of Yan Fu.[12] However, Kang believed that while the ability of humans to affect change was limited, human agency could promote and direct change. Hence, Kang did not merely propose political reforms in the 1890s; he explained exactly what made them possible. When the trends (circumstances; *shi*) are understood, they can be shaped. To Kang's mind, this was the role of the sage. Put more prosaically, it is what competent leaders do. The political sources for Kang's reformism were numerous: from China's long history—such as the reformer Wang Anshi (1021–1086) to examples of men who remade their countries in recent history, particularly Peter the Great and the Meiji Emperor.[13] Ultimately, it should be remembered, if Kang treated the monarch as an ally, it was the Teaching, not the monarch, that was sacred, and it was the role of the sage, not the king, to understand trends.[14] Still, it might be that the king and the sage were combined in one person, creating an enormous power for good. In his *Master Kang's Inner and Outer Chapters* of the late 1880s, Kang described a king wielding real power, not general magnanimity—getting things done through rewards and punishments, as described by the ancient Legalist thinkers.[15] But acting out of devotion to the people because he possessed a mind that could not bear to see suffering (not a Legalist view of rulership). The theme of suffering would become central to Kang's construction of the Great Commonweal.

As well, a link—or at least a simultaneity—between Kang's reform proposals and his utopian impulse was present from the late 1880s onward. The basis of Kang's reformism lay in his belief in the universal human capacity for intelligence (*zhi*) and ethical norms, which he thought Chinese institutions had suppressed, as Wen Yu convincingly argues.[16] Intelligence is by no means limited to sages, but finds its fullest expression among them. This implied that the revival of true learning would effectively legitimate the power of the literati class at the expense of officialdom. Educational reforms would also work to bring the common people into the political sphere. We may thus conclude that one way or another, progress for Kang was a product of human effort.

Historians have struggled to reconcile Kang the reformer and Kang the wild-eyed utopian. Some have dismissed Kang's utopianism as aberrant or unoriginal.[17] In the Chinese Marxist tradition, Kang's views were dismissed as "utopian socialism" and Kang himself as a representative of the bourgeoisie or perhaps enlightened landlords.[18] Another approach has been to problematize the relationship between Kang's nationalism and his utopianism.[19] Yet it may be better to see the relationship between Kang's reformist activism and his utopianism as two sides of the same coin. It is true that Kang's specific reform proposals were limited and can theoretically be divorced from his utopianism. Yet as Jianhua Chen has convincingly argued, Kang's reformism was infused with his sense of world revolution, including the French Revolution.[20] That is to say that Kang, even while opposed to self-proclaimed revolutionaries like Sun Yat-sen, had accepted the modern meaning of the ancient term for dynastic change, *geming*, now understood as regime overthrow. Kang was not aiming for regime overthrow, but he conceived his reform proposals, Chen argues, as amounting to remaking the imperial polity and thus as part of world revolution. Kang fully regarded himself in cosmopolitan terms as a participant—and a kind of leader—of the ongoing world revolution seen not only in France but in Russia under Peter the Great and Japan under the Meiji Emperor. At the very least, his faith in progress not only reconciled but linked the two sides of Kang's thought, and even explains why he thought the world was not ready to hear of his utopia. As a utopian, he was a realist. Kang's Great Commonweal was no eschatological break with human history. Rather, practical reforms to strengthen China were simply part of humanity's universal, linear progress that would gradually break down all boundaries dividing humanity from itself, dividing humanity from all life forms, and ultimately dividing humanity from the cosmos.

Saving the World

Kang was a deeply universalist thinker. He did not believe that distinct cultures would or should—at least ultimately—work out distinct social, political, and moral institutions. This is not to say he believed that all existing cultures and races were equal, but that cosmological laws applied equally to all humanity. Kang's universalism owed a great deal to his reading of the Classics and his faith that Confucius had foretold the course to be taken by humanity, not just the Chinese. If China's earliest thinkers had indeed envisioned something of a universal scheme, they had relied on a vision of a single civilized center surrounded by barbarian regions—regions that became more barbarian the farther their distance from the one source of civilization. This was a universalist vision insofar as the laws of civilization were universally true, just not practiced in full outside the center. Kang's vision, however, was of a borderless and hence entirely decentralized world. Hence, the Great Commonweal was to be composed of democratic federal political units. Kang found precedents for his sociopolitical vision in both the Three Dynasties and modern Western institutions, such as public education and community discussions of the public good (parliaments)—hints of the world still to come.

All human beings were equal in their capacity for intelligence derived from the cosmos. In the *Complete Book of Substantial Truths and Universal Principles*, written in the 1880s at about the same time as *Master Kang's Inner and Outer Chapters*, Kang sought to derive the principles of moral and institutional development from first principles that he called "geometric."[21] Universal principles (*gongli*), however, also had to be the product of human effort, not simply derived from something such as mathematical reasoning. Kang began his explanation of substantial truths by noting that everyone is allotted a share in the primordial substance of Heaven-and-Earth. As such, everyone has the "right of autonomy" (*zizhu zhi quan*) and is an equal member of society. Kang paid considerable attention to the family, emphasizing the importance of freedom and equality in marriage, while children should be reared in public nurseries. (These themes reappear in *The Great Commonweal.*) It is also worth noting that in spite of his devotion to Confucius, as noted above, Kang also stated that people should follow the truth, not the words of sages. In the political sphere, people should choose their sovereigns and their parliaments. Kang provided considerable detail about social relations, government, religion, education, and etiquette, prefiguring the detail provided in *The Great Commonweal.* However, the *Complete Book of Substantial Truths and Universal Principles* offered only prescriptions, with no indication about how these truths and principles were to be achieved and exercised. Nor did Kang yet speak of humaneness (*ren*). Yet we see here how Kang's thought was already making pragmatic reform proposals just as he was working out a metaphysics that explained them.

When we turn to *The Great Commonweal,* as Hao Chang has pointed out, Kang was not merely searching for a new order for society, but a new moral order, based on the ethics of humaneness (*ren*).[22] In fact, Kang had made the concept of humaneness central to his discussions in *Master Kang's Inner and Outer Chapters.* As Wen Yu paraphrases Kang's dense introduction to his chapter on the "Learning of Principles," Kang is already equating humaneness with a kind of universal empathy:

> As a part of nature, human beings, just like any other beings in nature, use whatever capacities they are endowed with to manage and protect themselves, and this is the way things are. Because human beings have a high level of spiritual consciousness, or psyche (*shenming*), they seek to extend themselves to connect with others, but they still only connect with their own kind. The sense of humaneness (*ren*) is the impulse to connect with others of their own kind, while the sense of righteousness (*yi*) is the impulse to make appropriate distinctions between themselves and others in making connections with each other.[23]

By the 1890s, humaneness had become a central concept in Kang's metaphysics, as well as a principle marking the progression from the Lesser Peace to the Great Commonweal. In Hao Chang's reading, for Kang, the moral ideal of humaneness was equated with Heaven and in effect encompassed the whole universe. At the same time, the universe was made up of *qi*, a quality both material and vital and which unified humankind. As Heaven produced human beings and all things, so the moral quality of benevolence "humanized" humans. The ethical order that produced familial and social relations, and that ultimately produced the political realm itself, was not the cosmic order. Kang's nationalism demanded he reform the state, but this kind of activity belonged to a category of moral behavior that was embedded in a larger moral cosmos. For Kang, then, the Lesser Peace described the temporal stage of the present day or the immediate future of a republican political order, marking the middle era of a motion from chaos to the true commonweal. But in a sense it also marked a spatial unit that was smaller than the cosmos and encompassed by the cosmos. Nationalism was a good, but not the ultimate good.

According to *The Great Commonweal*, the ultimate good (perfect humaneness) culminated finally in complete transcendence. But Kang began his work with a lengthy account of human sufferings, ranging from happenstance such as floods to social conditions such as poverty. He was also acutely aware of existential suffering such as old age. Kang then claimed that the cause of suffering resides in "boundaries," which ranged from nations and classes to species. Abolition of these boundaries would lead to unity, equality, independence, productivity, peace, and joy. Scholars have often pointed to the rationality and logic of the organization of the *The Great Commonweal*: Kang moved from individual, to family, to nation, race, and planet, following the same, relentless, homogenizing logic. Yet equally prominent is Kang's emphasis on the evolution of human institutions. Rooting these in history, he is able to see into the future.

For example, in the section on "Abolishing national boundaries and unifying the world," Kang emphasized historical processes that moved in linear fashion from one condition or stage to another. "The evolution (*jinhua*) of national boundaries from division to unity is a natural tendency," he proclaimed.[24] Kang traced the innumerable states (i.e., tribes) of China's legendary period to the three thousand states at the beginning of the Shang, to the two hundred or so states by the Spring and Autumn period, and so forth into the Qin unification of 221 BCE. He also traced the rise of the Persian and Roman empires, the end of feudal division in Europe, and the expansion of modern European colonialism. There was a tension in Kang's thought here, since he noted that much of this process could be explained by the conquest of the weak by the strong, or natural selection (he was not entirely immune to social Darwinism). The tension was between his desire for unity and its attendant homogeneity on the one hand, and his respect for the local and the individual on the other. Kang preferred the voluntary federalism of America or Germany to military conquest, but one way or the other his vision remained that of a politically unified world without national boundaries.

Kang listed the difficulties facing the program of world unification, but he predicted that in the future, as democracy spread, various states would form alliances, beginning perhaps with a unified western Europe and a unified northern and southern America, the probability of Russian domination, and so the gradual but steady unification of all parts of the world. He drew a chart listing how the world grows together in the three great stages of evolution. He posited the growth of world government to regulate the various states and pursue disarmament even before the final arrival of unification. Kang also noted that the world was contracting due to new forms of transportation such as airplanes.

Kang thus explained how a great commonweal would emerge out of present circumstances, however long and complex the voyage would be. He did not simply describe what the future would be like but analyzed the trends of history. These led him to the conclusion that as national boundaries were literally abolished, so the boundaries of class, race, and gender would disintegrate in time. Boundaries derived from human artifice and nature alike were to be dismantled brick by brick. Above all, public institutions would replace the private, such as the family. Women would be absolutely equal in status, rights, and professions. Couples, including homosexuals, would unite on the basis of one-year (renewable) contracts. Children would be reared in nurseries and schools, and seniors would be cared for in nursing homes.

Nowhere was Kang's egalitarian rhetoric more powerful than when he discussed the evils of the family and the inequalities of gender. America and Europe had begun to show the way forward, he said, though only just begun. At least women in the West could travel freely and choose their own spouses. Yet they still faced many disabilities and upon marriage assumed their husband's surname, a sign of subservient status.

Insofar as Kang premised gender equality on the abolition of private property (hitherto passed within the family), he presumably found little precedent in the West. He found that the West's lack of a clan system and neglect of filial piety, while emotionally harsh, was pointing the way forward to the abolition of the family. Since ultimately the family was a source of selfish partiality and inequality, its "boundaries" too would eventually disappear.

Most difficult of all the boundaries to dissolve, in Kang's view, was that of race. In essence, he foresaw a combination of ongoing extinctions of unfit races—in the social Darwinian struggle for survival—and the assimilation of races to be dominated by a kind of yellow-white synthesis created by miscegenation, climate adaptation, and better food and exercise. Here, Kang highlighted American prejudice against blacks, though a prejudice he found understandable based on Negroes' appearance and smell. Kang thought it likely that the black and brown races would be eliminated, and he thought the red race was already disappearing. But he was confident in the ability of the yellow race to adapt. Take for example, Kang said, a Chinese child being raised in Canada who was becoming more like whites in appearance as he ate meat and exercised in fresh air.

One way or another, then, the races will merge together. Jobs are all public. Residential work units are the basis of a democratic, federal system. Advanced technology solves many problems: robots will serve the food in the communal dining halls, which will also feature music and films. Kang was not alone in imagining how humanity might be freed from the necessity of labor. This was a major theme of nineteenth-century Western utopias, and also picked up by the Chinese anarchist Liu Shipei, for example. Liu's 1907 essay "On Equalizing Human Labor" proposed making everyone "independent" by abolishing their dependency on capitalist and familial structures.[25] This was another way of abolishing boundaries. Unlike Kang, Liu did not assume that suffering would one day be abolished, but he thought that the suffering imposed by social institutions could be ameliorated. At least, no one would suffer from a lack of goods or from the fear of such a lack.

While Kang assumed that illness and crime would be minimal in the great commonweal, he did not assume that human nature was necessarily good. He foresaw and sought to deal with problems of laziness, competition, idolization of individuals, and abortion. Like many literary utopias, there was a tone of realism in Kang's gritty descriptions of a functioning utopian society, however implausible, that dominates the book until its last chapters. Now Kang faced the question that all literary utopias face: Once the perfect society is reached, then what? Do time and history halt? If the great commonweal was the earthly manifestation of cosmic humaneness, perhaps there was no future. For Kang, humaneness was a transcendental ideal and therefore timeless. At the same time, he faced another question: Can a humanity mired in immanence really achieve transcendence? Kang's answer seems to have been yes and no. In the great commonweal, Kang left some room for individual differences but no further evolution. Yet beyond the great commonweal lay another realm, and here Kang moved beyond the ideal of humaneness.

> After humanity achieves equality, great humaneness (*ren*) prevails. However, the birth of absolutely everything is derived from the primordial substance [of Heaven-and-Earth], and people are but one species of such animals. When humanity first emerged long ago, people only knew how to cleave to their own kind and preserve them. If not of their kind, they would kill them. Therefore, to love one's own kind was a great principle, and throughout the world those who loved their own kind were labeled with humaneness (*ren*), while those who did not love their own kind were labeled with un-humaneness (*buren*).[26]

Yet was this true humaneness? It left the boundary of species intact. *The Great Commonweal*'s last two chapters went beyond this kind of humaneness to describe how people could "leave behind" the great commonweal—leave behind even their own humanity—to pursue the arts of achieving immortality, buddhahood, and finally roaming the heavens.[27] In abolishing the boundaries of species and of suffering, humanity finally transcends itself. In other words, Kang criticized humaneness as—at best—limited to human beings. This leaves even the sages as no better than tigers, who also kill other creatures. The killing of animals to survive had been justified during the age of Chaos, Kang said, but in the Great Commonweal when dangerous animals are all restricted to zoos, people will love all creatures equally.[28] All people will be vegetarians like the Hindus and Buddhists of today. Does the life of the great commonweal illustrate perfect humaneness, much less transcendence of all boundaries? Kang thought not. In the first place, even vegetarians ended up consuming countless living beings in the form of microbes.

This was to abolish—or at least begin to dismantle—the boundary of species, as Kang put it, and in effect the boundary of the body. The next and final step was to abolish the boundaries of suffering itself and achieve perfect joy.[29] Kang pointed out that primitive peoples found happiness in alleviating the immediate causes of their suffering: finding food, making clothes, taking mates, and so forth. But if the capacity for happiness is infinite, so is the capacity for suffering. Still, the evolution of society—through the contributions of the sages—has alleviated suffering and increased happiness. Here is where Kang pictured his most extravagant material fantasies. Yet if some of these fantasies have not come true, many have. We do not take our food in liquid form yet, but we have toilets that spray warm, scented water and even play music, as Kang envisioned. We certainly have hotels with air conditioning and a great deal of intercontinental air travel. Well-paid biologists of the twenty-first century are in fact searching for techniques to prolong life. Cloning and genetic modification are becoming widespread. We have not created beautiful clothing that says nothing about the wearer's individual status, nor does everyone shave off all their hair and bathe several times a day. But much of the world lives with a level of hygiene unimaginable at the turn of the twentieth century.

Certainly, a strand of Kang's thought included fear of impurity. This was perhaps one spur to his final prediction for the future of humanity freed from all bonds. The dogmas of Christianity, Islam, and Buddhism, no matter how useful previously, will no longer be necessary in the Great Commonweal.

> Therefore in the age of the Great Commonweal, only studies of [how to become] immortals and the buddhas are widely practiced. For if the Great Commonweal is the ultimate expression of the law of the world, studies of the immortals, and of eternal life, are an extension of the ultimate law of the world. Does not Buddhism leave behind the world as a state without birth and without death? And so in departing from the world we depart from the Great Commonweal. In reaching the point that we discard the human sphere, we enter the sphere of the immortals and buddhas. And thus do the

studies of the immortals and buddhas begin. . . . Thus after the Great Commonweal first comes studies of the immortals, the lower form of intelligence, then studies of the buddhas, the higher form of intelligence. And then after studies of the immortals and the buddhas comes studies of roaming the heavens, which I describe elsewhere.[30]

This mystical vision lies outside of the usual scope of utopianism, at least the secular utopianism of the twentieth century. But if nothing else, it expresses Kang's commitment to absolute freedom. It is worth noting that Kang's vision had something in common with one of the proposals of his intellectual enemy, the revolutionary traditionalist Zhang Binglin. Zhang's essay "On the Five Negations" of 1907 was a Buddhist-inspired polemic that began with a call to abolish government.[31] Since families might still exist and rebuild governments, Zhang then called for the abolition of the family. Then likewise of humanity, of life, and of the cosmos. Zhang, too, wanted to negate boundaries, or the institutions that divided people, and pursued his logic to a nihilist, reductio ad absurdum extreme. Kang's vision, unlike Zhang's, was of course highly detailed and did not demand the extinction of life itself. Rather, Kang demanded love for all life, not merely human. It may seem that while the earlier chapters of The Great Commonweal were based on a realistic critique of existing society, Kang moved from the present to celebrate the future of life in a thoroughly fantastic manner. Yet Kang was interested in astronomy, and, as Kung-chuan Hsiao points out, Kang's notion of "celestial peregrination" may have owed much to Neo-Confucianism's cosmology as well as contemporary science fiction.[32] This was a notion that is perhaps best interpreted metaphorically, as the power of imagination.

Suffering and Utopia

If we understand The Great Commonweal in three aspects—social arrangements, material civilization, and spiritual states—then it is possible that the first aspect was largely shaped by Kang's readings, likely that the second aspect was shaped by his travels, and evident that the third aspect was largely derived from Buddhism. This is to simplify, but it is important to note that Kang had much to say about America, Europe, and Africa as he discussed the nature of the Great Commonweal and the route to getting there. For the most part, America and Europe seemed farther ahead than China, while Africa was hopelessly behind. Kang's comments on America, Europe, India, and Africa could have been largely derived from his extensive reading through the 1880s and 1890s. However, we cannot rule out the possibility that the sharpness of those comments—on the backwardness of India, the American treatment of blacks, and the health of Chinese in Canada—was based on personal observation. Furthermore, what seems otherwise a curious emphasis on the importance of sightseeing (for gender equality, for example) may have derived as much from Kang's international trips as the tradition, for example, of visiting local temples.

In 1879, at the age of about twenty, Kang made a brief trip to Hong Kong, and was struck by "the elegance of the buildings of the foreigners, the cleanliness of the streets, the efficiency of their police. I was impressed by the organization and administration of the foreigners, and I realized that we must not look upon them as barbarians."[33] In 1882 he also visited the foreign concession in Shanghai, noting that "its prosperity gave me further insight into the firm basis of the Westerners' art of government." Kang's "thorough study of Western learning" then began.[34] However, not until he was exiled from China with a price on his head after 1898 did Kang undertake more extensive travels. First, he sailed to Hong Kong, Tokyo, and Canada. Then London, again North America, and after 1900 back to Hong Kong, Singapore, Penang, and India.

As Kang continued to revise *The Great Commonweal*, it is at least possible that some of the book's most science fiction-y elements were added later. In 1903 Kang traveled again through Southeast Asia to Hong Kong, and in 1904 he embarked on a new world tour. As Young-tsu Wong points out, "Kang sharply sensed the enormous material gap between the modern West and backward China. He thenceforth concerned himself with saving China by closing this gap."[35] Wong emphasizes that Kang used his direct observations of foreign technology and social institutions to urge that China adopt specific reforms. For example, that the Chinese not only build railroads but learn how to construct them and manage them themselves. Kang's political views did not change but his appreciation for "material civilization" undoubtedly deepened—"industrial manufacturing, steamships, electricity, canons, ironclads, and so on." As well, foreign examples confirmed Kang's preexisting belief that the way forward for China lay in becoming a constitutional monarchy with an elected parliament.[36]

His world tour, then, sharpened Kang's appreciation of the material accomplishments of the West and his understanding that their foundations lay in particular social and political institutions. What his world tour may also have done is provoke Kang's imagination of what the world of the more distant future could be like. Kang rhapsodically described the "new world" (*xin shijie*) where letters take seconds to arrive thousands of miles away over electric wires, while they might take years in the old word.[37] Telegraph systems, steamships, and railroads had already changed the very nature of time and space. Knowledge, as well, was transformed, for example by a new "abacus" that Kang saw in Washington and which could calculate three hundred numbers a second.[38]

Kang plainly broke with Confucian ethics in imagining a world without private property or family bonds. But in conceiving the Great Commonweal as the unfolding of humaneness, Kang's thought remained rooted in a Confucian metaphysics. As John Fitzgerald points out, Kang in effect granted subjecthood only to the world as a whole.[39] That is, individuals, nations, and classes possessed only temporary validity as historically contingent subjects. Or as Hao Chang notes, the cosmos, for Kang, was a living organism, and hence naturally subject to process and growth.[40] Progress moved on both the material and moral levels.

Kang was fully part of an era made optimistic by the spectacle of scientific and technological progress, though his moral concerns were ultimately paramount. These moral concerns, in turn, rested on empathy. It is not an accident that the first chapter of *The Great Commonweal* describes the "suffering of humanity." Kang described not distress over his own personal circumstances but the despair caused by his witnessing the suffering of others.[41] Kang saw in himself a soaring spirit with claims to transcendental powers and at the same time a man struck down by his sympathy for others. He wrote that it is the role of the sage to love humanity, and to love humanity is to feel its pains. Kang described a visit to his home village. What his description did not include was the cause of this visit: the French attacks on the coast that forced Kang to relocate in 1885. At any rate, he found in his village suffering, grief, misery, quarreling.

The sense of personal transformation that he experienced in his home village provoked Kang to think about how utopia could be based on notions of sagehood and empathy. In this sense, his great commonweal was founded on his reaction to despair, which gave him the desire to conquer suffering. The point of abolishing government, for example, was based on the charge that the government caused suffering. It caused suffering due to punishments, taxes, military service, and so forth. As we have seen, Kang's fundamental conception of abolishing "boundaries" stemmed from the view that they are sources of suffering. He saw the categories of nation, class, race, gender, family, and ultimately species to all be forms of boundaries. If we pursue this metaphor, it might seem that without boundaries there is simply undifferentiated mass. That is not what Kang meant; rather, his vision was of equality that left room for difference at the level of the individual. Indeed, it was, overall, a highly individualistic vision wherein that which separated individuals would be abolished but individuation would (somehow) continue to flourish, or indeed be allowed to flourish for the first time, unhindered by the boundaries that had hitherto suppressed the processes of individuation.

Where did Kang's serene confidence in the future come from? And was that confidence as confident as it seemed? There may be no way to answer these questions definitively. But we can turn to Kang's memoirs to see cracks in his normal complacency. Kang Youwei largely composed his "chronological autobiography" around 1896 with additions made in 1898 and apparently in 1927.[42] He began conventionally, situating himself in terms of (patrilineal) descent traced back to the Southern Song, with closer and proud attention paid to both maternal and paternal ancestors of the previous four generations or so. He was the first son, after two daughters. Significantly for our purposes, Kang claims to have been born after a pregnancy of eleven months.[43] Thus, in addition to Kang's pride in his family background and his own precocity, he hints at a kind of cosmic fate at work in his life. He sought to emulate himself on the sages of the past. Kang describes his childhood with a certain ironical detachment and self-knowledge. It is as if to say, in my reading, that "I know how exaggerated was my childish self-esteem, but at the same time, it was largely justified."

When Kang was ten, his father died after an extensive illness. Kang reports that at ten *sui* he would carry his father's cane and his basin and generally attend to him—all of which he remembers "as a dream."[44] Kang briefly described three reactions to his father's death: he accepted his father's dying charge to study hard, respect his elders, and take care of the younger members of the family; he wept from sorrow; and he took charge of the funeral arrangements "like an adult." In sum, Kang does not appear to have been especially hard hit by his father's death. He continued his education with his grandfather; and it was only upon his grandfather's death that Kang experienced strong grief.

> From the age of eight sui I was brought up by my grandfather. He gave me daily admonishments and taught me earnestly, and I had been close to him for more than a decade. When I heard the news, I was so grieved that for three days I ate and drank nothing and for a hundred days I ate only pickled vegetables. My uncles brought his remains back, and, weeping, we buried him at Xianggang, as recommended by a geomancer. After the funeral service the coffin was not interred but was left on a hill. My uncles and I constructed a grass hut close by, wore mourning garments, and abstained from eating meat for a year. At that time I had read the mourning ceremonials and had studied the three rites [the sacrifices to Heaven, earth, and the ancestral temple], and I carried out the rituals without an iota of deviation. Although many people scoffed at me, later my clansmen and fellow villagers respected me for this. In my youth I was firm in my purpose, and, as in this instance, I may have been too zealous in upholding my views. In the winter we buried my grandfather.[45]

Kang's performance of filial piety was exactly that: a performance for an audience that he was happy to have regard him as an eccentric. But it was also a performance for his own sake: Kang channeled his grief in ways he thought would contribute to his project of self-cultivation. Kang was, again, frank about his ambition to become a sage.

There is no reason to doubt Kang's distress over his grandfather's death. This sense of distress, if not despair, also applied to Kang's interpretation of public affairs. The personal, existential, and political aspects of distress bled into one another. The crisis Kang apparently experienced when he was twenty-one and gave up his studies for meditation was in fact relatively short-lived, though in its wake Kang began to play a more direct role in political affairs (establishing an anti-footbinding association) even while he remained restless. In his autobiography, Kang described how the Sino-French War caused him to return to his home village, and he again reported then achieving the intellectual and spiritual breakthroughs that would form the basis of *The Great Commonweal*.[46] Within a year, however, Kang reported the premature deaths of two of his daughters and a health crisis that was possibly psychosomatic (severe headaches) and gave rise to thoughts of death. He also failed to pass the provincial examinations.

Meanwhile, although Kang could always appreciate the pleasures of life, from this point on he writes of his concern for China's disastrous position in the world.[47] After the Sino-Japanese War of 1894–95, "national conditions had deteriorated, and if China were to recover, there were only a few years available to pursue fundamental reforms. Afterwards, it would be too late even if people wished to pursue them, and foreign pressures would intensify with no remedy possible." Although Kang did not often discuss the threat of racial extinction, by the 1890s the potential collapse of the dynasty was ever-present in his mind. This sense of urgency fueled the entire reform movement of the 1890s and beyond. It was not based on despair, insofar as despair would have led to counsels of defeatism rather than action. Nonetheless, the political vision that lay behind it was near to a despairing one: one in which China faced colonization or extinction. At any rate, Kang threw himself into quasi-public discussions of state affairs.

In 1887 and 1888, he reported, his criticisms of high officials and of the Empress Dowager for using public funds to rebuild the Summer Palace led him to fear for his life. He worried that he would be leaving his mother alone. In other words, he was possibly behaving unfilially in his own lights for the sake of his political ideals. "But then I thought, life and death are predestined. If I am to save the world, how can I withdraw now?"[48] On several occasions in the autobiography Kang recorded his belief that all his setbacks and dangers would be resolved by fate, or the will of Heaven. This seems to have given him the courage to face death. In 1893, Kang reported, he went into battle against local bandits and their gentry protectors. There were literally fights over control of the local self-defense organization, and Kang was slandered to higher officials. He later drew the parallel to 1898, the thwarted reform movement that ended in six executions. Others did indeed die, but not Kang.[49] In the wake of the debacle of the reform movement, Kang fled to Hong Kong under British protection while his mother managed to make it to Macao. In 1898 Kang told his mother how unfilial he felt to have risked her life for nothing. The autobiography also records that Kang's relatives and friends were persecuted. Kang reported the agony he felt over his brother's fate (though he kept it a secret from his mother, an act that Kang left unmentioned in his autobiography).[50]

Yet he reminded himself finally that in spite of the odds against him, he had not been fated to die.

Much of this sounds like egotism and complacency, but read against the grain, it also sounds like whistling in the dark. A belief in being chosen by Heaven was necessary to prevent the total collapse of his personality. After 1898 Kang was never again to play a significant role in Chinese politics, and, though he long remained a cultural force, he also became an object of ridicule in the years after the 1911 Revolution. This might have been as great a blow as the threat of death. But if Kang's convictions tended toward the egalitarian and liberal, he himself naturally fit into a role prescribed by the model of Confucius and other sages. Kang's self-appointed role as savior of humanity no doubt gave him strength, but he was able to channel his despair into long-accepted cultural patterns.

Kang in effect said that he suffered as humanity suffered because as a sage, his empathy was perfect. Compassion turned into horror. We can certainly ask if Kang were not projecting his own, personal distress onto innocent bystanders who wanted nothing to do with it. But in either case, Kang used the trope of suffering as the framework for building a utopia. Kang designed the entire structure of *The Great Commonweal* around the types of suffering that he witnessed. Great suffering and empathy were not disabling states but powerful levers for a transformation of sensibility and construction of the future. Kang's psychodrama of overcoming suffering irresistibly led to utopianism.

Kang and the Global Utopian

Kang Youwei's utopia was influenced, in its form and some of its details, by Edward Bellamy's *Looking Backward*.[51] Kang had obviously also read Darwin and Fourier, whom he cites, and at least a little Marxism.[52] But his utopian impulse was able to flower in a full-fledged speaking picture utopia because Bellamy had showed the way. An abridged version of *Looking Backward* was serialized in the *Wanguo gongbao* magazine in 1891–92.[53] Though perhaps better termed a chapter-by-chapter summary than even an abridged translation, it was enough to introduce the science fiction-y love story, the formation of the National Trust, the Industrial Army, compensation scheme, means of consumption (shopping), and other basic concepts of Bellamy's utopia. *Looking Backward* was published in 1888 to immediate and global success. In addition to the abridged Chinese version, translations appeared in the European languages, Russian, Arabic, Hebrew, and Japanese.[54] Notwithstanding earlier French utopian writers such as Fourier and Saint-Simon, Edward Bellamy was the first to imagine in such detail what a socialist future would be like to live in. Bellamy described not an isolated community but a historically embedded entire world.

My point here is not that Kang took his ideas from Bellamy, or even his basic utopian project, which, as we have seen, had its roots in Kang's concerns of the 1880s, but a comparison of *The Great Commonweal* and *Looking Backward* tells us something of the global utopian moment. Neither work was a utopia in the traditional or Renaissance form of a fantasy *place*. Rather, they put utopia in the *future*, a world to be created through time rather than imagined in space. It is widely recognized that the modern (Renaissance) utopia owed much to the discovery of the Americas and, if highly rational in form, also displayed a certain primitivism: utopias of the sixteenth and seventeenth centuries were travelers' tales of societies free of the decadence of civilization.[55] Utopias that are mediated through time rather than space, however, can free themselves of any primitive vestiges if they choose to do so. While Renaissance utopias were technologically and socially simple societies, by the nineteenth century, utopias were frequently imagined as lands of plenty, made possible by technological progress. Technology promised that humans would not have to labor (much) yet could still possess material wealth.

Furthermore, utopias of the future inevitably suggested themselves as projects, however fantastical. Neither *Looking Backward* nor *The Great Commonweal* proposed very specific plans for how to get from the here-and-now to the future they imagined, but both works sketched out the evolutionary progress of social institutions based on scientific principles. They postulated precise historical processes through which utopia would be reached, but neglected the political and social movements that might propel those processes. Popular movements were actually repudiated by Bellamy and described only casually by Kang. While notions of evolution were central to the structure of both works, Bellamy and Kang understood evolution in different ways. Bellamy's overall approach was deterministic and he explicitly denounced radical political action. Kang's voluntarism, in contrast, emphasized the historical role of sages in promoting progress. As well, while Bellamy's vision of the society of the year 2000 was based on an extrapolation of contemporary historical trends and just over a century away, Kang's utopia was based on a more mystical prophecy that the present world was not even prepared to hear, though just as inevitably fated to arrive in the far, far distant future.

Nonetheless, Kang as well as Bellamy understood social evolution as the expression of historical forces or trends. This created a theoretical dilemma: Does utopia come about by human agency such as social movements or sages, or does it come about willy-nilly? Neither man entirely answered this question. Concerning a second dilemma, they also produced different answers. If utopia promises a perfect society, does not stagnation necessarily follow? Or, does progress stop? Bellamy tried to imagine a space of continued cultural progress, but the institutions of his world of the year 2000 were essentially unchangeable. Kang's Great Commonweal, however, was more successful in incorporating the principle of progress in an almost dialectical fashion, so that innovations are unceasing (if increasingly fantastical).

If utopias of place are by their very nature set apart from the rest of the world, much less the real world, utopias of the future tend to be cosmopolitan. They rest on universal principles and forces. Yet for all his work's cosmopolitan premises, Bellamy simply was not much concerned with the rest of the world, but was content to focus on the United States. Kang's cosmopolitan utopianism was harder fought. Kang had to begin with the reality of imperialism and racial division, and work out a way to transcend the particularisms that seemed built into the modern world.

To compare a literary utopia—*Looking Backward* is a love story (if a wooden one)—to a lengthy expository argument may seem wrongheaded. Yet the novelistic framework of *Looking Backward* is quite flimsy, and most of the work consists of argumentation in the guise of dialog. The characters are one-dimensional, lack inner lives, and clearly exist either to explain the new society, exemplify its virtues, or (in the case of the narrator) represent the reader of the nineteenth century trying to understand how a society mired in the ills of industrialization, plutocracy, and class tensions could become a smoothly operating machine producing an equal and comfortable living for all its members.[56] In fact, most of *Looking Backward* consists of dry exposition, while the writing of *The Great Commonweal* often possesses real literary power.[57]

Looking Backward was a concentrated cry of protest against Gilded Age America. The entire book remains relentlessly focused on the problem of economic inequality. Bellamy's utopian longings thus revolved around a set of institutions designed to foster absolute economic equality. This system Bellamy called "Nationalism," since he wished to avoid the more natural term for his system, "socialism," which in America was already associated with European revolutionaries. Discussions of the means of economic production and distribution dominate *Looking Backward*. Bellamy envisioned a world (or at least an America) that was truly a cooperative society. All adults contribute to society by their best efforts, working from the ages of twenty-one to forty-five, and all receive exactly equal incomes for life. The notion that the fundamental institution of society was this "industrial army" was both metaphor and plan. All persons work, both for honor and out of the kind of loyalty a soldier feels for his comrades, now transferred to society as a whole. As in the army, there are a few malingerers, who will be punished. All workers are encouraged to explore their talents, while volunteers for more onerous or monotonous work will be rewarded with shorter hours. People can also retire early, if they accept less income; also, they can work on their own—writing novels, editing newspapers, or ministering to spiritual needs, for example—if they can persuade people in effect to pay them (although more precisely, as Bellamy insists, not paid by "subscribers" but supported by persons willing to indemnify the government out of their own credit for the artist's annual credit, since there is after all no private property).

As for what people do with their incomes, that is entirely up to them. Some will prefer fine homes while eating modestly, others will prefer fine foods while living in humbler quarters, and yet others will pursue moderation in both. Bellamy describes no topic in as much detail as the distribution and consumption of goods. The most imaginative descriptions in *Looking Backward* concern shopping expeditions—to grand but tasteful department stores full of sample goods to be ultimately delivered through pneumatic tubes from great warehouses—and dining halls or restaurants. But this world of plenty is predicated on the premise that efficiency and a degree of technological progress assure a society of abundance. Basically, Bellamy argued that ending the wasteful competition and class warfare of late-nineteenth-century capitalism would create efficiencies of production in the hands of the industrial army. Furthermore, by keeping track of what consumers demand, production will be planned to meet demands more precisely than markets can. Bellamy had less to say about the actual tasks of industrial production. Unlike the Chinese utopian writers, Bellamy did not really rely on technological breakthroughs to increase production but rather relied on rational planning.

Labor, for Bellamy, is an unpleasant duty; its hardships can be minimized, but the only goal of working is to maximize leisure. Instead of the nineteenth century's tiny leisure class maintained by the long and brutal labor of the large working class, the new society will equally share the burdens of labor and the pleasures of leisure. Ironically, Bellamy said relatively little about the "daily life" aspects either of labor, though he described its organization in detail, or of leisure, at least aside from shopping. He claimed that people of the twentieth century were happy because they could pursue whatever interests, studies, pleasures, and cultural pursuits interested them, but the novel presented few examples of this. Although he delighted in pneumatic tubes, telephony, and covered sidewalks, and although he lived in a period of technological breakthroughs, Bellamy eschewed anything that smacked of science fiction. Readers could not accuse him of imagining a world of abundance that depended on fantastic machines that might or might not be invented.

Looking Backward was not based on the principle of "from each according to abilities, to each according to needs" that formed the core of radical thought, but a purely mechanical distribution of labor and rewards regardless of contribution and regardless of need. Bellamy recognized that people's abilities were different, so the industrial army did not expect the same contribution from everyone—it expected the same effort. There was nothing pleasurable about work: Bellamy's dark vision of labor seems both realistic and unexpectedly grim. For one who could imagine such a total remaking of social organization, he failed to imagine any possibility of remaking work. Bellamy's vision of leisure seems almost as cramped as his vision of labor. And his vision of civic life seems even more cramped. As he praised leisure, so Bellamy referred to his citizens' vibrant social and civic lives. Yet all readers see in *Looking Backward* is a private family eating and shopping alone. Even sermons are consumed in the privacy of the home rather than in a congregation. Bellamy described a civic apparatus of tiered elections (though not universal suffrage), but officials had no real political decisions to make. *Looking Backward* has management but no politics. There are no lawyers and few laws. Nationalist society has the hierarchy of the (industrial) army; not the messy debates of a public sphere.

To many readers today and some in the 1890s, these limitations were real faults, and Bellamy's Nationalism smacked of authoritarianism. Nonetheless, Bellamy could argue that by giving humanity economic independence, he was allowing the mass of people for the first time to choose their own leisure, construct their own lifestyles, and discover their own spiritual resources. If Nationalism was to have a higher purpose than assuring a just and affluent society, this purpose perhaps lay in—according to a sermon preached toward the end of the novel—"the idea of the vital unity of the family of mankind."[58]

Looking Backward touches on many issues, including evolution, race, and gender. Bellamy's concept of social evolution is key to his whole scheme, because it explains how the new society is to be formed. Again, Bellamy insisted that to get from "here" to "there" required no class struggle—not even social reform movements—but was rather a natural process that observers of the nineteenth century could already see taking place. Essentially, Bellamy extrapolated from the growing numbers of trusts in such industries as steel, oil, and railroads. This concentration of capital led to great evils but great efficiencies as well. Bellamy thus foresaw that the trusts of the nineteenth century would soon merge into one single gigantic trust—"the final consolidation of the entire capital of the nation. . . . The industry and commerce of the country, ceasing to be conducted by a set of irresponsible corporations and syndicates of private persons at their caprice and for their profit, were intrusted [sic] to a single syndicate representing the people, to be conducted in the common interest for the common profit."[59] The "Great Trust" came about peacefully because public opinion saw its desirability. Bellamy's analogy was to the death of monarchy: just as the people had agreed that public affairs should not be left in the hands of kings, so they now understood that the economy should not be left in the hands of private capitalists (although Bellamy might have asked how many monarchies had been abolished peacefully). Bellamy thus posited both economic trends and a shift in "public opinion" which recognized the advantages of "trusts" and carried through a belief in those advantages to its logical conclusion: that there be one single great trust.

As for race, *Looking Backward* made no reference to the recently freed slaves. Nor did he mention the hot issue of Chinese immigration. Bellamy pictured a world in which most of the nations of the Americas, Europe, and Australia had built industrial armies and achieved a socialist order. These nations maintained their autonomy but cooperated closely. Not least of their cooperative projects was a "joint policy toward the more backward races, which are gradually being educated up to civilized institutions."[60] On the one hand, Bellamy seemed to assume that a single universal path was leading all nations to the final goal; yet on the other he stipulated that even after a century of progress only the West had reached that goal. Another section of *Looking Backward* stressed the advantages of a kind of eugenics wherein the women of Nationalist societies only reproduce with the "best and noblest of the other sex" to achieve "race purification."[61] Apparently Bellamy saw no tension between this goal and his vision of the "vital sentiment of brotherhood"—a vision that, in any case, he never took as a denial of the unequal physical, mental, and moral endowments of races and individuals.

Bellamy's casual paternalism extended to his attitude toward women. He assured readers that women would be perfectly equal in the Nationalist society, and he envisioned a world where most women could choose not to cook or launder for their families, as these tasks were performed by professionals of the industrial army. Women would be educated and have the same formal rights as men. Yet since women could not perform men's jobs, they would have their own industrial army. Bellamy proposed that women could love as readily as men and make the first moves in a relationship, including proposals of marriage. This was perhaps shocking stuff to Victorian readers. Yet what *Looking Backward* showed as a novel were female characters who were nothing if not demure and retiring. Dr. Leete explains how society works; Edith takes Julian shopping; Mrs. Leete stays in the background. Women even leave the men to smoke their cigars after dinner. It is as if Bellamy was torn between the principle of egalitarianism on the one hand, and an inability to imagine a world without patriarchal authority on the other. As individual and perhaps racial endowments differed, in Bellamy's view, so did those of the sexes.

Clearly, then, not all of Bellamy's concerns were those of Kang. Bellamy wrote in response to the evils of industrialization and was perhaps inspired by the military ideals of organization that had emerged in the Civil War. Not all of Kang's concerns were those of Bellamy. Kang wrote in response to the evils of the family and of national and racial discrimination and was perhaps inspired by the apparent efficiency and fairness of Western societies. Nonetheless, the secular social systems they envisioned were similar in many respects. They both emphasized equality of outcomes. They thought that people were motivated by honor rather than material gain, and deterred from wrongdoing by public shame rather than punishment. They assumed that egalitarian societies would have little crime. They both relied on a mix of social organization and technological fixes to minimize labor while maximizing production and hence providing a materially good life for all. They both assumed that some kind of highly expert central planning would take care of all economic issues.

Yet it is clear that the central metaphors or what might be called the core visions of utopia held by Bellamy and Kang differ considerably. Bellamy's was of "solidarity" based on the industrial army, a vision of hierarchical but voluntary cooperation, rather like the organization of social insects such as bees or ants (Bellamy never used this metaphor, but with some justification his critics thought it fit). Kang's core vision was of "abolishing boundaries" based on the contrast of human nature as pleasure-seeking on the one hand, and the reality of existential and contingent suffering on the other, though abolishing boundaries seemed to Kang's critics to threaten not only traditional cultural values but individuation as well.

Another fundamental difference in the two works lies in Kang's philosophical framework, which is simply lacking in Bellamy. Perhaps because he could base his social ideas on his metaphysics of cosmic humaneness, Kang's reimagining of social organization was more radical than Bellamy's. Unlike Bellamy, Kang abolished family life, while social life in the Great Commonweal was simultaneously individual and communal: individual in the pursuit of private pleasures (most notably, for Kang, lifetime study and spiritual discipline) and communal in its settings of work units, schools, and other institutions. Kang's approach was based on a more rigorous universalism than Bellamy felt required to pursue. For Bellamy, even though he advocated women's rights, family life in twentieth-century Boston was scarcely different from that of the previous century.

I would also emphasize the contrast between Bellamy's professionally managed, law-less society and Kang's civic realm of elections and public discussion. By no means was this an absolute contrast, for Kang gave little indication that people of the Great Commonweal would be debating fundamental issues. Still, he assumed the continued need for new policies and legislation. Perhaps Kang's appreciation for civic life was linked to his interest in the principles of republicanism and the project of democratizing China. But there was a more fundamental reason as well. One reason Bellamy failed to conceive of a civic sphere may be that he foresaw no need for any future change. But, as we have seen, the Great Commonweal continued to be devoted to development and progress.

These various contrasts between the two works highlight the different conditions the two thinkers were trying to work through, at roughly the same time, from their different positions in the globalizing capitalist system. It may not be surprising that in the world's foremost republic Bellamy dreamed of the end of politics, while in the last days of a decadent empire Kang dreamed of creating a civic realm. Both dreamed of an egalitarian social and economic order. Bellamy, of course, thought the American republic had become a plutocracy, while Kang knew that China was mired the autocratic decadence of the age of Chaos.

Bellamy's relationship to earlier utopian writers, perhaps especially Comte, and to Christian doctrine is obvious but indirect. He was well versed in European socialist texts, including Marxist writings, but in many ways rejected them, as he had rejected the Calvinism of his parents.[62] Bellamy's belief that the resolution of the social problem had to be solved at the level of the nation-state reflected new thinking about the nature of society, and his industrial army was derived from the experience of the Civil War. In a sense, Bellamy sought to enlarge capitalist organization, not destroy it.

Kang was also aware of modern socialist writings, including of course Bellamy. But his starting points were Confucianism and Buddhism. Rather than engage in the arid debate of whether Kang was more Confucian or more Buddhist, or the degree to which he transcended one or the other, it might be better to call *The Great Commonweal* a Buddho-Confucian text. At any rate, while Kang deliberately situated his work in relationship to both Buddhist and Confucian concepts, he just as clearly saw himself as making an original contribution to social thought.

Bellamy and Kang were thus not only responding to different circumstances with some of the same intellectual resources, they were also using strikingly different resources. Yet a comparison of their utopias demonstrates the appeal of communism across cultural borders and a shared belief in egalitarianism, if based on different premises. For all the differences in the two utopias, their commonalities suggest not the specific transference of ideas from metropole to periphery but something of a "global moment." The universalist thrust of both works even suggests a new concept of the global. Utopia cannot be located in an isolated backwater but represents irresistible forces working everywhere, at least one way or another.

Conclusion

Kang's ideas are deeply imbricated in modern Chinese history. Famously, Mao Zedong cited Kang as an inspiration in his youth.[63] While the thinkers examined in the next three chapters never acknowledged that they were utopian thinkers in the model of Kang, they reflected his egalitarianism and took socialist ideals for granted. Insofar as Kang's ideas were the inspiration for the 1898 Reform Movement, the reaction against them fueled the Empress Dowager Cixi's coup d'état and the catastrophe of official support for the Boxer Uprising. Yet the New Reform policies finally adopted in 1902 largely followed the proposals made in 1898.

Against this background, it matters little whether we label Kang a political failure or point out that the society of *The Great Commonweal* has not yet been achieved. Kang himself scarcely thought it would be achieved a mere century or so after he wrote it. It does matter whether we would want to carry out its ideals or find them abhorrent. Most utopias carry a whiff of the totalitarian. The great commonweal would unite the government and the teaching (*zhengjiao*) as in antiquity, or so Kang thought. It may be that his efforts to imagine a civic space in the great commonweal failed. But that is a matter for individual readers to decide for themselves. As Kang was a devoted cosmopolitan himself, it is little wonder that his utopianism can be seen as part of a global manifestation of the utopian impulse in the late nineteenth century. However, Kang's ultimate concerns were cosmological or spiritual, not political, moral, or aesthetic.[64]

For most of the twentieth century, Kang was remembered as a reformer dedicated to the renewal of the state, an activist whose career dwindled into irrelevance after 1898. His utopianism was pushed aside as an embarrassment. It is ironic, then, that the first decades of the twenty-first century have seen something of a Kang revival in the Chinese-speaking world. On what we might call the Left, the Hong Kong–New York film director Evans Chan has produced a docudrama and an opera emphasizing Kang's cosmopolitanism.[65] And, perhaps more remarkably, at least segments of the movement to return to Confucius have taken Kang to their bosoms. The New Confucians of the early twentieth century had little use for Kang, constructing a genealogy that began with Xiong Shili (1885–1968) and completely neglected Kang. This was a genealogy based on a definition of Confucianism as philosophy, and quite rigorous philosophy, rather than a Kang-style religion. After the 1911 Revolution, Kang led a movement to make Confucianism China's state religion along the lines of the established churches of Europe. The movement failed. But efforts to popularize Confucianism in the twenty-first century have brought about a new appreciation for Kang.[66] Some of today's Confucians argue similarly to Kang that China needs the ethical principles found in the Confucian tradition and the kind of national solidarity that a Confucian Church would provide. One wonders, however, what top Communist Party officials really think of the great commonweal.

3

Aesthetics and Transcendence

Cai Yuanpei

In 1904, Cai Yuanpei wrote a short story called "New Year's Dream." Cai pictured a democratic federal system in which all persons contributed to and benefited from social and economic cooperation on an equal basis. Cai's goals were "cosmopolitanism" and "liberty and equality," his quarry was Qing autocracy, and his faith lay in historical progress. The protagonist of "New Year's Dream" extrapolated the future from the current state of the civilized nations of the West and the rise of revolutionary parties around the world, as we will see further below.

This was to be Cai's only attempt to write a full-fledged, if brief, utopia. But in the 1910s and 1920s he thought more deeply about what had to change if something like utopia really was to be created. Cai's career revolved around educational reform and cultural reconstruction. Like Hu Shi, Cai was a scholar with broad interests in philosophy and the history of philosophy, and in liberal reforms. Like Kang Youwei, Cai balanced political realism with radical beliefs, so that he tended to appear excessively compromising. Like Chen Duxiu (who never compromised), Cai explored political ideas in occasional essays and speeches rather than trying to systematize his views.

Cai's vision was of a world that abolished all the boundaries between individuals, and we can best understand this, in spite of its religious overtones, as a secular utopian vision. If Cai was an unusual kind of utopian thinker, he was also an unusual kind of political theorist. Throughout his long career, he was primarily concerned with the theory and practice of education. Cai had been an outstanding student of the traditional curriculum, winning his *jinshi* degree in 1890 and being appointed to the Hanlin Academy.[1] He began a fairly conventional career with high bureaucratic prospects. Although he was on friendly terms with Liang Qichao, Cai remained aloof from the 1898 Reform Movement, but he was utterly disillusioned by the court's reactionary politics in the wake of the movement's failure. Resigning from his government posts, Cai began to participate in the revolutionary movement in Shanghai, though he maintained some of his official contacts. When in 1907 Cai was forced to flee China, he traveled to Germany with the new Qing minister. There he studied German for a year in Berlin, supporting himself with tutoring, occasional articles, and translations, which eventually included a translation of Friedrich Paulsen's *Principles of Ethics* (in 1909, albeit based mostly on a Japanese translation). Moving on, Cai then took classes at the University of Leipzig for three years, until the success of the revolution took him back to China at the end of 1911. His Leipzig studies brought Cai into close contact with modern Western trends in philosophy, psychology, and aesthetics. Cai's interests also included literature, history, and anthropology, and his studies even involved laboratory work. Perhaps the professors who had the most influence on Cai were Karl Lamprecht, a historian, and Wilhelm Wundt, who taught both psychology and philosophy.[2] With Wundt, Cai took courses on philosophy from Kant to the present day, as well as the history of "new philosophy" and psychology; with Lamprecht, Cai took courses on German "cultural history"; and as well he took courses in the natural sciences, literature (Goethe), the history of philosophy, art history, and aesthetics.

Cai can, in today's terminology, be called a public intellectual; he was also a scholar's scholar almost universally respected for his broad learning. Broad but not deep. In his otherwise admiring portrait of Cai, the literary historian Chen Pingyuan notes: "Cai Yuanpei has no prominent position in literature, historiography, philosophy, or ethics, and his published works are far from indispensible."[3] However, Cai was a prominent writer and speaker in his own time, and had much to say about political questions, ethics, and aesthetics, as well as education. For decades after "New Year's Dream," Cai's articles and speeches continued to promote "cosmopolitanism" and "liberty and equality," even as his faith in radical revolution waned. During the Republican period, Cai's moderate liberalism left no room for Kang-style teleology—Cai hoped for progress but he did not know history's final destination. In labeling Cai a "liberal," I am basically referring to his commitment to constitutional republicanism and freedom of inquiry. At the same time, Cai's liberalism was more a basic stance, or even instinct, toward the questions of the day rather than a full-fledged political ideology. This can be seen in his attitude toward education. At least in the realm of the university, Cai insisted on the autonomy of professors and students individually and collectively—the importance of freedom for intellectual work. As chancellor of Peking University for most of the period between 1916 and 1922, he famously advocated an inclusive toleration (*jianrong bingbao*). And as we explore below, he believed that aesthetic education was an essential method of cultivating the individual.

Cai both advocated modern citizenship, which presumed the identity of citizen and individual, and called for the abolition of all the boundaries between individuals. If Kang Youwei based his vision of breaking down boundaries on the basis of a kind of empathy that pervaded the universe, Cai argued that it was a true understanding of reality that broke down boundaries. While never denouncing Confucianism and indeed retaining some its moral concerns, Cai primarily rooted this vision in a metaphysics that he self-consciously derived from Kantianism. If Cai was not primarily a utopian thinker, he cannot be understood without a full appreciation of the utopian impulse. Cai's promotion of aesthetics education was the key to his utopian impulse to erase the boundaries that divided people.

Cosmopolitanism and Utopia

Before examining what Cai meant by aesthetics and aesthetic education, we should continue to look at his views on the social organization of labor and on historical progress. Like several late Qing intellectuals, Cai wrote a fictional "utopia" in the first years of the twentieth century. Unlike Kang (or Bellamy and other Western utopian writers), he was not interested in explaining precisely how the world gets from here to the perfect future, but simply offered a sketch of that future.

Cai's framed his utopia as a dream—"New Year's Dream." Cai was inspired by vision of pure cosmopolitanism, but the story largely focused on China.[4] The main character of Cai's short story is named, without subtlety, "China-Citizen" (*Zhongguo yi min*).[5] China-Citizen lived not in an era of world government but a recognizably colonial world.

China-Citizen moved to China's trading ports to learn English, French, and German before traveling to those countries, studying technology and philosophy. Making his way home through Russia after some fifteen years of hard work abroad, China-Citizen concluded that the world was not ready for a truly cosmopolitan order (*shijie zhuyi*). Rather, he carped, while peoples of the civilized world wasted half their strength on their own household and half on their nation, the Slavic and Chinese peoples do not even have nations but only their private households.[6] The first task was thus to create a new nation—the Chinese could do this simply by shifting their energies to public service. Yet, back in his homeland, China-Citizen was disgusted to see apathy around him even as Russia and Japan fought over Chinese territory.[7]

Next, home in bed, China-Citizen was awaked by the pealing of bells, which he followed to a large assembly hall. Here he found hundreds and hundreds of people—representatives of various regions of China—being urged by a speaker to fight for their country. The Chinese people cannot stand by while foreign powers fight over their country. And if the Chinese do not resist now, they might never again have the chance to build the China that they imagined. The speaker insisted on the one hand that the Qing policy of neutrality only reflected the view of a few idiots. But on the other hand, too many people thought only of their own families. The speaker incidentally noted the importance of democracy: "Of course we still cannot say that today's world is united, but the ideas of the majority are always stronger than those of the minority."[8] And also the importance of a quasi-socialist karmic principle: "If we want to completely get rid of the old methods, we have to establish a new rule: the amount of effort a person makes determines what benefits that person will receive; if people do not put forth the effort, they will not receive the benefits."[9]

In the next section of "New Year's Dream" China-Citizen was given a brochure that emphasized the need to understand China's natural resources, demography, geography, institutions, and economy—for example, details on how many people are employed, at what occupations, how many are disabled, how many are at retirement age, and so forth. The brochure suggested that along with farms, schools, and factories, China would build public dining halls, parks, hospitals, dormitories, nurseries, retirement homes, and so forth. The final sections suggested that everyone would be educated from the age of seven to to the age of twenty, work from twenty to forty-eight, and then retire, though allowed to work part-time, for example in education. The brochure further specified that the working day was to last eight hours, with equal time reserved for sleeping and leisure.

A question and answer period followed China-Citizen's reading of the brochure, and its idealism was put to the test. Who would be willing to take on hard jobs if their rewards were no greater than those for easier jobs? The answer was that people would choose the jobs they were most suited for—and also that machines could perform the most dangerous tasks while workers at truly arduous jobs would not have to work their full eight hours. But what about resistance from those who wield power today? Here the answer lay in the power of the majority over any such opposition of "public enemies."

"New Year's Dream" turned to a new brochure to raise the issue of imperialism and specifically the fight between Russia and Japan for dominance in Manchuria. This brochure proclaimed that a newly inspired Chinese army and militia could push back against Russia, while Chinese students appealed to Russian populists and Chinese diplomats found common ground with Japan. Chinese would be able to abolish the foreign spheres of influence in China once, following state reforms, they learned of their common identity. Chinese workers would refuse to work for the foreigners and the Chinese would announce that they were abrogating "uncivilized" treaties. Finally, all foreign trade in the future would be managed by the state; foreigners would be bound by Chinese law (instead of receiving extraterritorial privileges). If the foreigners did not recognize the justice of the Chinese case, the Chinese now had the resources, technology, skills, and of course righteousness to defeat foreign aggression.

So far, "New Year's Dream" encapsulated the major themes of late Qing revolutionary nationalism: the incompetence of the Manchu rulers; the capacity of China to strengthen itself through reform; and the appeal to rationality and justice (*gongli*). Then Cai imagined China attacked by the imperialist powers (excepting America and a revolutionary Russia). An attack China was now able to resist.

> Although we won the war, we didn't want to take advantage of this fact. With their armies scattered, we proposed a truce. We proposed establishing an international court and unifying the world's armies. The composition of the court and army was to reflect the population of each country. Aside from

domestic police forces, no one could maintain their own armies. If two countries quarreled, the case would be decided by the international court. In cases of disobedience, the World Army would deal with them; and in cases where the people of a country objected to the government, they could sue in the international court.[10]

"New Year's Dream" thus moved from nationalism to a distinctly cosmopolitan vision. Mr. China-Citizen has completely disappeared from the story by this point. It is China that has led the way to a world of peace and happiness, but China does not seek dominance.

As Cai reflected on how this world would operate, much of what he had to say resembled Kang Youwei's *Datong*. Marriage was made by contract—and prostitution and adultery disappeared. People had no more need of names—that is, family identities—and so identified themselves only by numbers. People who did not work were punished—but soon criminality disappeared. The technologies of communication and transportation improved—and language was transformed. (Here, Cai went beyond anything Kang had imagined.) Language evolved so that cursing disappeared. Also, adjectives such as *good* and *evil*, and nouns like *kindness* and *resentment*, disappeared, presumably because a perfect world required no need to make judgments. Perhaps most significantly for Cai's later thought, he proposed that expressions differentiating between "I" and "you" would disappear. Finally, and naturally enough, all countries agreed to abolish national boundaries; the international court and army fell into desuetude; humanity devoted itself to the conquest of nature, command of the weather, control of the atmosphere, and eventually colonization of the stars. The story ended with Mr. China-Citizen awakening to a world that was still dark, but he remained convinced that the new year was leading to a new world.

As with many utopias, the fictional framework of "New Year's Dream" is thin, and Cai never again tried to imagine a complete utopia. But at the same time, this vision of the dissolution of boundaries was to inspire much of his work as an educator, inserting a radical impulse into his moderate-seeming calls for intellectual toleration and inclusiveness, freedom of thought, and character training.

"New Year's Dream" was not Cai's first effort to imagine how boundaries could be abolished. A few years earlier, in a somewhat eccentric essay he wrote in 1900 as the Boxer Uprising was reaching its climax, he looked to Buddhism to "protect the nation." Cai seemed to argue that the true and original democratic impulse of Confucianism had long been lost and corrupted; much the same was true of historical Buddhism.[11] Cai's views owed something to the arguments of the 1898 reformers, especially Tan Sitong, though Cai's contempt and hatred of Christianity set him apart.[12] By 1900, Cai had begun to think his way through Chinese and Western traditions, and looked to the Shinshū sect of Pure Land Buddhism and the Japanese reformer and philosopher Inoue Enryō (1858–1919), who sought to make Buddhism compatible with modern science and to give it a role in the "protection of the state." The point here, however, is that while Cai, too, wanted to rid Buddhism of its superstitious elements and turn it into a modern educational tool, he ended his essay with a utopian view of evolution that would turn humans into literally spiritual beings. Cai not only called for vegetarianism, but he predicted that science would progress to the point we could abstain from eating living animals, and even plants, and even the microfauna found in a drop of water (a problem that had also exercised Kang Youwei). Before his encounter with Kant, Cai was searching for a means to achieve transcendence. In his discussion of the need to abolish marriage, Cai predicted that, as Herbert Spencer supposedly showed, evolution will progress beyond the material. In Buddhism Cai first saw a means to protect the state, but this led him to a vision of the elimination of the boundaries of the body.

> One day in the future when evolution reaches its highest point, people will be able to couple in a purely spiritual fashion, without bodily contact. When they have become eternal, without birth or death, there will be nothing to be gained by intercourse between male and female, and the custom of marriage will naturally disappear.[13]

The Ecstatic Moment: 1918

Cai accepted appointment as chancellor of Peking University under a warlord government in 1917. He fully partook of the general euphoria following the Allied victory in World War I and the Russian Revolution. Like many, initially at least, he saw that victory as a victory for the laboring masses of the world. In particular, Cai emphasized the "sacrality of labor," including mental labor. "Today's world is the world of workers."[14] The Allied victory represented the defeat of evil: in particular, social parasites such as the heirs to great fortunes, corrupt and traitorous officials, military officers, rapacious merchants, and the like. In an earlier lecture, Cai had already emphasized that a system of labor cooperation ultimately depended on its becoming a global system.[15] The Allied victory could thus be seen as contributing to the development of such a system. More generally, Cai noted the growth of cooperation through ascending orders of complexity, from the family, the simplest unit to raise the young and care for the old; to the community, which protected and educated its members; and now to provinces and countries, which provided better transportation and schools. This fundamental trend, Cai said, was leading to a global system where no place would be isolated, all burdens shared, rescue from natural disaster available, and war, whether commercial or military, abolished.

At the same time, however, Cai warned against excessive liberty and self-indulgence.[16] Cai sought balance. Liberties of thought, speech, domicile, occupation, and the like were all worth fighting for but should not become excessive. Self-indulgence was the enemy of liberty. In obtaining freedom from the dogmas of religion and the demands of custom, people had to rely on their consciences. Cai did not exactly explain what the conscience was, but he gave examples of how it worked. Cai said self-indulgence was when improper thoughts overcame one's conscience. Examples of conscience then included moderate habits versus overeating, drinking, and irregular sleeping; freedom of speech versus violating others' privacy or plotting evil; freedom of occupation versus adulterating goods or poisoning food. In sum, legitimate liberty lay in respecting the liberties of others. Cai praised the French Revolution but condemned Robespierre and Danton for bringing about an age of Terror. This was a case of self-indulgence turning into actual cruelty. Interestingly, Cai condemned the contemporary English suffragettes for similarly taking a good cause to extremes. Their threatening to burn mail and destroy artwork was, for Cai, another case of self-indulgence turning into violence.

But a balance between study and work offered one solution to the threat of excessive liberty. It is scarcely surprising that Cai would have welcomed the Diligent-Work Frugal-Study Society of 1915, one of a series of organizations founded by Li Shizeng that were devoted to the goal of combining work and school—in this case by sending workers to European factories during World War I. Cai began by noting the inevitability of the division of labor.[17] He emphasized that the exchange of goods is morally legitimate because (or when) it is mutual and does not involve exploitation. Humans cannot survive without labor, and, bringing the issue back to education, Cai pointed out that labor involves skills. Humanity has depended on teachers from ancient times, while today we have technical schools. Yet the pressure on workers to earn money was inherently unfair, and prevented them from studying. Hence the desirability of organizations that promoted work-study. Cai concluded with a reference to the anarchist utopian ideal of "from each according to ability, to each according to need," contrasting this to the reality of the present day. However, the real utopian thrust of Cai's vision of education lay not in the mere hope that workers would require better skills, much less that students would become workers, but rather derived from the thought that the best technical education was insufficient to living a good life. All branches of learning, Cai said, were relevant to the various jobs.

> Life has limits, but knowledge is limitless. We can live by eating and drinking, but the hunger and thirst of its principles may lie deeper than eating and drinking. To like beautiful colors and to detest ugly smells is enough to provoke feelings, but the impulse behind aesthetic feeling lies beyond color and smell.[18]

Cai thus advocated general education that would effect an impartial love of learning.

Cai rejected social Darwinism, believing that social evolution depended less on competition and raw power, and more on mutual aid as theorized by Kropotkin. He called the Allied victory of 1918 a victory of right over might, of light over darkness.[19] Although many Chinese initially regarded the European War as a fight between imperialist powers in which China had no direct stake, China had eventually joined the Allies, declaring war on Germany in 1917. While not engaged in the fighting, more than one hundred thousand Chinese workers were sent to England and France to work in factories and transport. The Allied victory was thus a Chinese victory. Cai was not alone in regarding the end of the war as proof that "the strength of justice is truly omnipotent." He gave a speech supporting students' efforts to organize education for the common people—itself an expression of the utopian idealism of the day—titled "The Ebb and Flow of the Dark and the Light." Cai cited the Zoroastrian struggle of light and dark, which light ultimately wins.[20] Thus, "the evolution of the world." Individual victories may be small, but they build up. As for big victories, the French Revolution abolished inequality in French politics, and the Allied victory of 1918 would abolish international inequality.

Cai discussed the "victory of light" in four aspects. First, the rise of the theory of mutual aid, which Cai, in effect, believed linked morality to biological evolution. Darwinian versions of competition left no space for justice (*gongli*), but the fossil record actually proved that individually weak but cooperative species such as bees and ants survive while species of isolated individuals, even if those individuals were strong, were eliminated. In the war, Cai thus concluded, Germany represented might and the Allies represented mutual aid.

Second, Cai found that conspiracies to dominate had been defeated by righteous, open alliances. Third, the war had led to the elimination of autocracy (*wuduan zhuyi*) and the development of mass democracy (*pingmin zhuyi*).[21] The German and Russian autocracies had both crumbled, while President Wilson's Fourteen Points, Cai thought, represented the global trend of democratization.

Cai finally concluded, fourth, that the elimination of racial prejudice and the Great Commonweal (*datong zhuyi*) were at hand. Following the historical ethnology of the day, Cai said that primitive peoples regarded all who were not members of their own clans as animals. They even practiced cannibalism. But then, gradually, culture progressed and the scope of human vision grew to encompass human equality. Cai also described a link between the advancement of knowledge and the enlargement of the scope of love (*ai*), that is, a creed that recognized the humanity of others. But in spite of such enlargement, he said, the distinction between self and others persisted, at least outside of the ivory tower of scholarship. Love—that is, equality—in the world of learning is universal, but boundaries persist outside that world. Indeed, the rotten roots of racial prejudice had persisted into the twentieth century, Cai said, inspiring the German attempts at world domination, for the Germans preached the doctrines of the "Yellow peril" and followed "blood and iron" policies.[22] They regarded whites as superior to blacks, Aryans as superior to Jews and Poles, and the German Teutons as superior to Anglo-Saxons and Latins. Therefore, Cai triumphantly concluded, the Allied victory brought together yellows and blacks along with whites to defeat the Germans. As various groups fulfilled new duties, their rights were gradually being equalized. Ireland has won home rule; Poland was recovered; the United States was recognizing the rights of blacks. The "national self-determination" preached by Wilson was already a success, Cai somewhat prematurely announced. "Does this not present us with the opportunity to build a perfect world (*datong zhuyi*)?"[23]

However, the elation of victory soon turned to disillusionment as the Versailles Peace talks dragged on in 1919, and it became clear that "national self-determination" did not apply to Asia or Africa or the Middle East or the Pacific. Nor did the end of World War I mean the end to the struggles of warlords in the divided China that had emerged after the 1911 Revolution. Chinese students were particularly angered by the victorious Allies' decision to turn the former German concessions in Shandong Province over to Japan—an anger that only intensified when it became apparent that the warlord regime in Beijing was complicit. A student demonstration in Beijing on May fourth led to a nationwide movement of demonstrations and boycotts, and in the end the Beijing government did not sign the Versailles Treaty.[24] From Cai Yuanpei's perspective as head of Peking University, the students, however justified their cause, threatened the intellectual life of the university. In a somewhat unfocused talk in March 1919, Cai urged students to consider the advantages of "scientific personal cultivation."[25] Conscience, at least in a purely natural form, was apparently an insufficient guide to action. But in the end Cai did not seem to have much faith that people were prepared to engage in scientific personal cultivation either. By cultivation, he meant a kind of training to learn how to make instant decisions as to right and wrong. Normally, there is time to consider what one should do, but sometimes one must decide immediately. In that case, one has to follow rules. Cai pointed out that all societies provide such rules, though they necessarily evolve over time. His first point was that we can no longer rely on the morality of the Neo-Confucianism of the Song and Ming; if the Neo-Confucians had devoted a great deal of thought to appropriate methods of self-cultivation, they had nonetheless had failed to make make people good. Cai seemed to feel at somewhat of a loss. His second point was that the old rules were no longer applicable, and retreat from the world is impractical. Yet modern pressures and responsibilities leave little time for spiritual cultivation. Presumably, Cai found some hope in the prospect of a scientific approach, but he seemed less than confident.

Two years after the war, Cai was even more cautious. But his fundamental teleology had not shifted. In a discussion of the development of education, he twinned the progress of knowledge with that of social organization: from clans to kingdoms to constitutional states.[26] The latter recognized both the liberties of its citizens and the duties they owed. Therefore, Cai said, education both had to foster "individual nature" so individuals could properly enjoy the liberties of thought, speech, and assembly, and had to foster "group nature," or the duties to pay taxes and serve as soldiers. Such was citizen's education (*guomin jiaoyu*). However, Cai found this inadequate. Education in the name of a militant citizenry, aristocracy, religion, or utility—that is, capitalism—could not provide true education in individualism. It was limited to civic rights (*minquan*) rather than human rights (*renquan*). Under this scheme, the entity to which duties were owed was the state. Progress, however, was leading humanity to transcend the state to become truly cosmopolitan. As evidence, following Kropotkin, Cai cited international organizations working in the fields of labor, agriculture, and charity. The proper goal of education, as far as Cai was concerned, was the development of the complete personality.

Cai's optimistic view of history thus revealed a strong utopian impulse. Cai did not believe that progress was driving humanity to a clear final goal. He did not share Kang Youwei's teleology, though he found "great commonweal thinking" (*datong zhuyi*) attractive. Cai's condemnation of the boundaries dividing people is also derived from Kang. But so far, we have only seen Cai's secular understanding of history. Grounded in a certain utopian impulse, but secular. Cai turned to metaphysical speculation to answer two further questions. First, why were boundaries wrong? And second, how can humanity abolish them? Cai's answers here were distinct from Kang's. Cai linked practical educational reforms to his metaphysical solution to the problem of the boundaries dividing humanity. Class, gender, nationality, and clan tottered before Cai's vision of individuation.

Aesthetics Education and the Noumenal

It may seem that Cai's commitments to cosmopolitanism and individualism left little basis for group solidarity. Indeed, while Cai did not deny the need for nationalism to accomplish certain immediate tasks, he criticized this limited solidarity. Nonetheless, he sought a higher solidarity. Individuation and self-cultivation were meant ultimately to show individuals how to recognize their common nature with all humanity.

Essentially, Cai believed that aesthetics education offered a way to bridge the conventional, temporal or "phenomenal" world (*xianshi*) and the world of fundamental reality or the "noumenal" world of the "thing-in-itself" (*shiti*).[27] And across this bridge, the illusionary distinction between self and other may be destroyed. What then opens up, presumably, is a kind of path toward ever-improving social consciousness and higher individual consciousness as well. This utopian view of the possibilities of the transformation of the self led Cai to an ambivalent view of the realm of the political. Cai cited Kant—whose understanding of aesthetics "no later philosophers have ever rebutted"—and Cai found in aesthetics both beauty and "awe" (*zunyan*), or the sublime (Ger. *Erhabenheit*). Cai discussed the possibility of achieving a state of transcendence through aesthetic appreciation in an essay he wrote when he became Minister of Education in the provisional revolutionary government of 1912.[28] Although evidently written with an audience of professional educators and bureaucrats in mind, "Some Opinions on the Direction of Education" dealt with matters usually considered far outside ordinary schooling.

Cai began by distinguishing between political education and education that goes beyond the political. His attitude toward political education was ambivalent. First, he equated it to the era of autocracies where educators simply followed the government's directions.[29] This is in contrast to the education of the republican era wherein educators based their standards on the position of the people: the first step of going beyond the political. But Cai also acknowledged the importance of "political education." Second, Cai noted that the educational reforms started by the Qing government in 1904 had begun with the goal of fostering a "militant citizenry," a goal now being superseded by socialism abroad, but a goal still necessary for self-defense in the case of a China under assault by stronger powers. And indeed Cai suggested that only a militant citizenry could now, in the wake of the "military revolution" of 1911, prevent an officer caste from coming to power. And third, Cai held that practical or vocational education was also necessary in a world of competition—and even that military power basically stemmed from economic might. This had also been one of the explicit goals of the Qing's political education, more or less directly training people for jobs. With other countries emphasizing vocational education, China—mired in poverty, its industries immature, and its resources undeveloped—could not ignore it.

A militant citizenry and vocational education, Cai said, represented the ideology of "strong army-wealthy country"—a phrase that had dominated Chinese political discourse for decades. But a strong military, Cai warned, had the potential of committing aggression while a wealthy country might increase the gap between the rich and the poor and end in a tragic struggle between capitalists and workers. Thus, "civic education" was needed to tame, in effect, the dangers of strength and wealth. For Cai, civic education consisted of the liberty, equality, and fraternity proclaimed in the course of the French Revolution. He then implied through a flurry of classical quotations that ancient China had produced equivalent moral ideals. "Righteousness" (yi), "reciprocity" (shu), and "benevolence" (ren) paralleled liberty, equality, and fraternity. The following represented *liberty*, which Cai said the Confucians had called "righteousness" (yi):

* Confucius—"The will of even a common man cannot be taken from him."[30]

* Mencius—"Great men are above the power of riches and honors to make dissipated, above the power of poverty and mean condition to make swerve from principle, and above the power of coercion and force to make bend."[31]

Likewise, according to Cai, *equality* was what the Confucians had called "reciprocity" (shu):

* Confucius—"What you would not have done unto yourself, do not do unto others."[32]

* Zigong—"What I do not wish men to do to me, I also wish not to do to men."[33]

* "Great Learning" chapter of the *Liji*—"What he hates in those who are before him, let him not therewith precede those who are behind him; what he hates in those who are behind him, let him not bestow on the left; what he hates to receive on the left, let him not bestow on the right."[34]

Here, Cai commented that individual liberty was subjective, but, with respect for the liberty of others, it becomes objective. Equality was objective, but it becomes subjective as a matter of treating others equally and insisting on equal treatment for oneself. Viewed as negative virtues, according to Cai, liberty and equality complement one another. But unless they are treated as a positive morality, natural deficiencies and conditions will prevent their practice. And the following notions, according to Cai, represent *fraternity*, which the Confucians called "humaneness" (*ren*):

> * Mencius—"Four classes of indigents, who had no one to speak for them, were officially recognized: the elderly man with no wife, the elderly woman with no husband, the elderly who had no children to support them, and the young who had no parents."[35]

> * Zhang Zai—"All under Heaven who are tired, crippled, exhausted, sick, brotherless, childless, widows or widowers—all are my siblings who are helpless and have no one else to appeal to."[36]

> * Confucius—"The man of perfect benevolence, wishing to be established himself, seeks also to establish others; wishing to be enlarged himself, he seeks also to enlarge others."[37]

And Cai further found worthy exemplars of this principle in the (mythical) sage-kings. Yu said that if anyone in the kingdom were drowned, it was as if he drowned them; and Ji said that if anyone in the kingdom went hungry, it was as he himself starved them; and the minister Yi Yin thought that among all the people of the kingdom, even the private men and women, if there were any who did not enjoy such benefits as Yao and Shun conferred, it was as if he himself pushed them into a ditch.[38]

    Why did Cai try to explain the ideals of civic education in terms of the French Revolution and the ideals of the French Revolution in terms of the Confucian Classics? It may be that Cai's mind ran naturally to synthesis; as well, given his audience of often conservative educators, he may have been trying to find a legitimate pedigree for modern civic education.[39] It should be noted that Cai was *not* claiming that these Western ideals were derived from earlier Chinese discoveries, as the familiar "Chinese origins" theory (*Xixue Zhongyuan*) proclaimed. (This approach to Western concepts, seen often since the late Qing could be a form of special pleading.)[40] Rather, Cai was offering *interpretations* of the Western concepts of liberty, equality, and fraternity. He seemed to be saying that Western concepts could be understood in Confucian terms. The result was a hermeneutics whose goal was to provide explanations, not equivalences. Thus, liberty, which would seem at first glance to have very little to do with *yi*/righteousness, is a highly moral concept as seen through the Confucian lens. It refers to the individual will, quite specifically the will to hold steadfast to the good. To adopt Isaiah Berlin's famous distinction, Cai believed in "positive liberty" (self-ful-fillment and agency) and was not speaking here to "negative liberties" (freedom from external restraints).[41] Insofar as equality rests on respect for others, or an acknowledgment of their humanity on a par with one's own, it serves as a check on liberty (negative liberty). Fraternity, in this Confucian perspective, represented a kind of extension of equality, but rooted in a clearer sense of common humanity, especially empathy for the oppressed. Fraternity was a moral demand to take responsibility for others' suffering.

Similarly, the term *shu*/reciprocity does not *translate* "equality" but rather explains its moral basis in terms of mutual respect. Cai's audience would have recognized the original contexts of his citations, which were based on discussions of the meaning of virtue and of how rulers can secure their legitimacy. *Ren*/humaneness does not translate "fraternity" (which Cai actually translated as "intimacy," *qin'ai*), but interprets it as impartial empathy. Again, Cai's audience would have recognized the original contexts of his specific citations of this central Confucian concept, citations that emphasized the universality of *humaneness* (as opposed to other strands of "humaneness" in the tradition). By the time Cai was trying to think through the question of what a republic needed from its schools, much of his audience would also have been familiar with the late Qing turn to humaneness/*ren* as a kind of cosmic force.

Cai explained what the new republican government would and would not adopt from the existing Qing system. In 1906, the Qing's new Ministry of Education had announced five central goals for the embryonic school system: fostering loyalty to the emperor, honoring Confucius, public-spiritedness, militant citizens, and practical learning. While thus accepting, up to a point, the last three goals, Cai explicitly rejected the first two of these goals.[42] Loyalty to the emperor obviously had no place in republic. For Cai, Confucianism was more complex. He was careful not to reject Confucius or Confucianism; rather, his point was that "honoring Confucius" violated the tenets of religious freedom. At the same time, Confucian scholarship, as distinguished from a Confucian religion, could be dealt with separately.

So, having accepted the last three goals of the Qing system, Cai returned to his key distinction—between political education and education that goes beyond the political—in order to emphasize the limits of civic education.

> It may seem that education reaches its final goal in civic morality, but this is not the case. Education in civic morality is still unable to go beyond the political, and even what are considered to be the best political forms limit their goals to the achievement of the greatest happiness for the greatest number. Now, the greatest number is made up of the accumulation of individuals. The happiness of an individual stems from having good clothing and enough food and avoiding disaster and hardship—but this is simply the happiness of the phenomenal world. When the happiness of individuals accrues to form the happiness of the greatest number, this is still its goal. The discussions of a legislature, the actions of an executive, and the safeguards of a judiciary are simply this as well. And even if we progress to the point we can approach [such good political forms as] the public spirit of the Datong of the "Liyun," the golden age of the future of the socialists, and "from each according to abilities and to each according to needs," these are all still essentially no more than the happiness of the phenomenal world.[43]

Cai did not think that that there was anything wrong with happiness in the phenomenal world. Adequate material wealth is a necessity. But it is not sufficient. The basis of Cai's criticism of utilitarianism was not that the goal of happiness was wrong but that it did not take the noumenal world into account. He pointed out that happiness (in the phenomenal world) is inevitably extinguished upon death. That rule applies to nations and the whole world as well as to individuals; so, Cai asked, What is its value? Even here, Cai was not criticizing happiness or material good as such: he was simply warning that they could not be made into ultimate goals. People and institutions need a way to see beyond their immediate interests. The goal of fostering this "happiness" is the realm of politicians, not educators.

What, then, was the proper concern of educators? For Cai, their proper concern lay in opening a way to the noumenal world. He emphasized that there were not in fact two distinct worlds but only one—

phenomenal and noumenal are like two sides of a sheet of paper. There is no contradiction between them, and it is not necessary to reject one in order to achieve the other. It is probable that Cai conceived of the phenomenal world as the site where the political goal of happiness was properly pursued, and the noumenal world where, say, spiritual insight could help to emancipate people from the phenomenal world. It is certain that Cai believed that if people grasped the noumenal world, they would radically change this phenomenal world.

In spite of his emphasis on the unity of the phenomenal and the noumenal, for Cai, the noumenal was the higher, superior realm, even while it was somehow rooted in the phenomenal—the "happiness" of the latter necessary to approach the more basic goal. At least, it was useful to discuss the phenomenal and the noumenal as if they were in fact separate worlds: the world of phenomena or everyday reality is "relative" while the noumenal world is "absolute," Cai said. For the phenomenal world is regulated by cause and effect, while the noumenal world transcends cause and effect; the former is inextricably bound by space and time, the latter is free of space and time; and the former is subject to experience, the latter is felt intuitively. And the noumenal world is ineffable, though as a kind of concept it has to have some kind of name: Dao, Supreme Ultimate (*taiji*), God (*shen*), "dark consciousness," and "unconscious will"—for Cai, these terms were all feeble expressions of the same concept. Although Cai was often critical of religion, in this essay he gave it equal status with philosophy as possessing a grasp of the noumenal. Equally, he condemned world-denial, whether religious (Buddhism?) or philosophical (Schopenhauer?). But why did some people find a contradiction between the phenomenal and the noumenal in the first place? Cai explained:

> There are simply two forms of consciousness that block the noumenal world from within the phenomenal world. First, the distinction between self and other. Second, the search for happiness. Because everyone's ability to defend themselves differs, there are the strong and the weak; and because everyone's ability to prosper differs, there are the rich and the poor. These differences give rise to the distinction between self and other. The weak and the poor suffer from lack of happiness and so the consciousness of seeking happiness arises. Thus amid the various phenomena, multifarious boundaries divide

the self from others, contrary to the noumenal world. When the search for happiness fails, the suffering is endless. When it succeeds, too much searching swirls through the phenomena, and becomes divided from the noumenal world. If balance can be achieved and biological needs satisfied according to nature, then the seeking in the realm of consciousness is extinguished and the view of self and others transformed. When every distinct consciousness of the phenomenal world is blended together, then they can unite with the noumenal world. Therefore, it cannot be doubted that the happiness of the phenomenal world is a kind of function enabling unhappy humanity to approach the noumenal world. The ideals of a militant citizenry and vocational education improve people's ability to defend themselves and to prosper, while moral education enables them to support each other and cooperate with each other. All three ideals thus act to destroy seeking and to forget the distinction between self and others. From here, we can progress to promoting education in the concept of the noumenal.

What are the methods of promoting the concept of the noumenal? The negative method is to approach the phenomenal world with neither denial nor with attachment. The positive method is to wish for the noumenal world and gradually become enlightened. Following public practices of freedom of thought and freedom of speech, and avoiding the shackles of a single school or sect, our goal is only an unbounded and infinite worldview. I cannot name this kind of education, but it might be called "worldview education."

However, worldview education cannot be achieved simply by calling for it. Furthermore, its relationship to the phenomenal world is not such that it can simply be captured in a few tired phrases. How, then, can it be achieved? The answer is: through aesthetics education. Aesthetic feeling encapsulates both beauty and awe, and it forms a bridge across the divide of the phenomenal and noumenal worlds. It was created by Kant, and no philosopher since has differed from him. In the phenomenal world ordinary people all experience feelings of like and dislike, surprise and fear, delight and anger, sadness and happiness—and then the phenomena of separation and unity, life and death, and disaster and good fortune spread. As for art, it uses these phenomena as its raw material and allows those who experience it nothing except their own aesthetic pleasure. For example, gathering lotuses and cooking beans are a question of eating, but once they are in a poem they become of interest. Volcanic fires and storm-tossed boats are terrifying sights but once in a painting they become enjoyable. This is the meaning of having neither denial nor attachment in regard to the phenomenal world. If we can leave behind the relativistic feelings of all phenomena and turn them all into aesthetics, then we can become what is called friends with the Creator and touch the concept of the noumenal world. Therefore, educators who wish to approach the concept of the noumenal world from the phenomenal world must use aesthetics education.[44]

Cai thus laid out a vision of education that claimed certain con-tinuities with late Qing goals and the entire Confucian tradition but also staked out new ground. The five areas that Cai wanted schools to emphasize—military, utilitarian, ethical, worldview, and aesthetic educa-tion—would, taken together, produce good citizens who also understood the existence of something beyond everyday life.[45] By "worldview edu-cation" (shijieguan jiaoyu), Cai was evidently referencing the German "Weltanschauung," which had become associated with the ideal of a general humanistic education. Cai's "New Year's Dream" had found a plan and a transcendental goal. Cai's foray into Buddhism had hinted at a desire to transcend the body and reach a spiritual state. His 1912 essay on the goals of education combined Kantian perspectives on aesthetics and on the noumenal to promote abolishing the final boundary—that of selfhood.

In the following year, 1913, notwithstanding political defeats and dangers, Cai was cautiously optimistic that people could bring the phenomenal and noumenal worlds together.[46] His essay on "Worldview and Lifeview" was written in a more metaphysical vein, though from an evolutionary point of view. Cai started with the observation that individual human beings were limited entities that could not transcend their particular times and places. However, they shared a common nature precisely as elements in a larger world. It is human consciousness (yishi) that links all the individual entities of the world. Now, human consciousness takes materiality and form, but the will (*yizhi*) can transcend materiality and form and is unrestrained. Cai thus claimed that the will represents the common nature of every human and that this was also the fundamental nature of the world.

Cai asserted that as long as individual human wills were devoted to achieving certain objectives, they took material form and were bound by the laws of cause and effect. However, all of these wills did tend toward the noumenal world. In the noumenal world, the will has no objectives but is "dark" or "blind." The "final great goal," then, "is to unify all the individuals of the world in a tight relationship so that differences between self and other never arise again, and the phenomenal world and the noumenal world intersect at a single point."[47] Cai was not saying, in my reading, that humans should live in the noumenal world but that in recognition of the fundamental identity of all the elements of the world, the phenomenal and noumenal meet. Cai said that religion promised that people could make a sudden leap to achieve the collective identity or "great self" (*dawo*) of the noumenal world. However, at this time, our use of language limits us to gradual methods—pursuing small steps in an incremental process, or "evolution."

Cai's view of evolution was distinctly orthogenic.[48] The progress of human consciousness is leading toward the intersection of the phenomenal and the noumenal worlds. He pointed to inorganic matter, whose particles are unrelated to one another but which evolved into plants, whose cells in effect cooperate with another, and animals, which develop relationships of kinship and friendship. Then the human species developed ever-increasing forms of mutual relationships—from kinship and societies to nations and global organizations. This is the march toward growing interconnectedness (*tong*), and undifferentiatedness (*tong*).[49] Cai celebrated the growth of material civilization and scientific knowledge. This has led humans to recognize their common humanity, and even the commonalities they shared with animals. Cai pointed to vegetarianism as an example of consciousness that transcended previous distinctions such as those between kin and non-kin, and between human and animal. He directly linked material progress to cultivation of the spirit—a theme that was to become central to the utopian impulse that shaped Hu Shi's thought. Cai insisted that science and art were in the midst of becoming "universal." Ultimately, then, "Science is what will eliminate the obstacles of the phenomenal world and bring about enlightenment. And art is what will describe the phenomena of the noumenal world and spark people into enlightenment."[50] Finally, then, evolution is directed toward the group, not the individual; toward the future, not the present; and toward the spirit, not the body. Cai's rejection of everything associated with Darwinism at the time could not be clearer.

In later years—exile again, triumphant return to head up Peking University, stalwart supporter of the Guomindang, founder of Academia Sinica, and disillusioned liberal—Cai frequently spoke of the importance of art and aesthetics education in shaping the moral individual and a good society. Not as often, but sometimes, he still referred to the power of aesthetics to break down the "bias" of the self-other distinction. Writing at the end of 1919 to again warn students against extremism in their "culture movement," Cai began by pointing out the complexity of culture.[51] In effect, he urged students to use science to understand the nature of culture and to use aesthetics learn how to "practice" it.[52] Aesthetics education was necessary "to raise interest in transcending personal interests, unify the partiality of the distinction between self and others, and maintain a sense of perpetual harmony"—otherwise the cultural movement would become corrupt.

Even in the tumultuous year of 1919, Cai saw the need to commit to a long process of building civilization. There would be specialized schools; in addition to the sciences, there should be schools and graduate schools devoted to art, art history, music, acting, crafts, and so forth. Next would come a whole world of public museums displaying art loaned by private collectors or purchased with public funds, as well as art exhibitions, musical concerts, and plays. People would live on streets lined with trees and flowers, with public plazas, fountains, and sculptures. Cities would have parks to preserve natural environments. Capable artists would produce not only beautiful public and private architecture, but utensils, printing, and even advertisements.

In other words, according to Cai, living amid beauty people would experience lively and uplifting sentiments. This perhaps represented a secular view of utopia that we will return to below. Here, it is only important to note that as late as the 1930s Cai at least occasionally revisited the metaphysical notion that aesthetics could nourish the dissolution of the distinction between self and other.[53] This startling, even bizarre proposal was based on Cai's understanding of Kantianism as he had come to learn of it through Friedrich Paulsen, some of whose works he translated, as well as his teachers Lamprecht and Wundt.[54] Perhaps one of the appeals of Kropotkin's theory of mutual aid to Chinese intellectuals like Cai was that it tempers the meaninglessness of Darwinian selection with a kind of morality. (That Darwinian selection was often regarded as goal-producing in the form of hierarchies of races and species, as taught in social Darwinism, is besides the point here.) And perhaps one of the appeals of the Kantian notion of the noumenal or thing-in-itself was that it seems to temper the harshness of a purely material, atomistic world with the promise of higher meaning.

Cai and Kantianism

Chinese thinkers were initially unsympathetic to Kant. What Joachim Kurtz has called the "Kantian challenge" lay in the epistemological problem whereby "Chinese thinkers understood the limits of human knowledge delineated in Kant's *Critique of Pure Reason* as a potentially lethal threat to the ethical maxims enshrined in classical Chinese texts."[55] A key problem for certain Chinese was precisely the Kantian notion of "thing-in-itself" (*Dinge an sich*) or "noumenon." They distrusted the notion of a gap between phenomena (which are known to the senses and understood through mental processes) and noumena (which may exist but cannot be known directly). For if we cannot have direct knowledge of the world of noumena, how can we trust our moral intuitions? However, neo-Kantianism came to dominate the field of philosophy in Meiji Japan, and many Chinese students began to absorb Kantian concepts there. Cai went closer to the source. Cai's use of the term *shiti* (true body, fundamental substance) to represent Kant's "noumenal" was one of several common translations, including that of the greatest of the early Chinese scholars of Kant, Wang Guowei. To Chinese thinkers, *shiti* implied a world of "reality" not entirely suitable to the degree of doubt that Kant seems to have surrounded the term with. However, Cai's emphasis on the unknowability of the world of *shiti* reflected Kant's own emphasis. It was in their use of the concept that they differed: Cai was committed to the idea that knowledge of the noumenal world could remake the world of phenomena, the everyday world.

According to Cai's own account, it was at Leipzig under the instruction of Wundt that he encountered Kant's theory of the transcendence and universality of aesthetics.[56] It is not my purpose to delineate specific influences on Cai's thought but rather highlight common themes and divergences.[57] The following highly partial discussion of Kant highlights elements of Kant's aesthetics that seem to have particularly impressed Cai. Ironically, while Cai had little original to say about aesthetics, he had a great deal to say about art education, while Kant neglected what we might call the practical applications of his theory of aesthetics.[58]

According to scholars of Kant, his aesthetics is inseparable from his view of the possibility of judgment and his teleology and was, indeed, basically formulated to solve problems that his earlier work on "reason" had raised.[59] Cai's interests lay more in the relationship between aesthetics, morality, and transcendence, but he could not ignore the question of the validity of taste. Kant began with the subjective sense of pleasure. This was a kind of natural response to beauty (and the distinction from ugliness), whether found in nature or art. "Four moments" of the judgment of taste refer to quality, quantity, relations, and modality. Eva Shaper summarizes the development of taste according to Kant: "That is beautiful which is felt with disinterested pleasure (first moment). Calling something beautiful we deem it an object of universal delight (second moment). We discern in it 'the form of finality perceived without the representation of a purpose' (third moment). And we claim not only that it pleases but that it does so necessarily, and without concepts (fourth moment)."[60] For beauty to reflect an aesthetic judgment, the pleasure one takes in it must be disinterested, and it is enjoyed for its own sake through both imagination and understanding. Such is not necessarily true of the simply "agreeable," which reflects (subjective) sensory gratification. Beauty is subjective insofar as its experience is internal, but it is universal insofar as all who experience it have the same feeling.

This gives rise to the obvious paradox that a subjective sense can be a universal judgment. Ultimately, Kant seems to suppose that, first, judgments of taste must be correctly made—that is in a disinterested way; and second, that under these conditions everyone will share the same tastes. "For the fact of which every one is conscious, that the satisfaction is for him quite disinterested, implies in his judgment a ground of satisfaction for every one."[61] Key to Kant's argument is the fact that people can communicate that which is produced by the play of imagination and understanding (taste), and hence taste is shared. Appreciation of beauty is not, then, entirely subjective as if it were privately sensed, but rather a public act in which everyone is taking into account the judgments of everyone else. Nonetheless, Kant begins with neither the development of good taste in the individual or the culture but rather a kind of instinctive response: a pleasure or satisfaction that, whatever it requires, does not require thinking. Beauty does not rest on concepts; it is in a sense a priori, which helps to explain its universality.[62] But our pleasure in beauty, resting on the play between imagination and understanding, is also universal since cognitive powers work the same way in all persons. Beauty still requires judgment, which stems from reflection on the origins of pleasure. And finally, as Paul Guyer summarizes, "It is on the basis of this reflection on one's pleasure that a claim of taste can be erected, for it is precisely the attribution of a particular feeling of pleasure to the harmony of the faculties which licenses the attribution of the pleasure to other persons, or a claim of intersubjective validity for the pleasure—the actual content of an aesthetic judgment."[63]

Kant considered that although the "sublime" was distinct from the beautiful, both represent aesthetic judgments. Both give rise to feelings of pleasure; both are based on reflection rather than cognition; the pleasure taken in both stems from the interplay of imagination and understanding; and both are universal. But unlike beauty, sublimity does not stem from form, for it is "limitless," and gives rise to "negative" pleasure or awe rather than a simpler sense of pleasure. Kant's distinction between the beautiful and the sublime rested on his teleology, or at least a sense of "purposiveness":

> Susceptibility to pleasure from reflection upon the forms of things (of Nature as well as of Art), indicates not only a purposiveness of the Objects in relation to the reflective Judgment, conformably to the concept of nature in the subject; but also conversely a purposiveness of the subject in respect of the objects according to their form or even their formlessness, in virtue of the concept of freedom. Hence the aesthetical judgment is not only related as a judgment of taste to the beautiful, but also as springing from a spiritual feeling is related to the *sublime*.[64]

The sublime, for Kant, seems to be something uncontrollable (formless, boundless), yet "is produced by the feeling of a momentary checking of the vital powers and a consequent stronger outflow of them." And "the satisfaction in the sublime does not so much involve a positive pleasure as admiration or respect, which rather deserves to be called negative pleasure."[65] As the mind controls, so to speak, or gets some handle on, the uncontrollable, sublimity is produced. Eva Schaper suggests that Kant felt that the sublime could intimate noumenal reality.[66] At any rate, the sublime, being formless, forces the mind to impose unity or "totality" on it. The sublime pleases as it causes "the mind to abandon sensibility, and occupy itself instead with ideas involving a high finality."[67] Certainly, Cai believed in the power of the sublime.

Kant distinguished between the "mathematically sublime" and the "dynamical sublime" in a way that focused on the subject rather than the object. Thus, the mathematically sublime referred to the "absolutely great" so that "the sublime is that in comparison with which everything else is small."[68] Although there is nothing in nature that is absolutely great in this sense (there is always something greater), such objects nonetheless can inspire a sense of the absolutely great and therefore the thought of the sublime. Or in Kant's terms, inspiring a vision (imagination) of the totality as infinite, which is beyond the senses, and which is indeed a reference to the noumenal. Thus, "Nature is therefore sublime in those of its phenomena, whose intuition brings with it the Idea of their infinity. . . . As this, however, is great beyond all standards of sense, it makes us judge as *sublime*, not so much the object, as our own state of mind in the estimation of it."[69] An example of this mathematical sublime is consideration of the infinite (boundless) vastness of the universe, which is essentially beyond imagination, but not beyond our reasoning abilities.

> The feeling of the Sublime is therefore a feeling of pain, arising from the want of accordance between the aesthetical estimation of magnitude formed by the Imagination and the estimation of the same formed by Reason. There is at the same time a pleasure thus excited, arising from the correspondence with rational Ideas of this very judgment of the inadequacy of our greatest faculty of Sense. . . . The mind feels itself *moved* in the representation of the Sublime in nature.[70]

The dynamical sublime, for Kant, refers to nature. For nature, insofar as it is sublime, excites fear, but a fear that in turn inspires resistance. Fear itself is meaningless or counterproductive if it only induces terror and retreat. But if it is, in effect, managed—through resistance, or courage—then a different kind of gap is created between what is sensed and what can be understood. Finding sublimity in nature is not so automatic, so to speak, as in the case of finding beauty, because culture plays a larger role. In Kant's words, "In fact, without development of moral Ideas, that which we, prepared by culture, call sublime, presents itself to the uneducated man merely as terrible . . . he will only see the misery, danger, and distress."[71] Nonetheless, Kant continues, the sublime "has its roots in human nature" and ultimately practical ideas and hence moral feeling. Given the existence of any culture at all, then, all humans develop moral feeling, and the sense of sublimity is universal. Simply put, in its dynamical form, sublimity arises in the mind when it is threatened with overwhelming force:

> Bold, overhanging, and as it were threatening rocks, clouds piled up in the sky, moving with lightning flashes and thunder peals, volcanoes in all their violence of destruction, hurricanes with their track of desolation; the boundless ocean in a state of tumult; the lofty waterfall of a mighty river, and such like; these exhibit our faculty of resistance as insignificantly small in comparison with their might. But the sight of them is the more attractive, the more fearful it is; provided only that we are in security; and we readily call these objects sublime, because they raise the energies of the soul above their accustomed height, and discover in us a faculty of resistance of a quite different kind, which gives us courage to measure ourselves against the apparent almightiness of nature.[72]

And sublimity lies in "a superiority to nature even in its immensity," because, although human beings are physically impotent in comparison to the might of nature, our judgment remains independent, and thus we are not subject to its "dominion." Kant also considered the sublimity of religion, concluding that fear of God did not mark the sublime, but true reverence and commitment to a good life marked a sublime state of mind. Sublimity resides in security. "*Astonishment*, that borders upon terror the dread and the holy awe which seizes the observer at the sight of mountain peaks rearing themselves to heaven, deep chasms and streams raging therein, deep-shadowed solitudes that dispose one to melancholy meditations—this, in the safety in which we know ourselves to be, is not actual fear, but only an attempt to feel fear by aid of the Imagination."[73]

For the most part, Kant regarded aesthetics as an autonomous realm, and therefore not a guide to morality. He did speak of beauty as "the symbol of morality,"[74] and of the "ideal of beauty" or, in Paul Guyer's description, "a sense of harmony between the outward form and the invisible moral virtue of a human being."[75] But this was only one aspect of beauty and not a very substantive link to morality. Rather, aesthetics and morality were analogous to some degree, but distinct. A key reason why morality and aesthetics were distinct lay in the disinterestedness of the latter. In Kant's words, "The Beautiful, the judging of which has at its basis a merely formal purposiveness, *i.e.* a purposiveness without purpose, is quite independent of the concept of the Good; because the latter presupposes an objective purposiveness, *i.e.* the reference of the object to a definite purpose."[76] However, Paul Crowther argues that Kant regarded the *sublime* itself as a moral concept.[77] And indeed Kant noted that "a feeling for the Sublime in nature cannot well be thought without combining therewith a mental disposition which is akin to the Moral."[78]

For our purposes, it seems fair to conclude that if Cai Yuanpei regarded the sublime as possessing moral implications, he was not betraying Kant. Nonetheless, whatever Kant's views, Cai had no interest in dividing aesthetics as a whole from morality. Nor was Cai much concerned with what was perhaps Kant's central problem: how can a sense of beauty, which is inherently subjective, lay claim to any kind of universal truth?[79] Indeed, many of Kant's concerns—including larger questions of judgment, the realms of cognition and morality, the Christian religion, the entire system of transcendental idealism; and even aesthetic concepts such as the notion of genius in art, the distinction between fine arts and nature, and the like—were of relatively little interest to Cai. For Cai, what mattered was the notion that beauty—and perhaps especially the sublime—provides a universal experience. However, he could not derive from Kant the notion that the sublime actually erases the boundaries between self and other. Rather, Cai seems to have had confidence in the knowability of the noumenal world, or at least that the noumenal world was sufficiently knowable to provide a basis for practice.

Distinguishing the realm of aesthetics from the realms of science and morality, Cai borrowed a Buddhist term for the "self" to explain Kantian aesthetics.[80] However, it is not entirely clear what Cai meant by concluding that the concept of self-as-illusion (*woxiang*) is the thing-in-itself (*benti*) of the unimaginably powerful sublime. Perhaps this was a reference to the neo-Kantian view that experience of the sublime leads to self-forgetfulness as the self is overmastered by an outside force.[81] Cai believed at least in some sense that that the concept of the self is a delusion, blocking realization of the unity of self and other. This is why he looked to aesthetics, particularly the sublime, to provide a kind of route into the noumenal. In Buddhism, selfhood—at least the reification of the self as opposed to self-nature—is an obstacle to enlightenment. The term *woxiang* is central to both the *Diamond Sutra* and the *Sutra of Perfect Enlightenment*. The *Diamond Sutra* was a very early Sanskrit text first translated into Chinese at the beginning of the fifth century. In it, the "concept of self" is the first of four concepts, or "marks" or "traces," that enlightened beings and Buddhas know not to exist, along with concepts of others, sentient beings, and life.[82] The tone in the *Sutra of Perfect Enlightenment*, probably an early eighth-century Chinese work, is slightly different. It notes that the "concept of self" is the first of four delusions that prevent one from achieving enlightenment: "From beginningless time all sentient beings deludedly conceive and attach to the existence of 'self,' 'person,' 'sentient being' and 'lifespan.'"[83]

For Cai, then, it is not meditation or some other discipline that leads one to abandon selfhood; rather, it is aesthetic experience that leads one to transcend selfhood.[84] What Cai seemed to be driving at was the sense that, when the ego is overpowered by an aesthetic experience, it feels oneness with the cosmos. Cai began by referring to Kant's definition of aesthetics in terms of four categories: transcendence, or complete disinterestedness; universalism, or that which is common to all persons; patterns, or entirely intrinsic purpose; and necessity, or that which is inherent in humanity. Now, Cai said, the need to develop humanism is widely acknowledged, but it is blocked by the ego (*zhuanjixing*). But the transcendent and universal can conquer the ego. For aesthetics refers not merely to the delicately beautiful but to the "beauty of the overmastering." When one encounters that which is great beyond any calculation and strong beyond any resistance, one does not at first feel aesthetic appreciation, but one intuitively and even unconsciously comes to realize in the face of its power how tiny and weak is one's small self.

If Cai could not directly derive his belief that the distinction between self and other could be surmounted by using Kant's aesthetics, Friedrich Schiller (1759–1805) directly or indirectly could have supplied Cai with some of the conceptual apparatus he needed to link beauty, freedom, and goodness.[85] Schiller's gestures toward the infinite and absolute may have confused Kant's distinction between the beautiful and the sublime, but they helped Cai to attribute great power to aesthetics as such. Deliberately or not, Schiller's *Letters on the Aesthetic Education of Mankind* (1793–96) moved beyond Kant.[86] Without attempting the probably futile task of providing a systematic explanation of Schiller's thought (or even highlighting his main concerns), it is worth noting a tension in Schiller between individuation and cosmic unity. If the Buddhist notion of the illusion of distinctions probably lay behind some of Cai's thinking, the Christian notion of the immortality of the soul certainly lay behind Schiller's. In Letter Eleven, Schiller refers to the eternal aspect of the person in these terms: "It is not because we think, feel, and will that we are; it is not because we are that we think, feel, and will. We are because we are. We feel, think, and will because there is out of us something that is not ourselves." In the following Letter Twelve, Schiller distinguished physical existence (the sensuous instinct) from absolute existence (the formal instinct), linking the latter to rationality, harmony, and freedom.

> Accordingly, when the formal impulse holds sway and the pure object acts in us, the being attains its highest expansion, all barriers disappear, and from the unity of magnitude in which man was enclosed by a narrow sensuousness, he rises to the unity of idea, which embraces and keeps subject the entire sphere of phenomena. During this operation we are no longer in time, but time is in us with its infinite succession. We are no longer individuals but a species; the judgment of all spirits is expressed by our own, and the choice of all hearts is represented by our own act.

If this delirious prose is not specifically picturing the collapse of the distinction between self and other, it comes close to dissolving the self in some kind of universal flow.

Schiller also treated the division between humans and nature with great ambiguity. In Letter Twenty-five, he noted that, through the senses, the world appears as an objective reality that the personality may be "severed" from. That might be regarded as the first stage of aesthetic appreciation. But then, "That which first connects man with the surrounding universe is the power of reflective contemplation. Whereas desire seizes at once its object, reflection removes it to a distance and renders it inalienably her own by saving it from the greed of passion." Reflection, in turn, leads to command, through the freedom (not least freedom from terror) to mold nature, having understood it.

It thus seems that for Schiller, aesthetics refers to the transformation of nature into art. Probably here he was thinking of what Kant called the sublime, but perhaps he was thinking of all forms of beauty. At the same time, if not dissolving humans and nature into one another, Schiller does find in beauty the basis of social life. In Letter Twenty-seven he commented that "taste alone brings harmony into society, because it creates harmony in the individual. All other forms of perception divide the man, because they are based exclusively either in the sensuous [physical] or in the spiritual [absolute] part of his being. It is only the perception of beauty that makes of him an entirety, because it demands the cooperation of his two natures." It is beauty alone that can and does unite humanity. In Cai's hands, this view became the basis of this pedagogy. Cai may have read Wilhelm Windelband's history of philosophy, which treated Schiller as extending Kant's own theory of aesthetics by linking art and ethics more closely.[87] In Windelband's view, the *Letters on the Aesthetical Education of Mankind* taught that the "aesthetic condition, or state, because it is the completely disinterested state, destroys the sensuous will [working in the phenomenal world], also, and thus makes room for the possibility of the moral will; it is the necessary point of transition from the physical state, ruled by needs, into the moral state." For Windelband, Schiller was not so much departing from Kant as completing him; we might make the same claim for Cai.[88]

Mind, Aesthetics, and Religion

In a lecture given in the midst of World War I, Cai distinguished among "desirous beauty" (*yumei*), "true beauty" (*zhenmei*), and the sublime (lit., lofty, *gao*).[89] Desirous beauty worked through an appeal to the erotic. True beauty lay in the pleasure derived from descriptions that captured the true spirit of things, such as the light of the moon and sun, the clarity of clouds, and so forth. And the sublime was the artistic expression of terrifying phenomena, such as steering a ship through tumultuous seas and volcanic explosions—phenomena that conveyed terror. The sublime conveyed a kind of strength or power, but also, Cai seemed to be saying, a power that was tamed. But in the long run Cai was not much concerned with the distinction between the beautiful and the sublime: both could transform people.

Given the enormous power of beauty and the sublime, Cai believed that art should provide some of the functions traditionally held by religion—following a direction pioneered by Schiller. In Cai's 1917 essay "Replacing Religion with Aesthetics," he again noted that "pure aesthetics" could eliminate the distinction between self and other, and he explicitly emphasized the social utility of aesthetics.[90] Cai began with a standard New Culture critique of religion, dismissing contemporary religious practice as merely a relic of habit. Science was solving old religious questions, and religion itself had nothing to offer China today, whether in the form of Christianity or Confucianism. Nonetheless, in "primitive times" religion had met three spiritual needs: knowledge, will, and sentiment. It had answered basic questions such as the origins of the universe (through knowledge, *zhishi*). It had helped end a period of pure exploitation with doctrines of altruism (through will, *yizhi*). And it had fostered music, dance, and art (through sentiment, *qinggan*). However, the progress of knowledge demonstrated that religious answers were partial at best. People further came to realize that supposed mandates of the gods did not provide a sound basis for morality. Rather, numerous factors depending on time and place clearly formed moral beliefs. In time, then, the religious functions of knowledge and will decayed. Cai believed that the aesthetic spirit of religion continued longer. But the evolution of aesthetics had also moved beyond its religious origins. Tang dynasty poetry and Renaissance art had become more secular, while today it is schools, theaters, and museums that provide the highest expression of architecture.

In particular, Cai felt, links between religion and autocracy made religious aesthetics inappropriate for a republic. Religion also aroused the emotions in ways that could become pathological. Aesthetic education, on the contrary, could do what religions may have sometimes glimpsed but largely failed to accomplish.

> Through molding the sentiments of the people with pure aes-
> thetics, noble and pure habits will be fostered, and the view
> of self and other that seeks to benefit the self at expense of
> others will be gradually eliminated. And as beauty becomes
> universal, the view of the distinction between self and others
> will have no entry point. The food I personally eat cannot
> feed others, and the clothes I personally wear cannot warm
> others: this is because they are not universal. But beauty is
> not like this. For example, I have traveled in the hills west
> of Beijing, and others have also traveled in them: we have
> not inflicted any losses on one another.[91]

Cai claimed that beauty had been helping to extinguish the distinction between self and others for thousands of years, as people experienced aesthetic pleasures together. In ancient times, Egyptian pyramids and Greek temples; today, public museums, concerts, and theater.

At this point, Cai had not clearly distinguished between aesthetics or aesthetic education on the one hand, and art works on the other. But in 1930 Cai complained that people had misunderstood his call for aesthetics education to replace religion for the claim that art itself could replace religion.[92] Art itself was too limited to do any such thing, Cai pointed out. But aesthetics education was much broader. It included the arts such as painting, sculpture, and architecture, as well as music and literature, and also museums, theaters, movie houses, parks, cemeteries, city planning, and even the appearance of individuals and the organization of society, as well as opening sites of natural beauty to the public—everything that might be to some degree beautiful. Here, Cai was content to simply point out that the various social functions previously held by religion had been superseded by the arts broadly understood. He did not refer to a higher communal identity that aesthetics could provide. Cai merely stated that today science provides knowledge, while history and sociology guide morality, and so with all the modern disciplines. Religion still provides a source of beauty—in its buildings and music, for example—but only in ways bound to untenable claims. Only aesthetic education represented liberty, progress, and universalism.

Fifteen years after his first essay on the subject, Cai gave another lecture with the same title, "Replacing Religion with Aesthetics." In his 1932 version, Cai began by noting again that aesthetics or aesthetic education should not be confused with art itself.[93] Furthermore, he noted that "art" was limited to the visual and the auditory—pictures, architecture, music, and the like—and did not include the other three senses. But aesthetics was a broader category also including parks, landscaping, urban planning, village planning, and even individual activities, social organizations, scholarly groups, and every kind of social expression: all can be beautified. Aesthetics appealed to all the senses. As for religion, Cai again granted its original pedagogic function giving primitive people a sense of knowledge, morality, and even aesthetics. But today religion supplies nothing appropriate for a modern society. It offers only temporary comforts. Today, even morality should be studied scientifically, and religion is not a necessary basis for morality. As for aesthetics, Cai could not deny that religions had produced much beauty. But, "the materials that religion offers for aesthetic education are limited, while aesthetics is limitless. Aesthetics should have absolute liberty to nourish human sentiment. . . . Aesthetics must be completely independent, and only then can it preserve its position."[94] Religion is not only conservative but it is divided among various sects, while aesthetics evolves and is universal.

Cai based his insistence on the centrality of art to life on three aspects of human consciousness: aesthetics, science, and morality.[95] In a 1920 essay he rooted aesthetics in a sense of delight, science in knowledge, and morality in the will. Science lies in investigation and so distinguishes truth from falsity based on logical deduction. Morality lies in actual behavior, and so distinguishes the good from the bad based on ethical judgments. And the sense of beauty (*meigan*) lies in careful appraisal, and so distinguishes the beautiful from the ugly based on aesthetic judgment. The Kantian insistence on appraisal and not simply intuitive reaction to art also allowed Cai to unite these three aspects of consciousness while giving aesthetics a special place. In Cai's new formula, aesthetic pleasure diminishes consciousness of the self and so gives rise to humanism (*rendao zhuyi*).

In contrast to the scientism of the New Culture movement, Cai warned that science might lead to a purely mechanistic view of the world that left no room for freedom and will.[96] But properly understood, science plays an indispensible role in determining what was true, a necessary step in constructing a moral system. This approach is seen in another version of this tripartite division of human consciousness that Cai wrote about: truth, goodness, and beauty.[97] All people, Cai said, possessed a critical sense of right and wrong, good and evil, and beauty and ugliness. This is due to the psychological functions of knowledge, will, and sentiment, which seek, in effect, truth, goodness, and beauty. Of these three, goodness is central, while truth and beauty help to establish it. Thus, it is the will that forms a person. That said, all three "functions" are equally necessary. Goodness without truth tends to evil; while without beauty, goodness may be knowable but impossible to practice. Cai offered a little parable. People walk down a road to reach goodness, but they need lights (truth) to reach their goal at night, and pleasant songs and scenery (beauty) to combat their fatigue. Here, Cai did not privilege aesthetics, but rather criticized the pure aestheticism of artists who attempted to ignore morality.[98] (Just as scientific discoveries kill people as well as help them.) Cai cited Comte in tracing the search for the true, the good, and the beautiful to three stages of civilization: the theological, metaphysical, and scientific (or positivist), but he argued that for all the progress it had made, science could not resolve all the questions of the true, the good, and the beautiful. Cai concluded that both science and philosophy were needed.[99]

Nonetheless, Cai continued to insist that morality—that is, behavior as a function of will—could not be supported without aesthetic education.[100] Rational calculation (knowledge or science) was necessary to provide a basis for how to perform such tasks as self-preservation or defense of the nation. But Cai focused on the other side of morality, so to speak: willingness to undertake self-sacrifice and even death. That is, the sentiment nourished by aesthetic education. Cai found numerous examples of such education, in China and the West alike, but he said that the actual study of aesthetics only began in the eighteenth century with Alexander Gottlieb Baumgarten (1714–1762), followed by Kant and Schiller. In this essay of 1930, Cai was not concerned with the power of aesthetics to erase the distinction between self and other, but he continued to outline how aesthetics could create a utopian society. School, family, and society all have a role in aesthetics education. Cai predictably discussed how, in addition to art classes, school subjects such as language, history, and the sciences all have aesthetic aspects. For example, families should try to keep their homes clean and neat, ideally with yards full of plants and room for exercise.

But it is in his discussion of infrastructure that Cai leaves behind bourgeois respectability to envision how planning could help create "civilized people."[101] City planning was key. Cities needed water pipes and sewers attached to houses, not so much for hygiene as to keep from spoiling beauty sites. A mix of boulevards and small streets would meet at plazas, where the flower displays would be changed according to the season, and with fountains and art works such as statues of famous people or of myths and stories. Streets would be lined by trees, with sidewalks separated from the traffic. And while individuals had the right to build, their plans would need government approval. There would be public housing for the poor, and in addition to public schools, day care would be provided for orphans or children whose parents both had to work. As well, signage and shop displays must accord with regulations designed to avoid the unsightly. Cai hoped that motorized vehicles would be used; if this was not possible, draft animals should be in good shape, and rickshaw pullers only allowed to carry light goods, women, and the ill. Cai's concern was less for the suffering of the individual animal or laborer and more for the distress their sight might cause onlookers. However, it is unfair to accuse Cai of prissiness; rather, he was trying to describe a working totality. He did not want begging either, but he assumed begging would not be necessary because the poor and the handicapped would be trained in crafts to the best of their ability. Cemeteries would be nicely laid out with trees, flowers, and grave markers according to regulation. Private burial plots would be prohibited. There would be parks at appropriate distances, with ponds, pavilions, and trees and flowers for people to enjoy after work; botanical gardens, zoos, natural history displays, art museums, historical museums, ethnic museums, art fairs, concert halls and music in the parks, cinemas, theaters, and so on and so forth.

Cai highlighted the educational functions of all these institutions. Vulgar and obscene materials would be banned, since they ran contrary to a "true sense of beauty." In this spirit, weddings and funerals would be reformed to make them simpler. Cai's cultural puritanism, like his disdain of "superstition," reflected a certain elite contempt for the messiness of popular culture. But his faith in the power of an environment filled with beauty to improve the lives of the people can hardly be called puritan.

Notwithstanding such a secular approach to a utopian built environment, Cai maintained his faith that aesthetics provided the basis for extinguishing the distinction between self and other. In an unpublished piece from 1931, Cai argued that while the will itself was blind, it was shaped by both knowledge and sentiment.[102] In one regard, knowledge and sentiment work together, since neither logically nor emotionally is it possible for one person to survive in solitude, in isolation from the rest of humanity. The willingness to sacrifice oneself for the sake of humanity lies precisely in forgetting the very distinction between self and other. But that willingness depends not on just any sentiment, but on sentiment of strong motive force. And the strength of that motive force needs to be molded and nourished through aesthetic education. Beautiful objects have this power because they are both universal and transcendent. Cai's "universal" (pupian) was different from Kant's notion of the universal in art; rather than a quality of judgment, Cai was referring to the human ability to share beauty, which is not simply consumed and extinguished but is potentially eternal. Again, Cai stressed that everyone can tour natural wonders, enjoy the sun and moon, and view statues in parks or paintings in museums. As for the "transcendental," Cai was referring to the human drive to create beautiful objects that were not merely functional or indeed functional at all.

Cai and *Kultur*

During the first years of the twentieth century, Cai Yuanpei reacted with sensitivity to what he saw during his years in Germany, which included considerable travel around western Europe. German philosophers and writers had established links among enlightenment, culture, and cultural education over the course of the eighteenth century.[103] These ideas—really values—rapidly spread through literature and theater among the middle classes, especially perhaps "culture" and its emphasis on aesthetics. If German in origin, these values had spread across Europe by the nineteenth century. And by the end of the nineteenth century, the importance of city planning was also being recognized, perhaps nowhere more than in Germany.[104] The purposes of planning were not limited to hygiene and control, but included the promotion of aesthetic values as well. The Arts and Crafts movement was peaking at the time of Cai's sojourn in Europe, seeking to elevate daily life with good design.[105] In an age of secularization, it is not surprising that the notion of replacing religion with aesthetics—derived, if possibly vulgarized, from Kant and especially Schiller—seemed a way to continue to find meaning in an otherwise disenchanted world.[106]

Knowledge, Beauty, and Will—or science, aesthetics, and morality—were the touchstones of Cai's view of human faculties in his mature thought. In this regard, it is interesting that as early as 1903 Cai had translated Oswald Külpe's *Introduction to Philosophy*, based on a Japanese version of the text.[107] It is interesting that Külpe, a student of Wilhelm Wundt, observed that Plato in effect treated philosophy as comprised of three fields: dialectics, physics, and ethics. Perhaps, Külpe said, Plato's division was derived from Aristotle's fields of the theoretical, practical, and poetic. But in any case, the echo with Cai's tripartite division is worth noting. For Külpe, as well, the discipline of metaphysics was based on understanding, feeling, and will that any theory of the universe must satisfy.[108]

As for ethics and aesthetics, Külpe treated these fields as related, at least insofar as, unlike other fields of philosophy, neither rested on outside disciplines such as the natural sciences or psychology.[109] Cai was not to agree with this view of outside disciplines, but he certainly agreed that ethics and aesthetics were intrinsically related. For Külpe, the "art of conduct" is normative, but it also has to be based on historical development to rationalize certain ideals: it is not and cannot be arbitrary. Then, in tracing this history, Külpe returned to Plato's notion of Beauty: "All that is good comes, in the last resort, from God; and true happiness is found only in the immaterial world of pure ideas. Beauty alone can give sensible knowledge of the imprint of the good, of moral value, and so enable us to catch a glimpse in it of the higher beyond it."

At the same time, Külpe seems to have wanted to separate ethics from aesthetics insofar as each was, after all, an independent "science" or field. "Aesthetics, like ethics, is concerned with the investigation of particular facts; it is not a critical appendix to some special science, whether the history of art, as Vischer believed, or any other. The aim of modern aesthetics, then, must be the same as with that of modern ethics: to become a positive science."[110] Aesthetics focuses on: first, aesthetic judgments of pleasure and displeasures; and second, art and artistic production. Now, according to Külpe, modern work suggests that Beauty is not any kind of knowledge but rather feeling. Kant also wanted to separate aesthetics from ethics, logic, and pleasure (sic, at least according to Külpe). Rather, Kant thought that Beauty was a priori: "the assumption of the communicableness of aesthetic impressions, and of a teleological harmony between the faculties of knowledge,—imagination and understanding or reason. Beauty is disinterested pleasure in forms and relations; sublimity is direct pleasure in something that baffles the interest of the senses, i.e., whose magnitude or power puts it beyond the grasp of sensibility. . . . The beautiful and sublime derive their greatest value, however, from their character as perfect symbols of the moral and good."[111]

Külpe noted that, following Kant, Schiller placed greater emphasis on the beautiful than on the moral. Romanticism sees art almost everywhere, exaggerating an aesthetical point of view, and, "Lastly, Schopenhauer looks upon the state of aesthetic enjoyment as the highest form of earthly existence, the one condition in which we can conquer the cause of all suffering—will." For Külpe, Schopenhauer's lunge into metaphysics did not seem to be a positive step.[112] But he thought that the most recent empirical approach to aesthetics might lead to a more scientific understanding of Beauty. Külpe seemed to be suggesting that in spite of divergences of taste, aesthetic judgment could be founded on a universal basis. As for ethics, Külpe rather cautiously concluded that the pursuit of individual benefit was often more or less compatible with altruism or universalism.[113] Acts benefiting an individual or a small group were not necessarily less moral than those benefiting larger groups. However, it seems that, notwithstanding Kant's categorical imperative or Christian universalism, Külpe believed that no simple rule could cover all cases of conflict, such as when the good of the individual conflicted with the good of society. This concession to relativism was made frankly.

Cai's views certainly differed from Külpe's in key respects, but as early as 1903 Külpe had presented him with the issues he would wrestle with for the rest of his life. Cai's second major translation, also from the Japanese version, was of Friedrich Paulsen's *System of Ethics*, which he probably began in 1907 and published in 1909.[114] This was a massive monograph; here, we will simply note that Paulsen's relatively brief discussion of aesthetics compared art both to philosophy and to play.[115] Like philosophy, art was based "partially at least, on pure contemplation," and since art, unlike work, was not intended to produce an "external end," it was, like philosophy, a form of play. One may wonder what professional artists would have thought of this formulation, and Paulsen certainly noted the economics of art production. But he insisted that at least the fine arts represent "playful and purposeless exercise of sensual-spiritual powers." The audience, too—and perhaps more significantly—has no special object in mind beyond following the "'play' of imagination" produced by the artist. Paulsen insisted that art and play were closely related (perhaps more so than play and philosophy), as shown by primitive peoples and children. But Paulsen also highlighted the emotional effects of art. "Art is also partially rooted in *feeling and willing*. Every strong emotion is accompanied by the desire to express and communicate itself."[116]

Paulsen discussed art production not in terms of the individual artist but as the expression of a people and an age—the Finnish epic, the German fairy tale, Gothic art—and so: "It is the highest function of art to shape and express the ideals which the spiritual life of a nation creates."[117] For Paulsen, the relationship between art and religion was particularly close. It seems Paulsen is saying that art's representations of perfect images of the "supermundane-superhuman world" are simultaneously religious in nature, illustrating ideals of perfection, and aesthetic, fulfilling sensual needs.

We may therefore describe the *effect of art* upon the soul as follows: (1) It exercises our sensual-spiritual powers and so fills our leisure moments with the purest and most beautiful recreation and pleasure. (2) It satisfies and quiets the cravings of the emotions to express themselves, by providing them with the necessary stimulus and affording relief. (3) It raises the soul above the world of work and need, struggle and misery, to a world of freedom and ideals, and purifies it from misery, to a world of freedom and ideals, and purifies it from the dust of base feelings and passions with which the affairs of daily life cover it. The inner uniformity and harmony which constitutes the essence of all art also brings uniformity and harmony into the soul. Finally (4) it binds together and unites the members of the nation, nay, all the members of a sphere of civilization; all those who have the same faith and the same ideals.[118]

In other words, art dampens the interests and emotions that divide people and reminds them of what they have in common. Paulsen does not seem to have believed that art produces a transcendent experience, but it does not work through reason either. At least temporarily, art "fills all hearts with the same feelings and makes the popular soul conscious of its unity." Clearly, Paulsen's subject has tacitly moved from "contemplation" of the fine arts to popular arts, public festivals, and group participation. Paulsen recognized this, deprecating the inaccessibility of art faced by ordinary people, and the irrelevance of art even to most of the elite. If new scientific discoveries can only be understood by persons with sufficient training, art should be understandable and enjoyable—if to different degrees—to all. Historically, this had precisely been the case, Paulsen claimed, for Greek drama and the medieval arts that were created for, and sometimes by, the people. The problem, as he saw it, was a lack of "national feeling" that stemmed from interruptions and repudiations of the past. Both the initial conversion to Christianity and then the Renaissance and Reformation brought benefits, but they also drew an unfortunately sharp line between present and past. And, Paulsen continued, the Renaissance further divided German society itself by creating a small classically educated class whose culture was sharply distinct from that of the masses. Thus, German culture could not be truly national and the arts could not not satisfy most people. The result was that popular entertainment is vulgar, while the higher arts degenerate into mere luxury goods.

Paulsen's jeremiad led him some distance from any direct consideration of ethics, although he was disturbed by the degeneration of the customs of both the masses and the educated classes. If Paulsen's concluding vision of art was in a sense utilitarian and nationalistic, this was abhorrent to Cai Yuanpei. But if Paulsen's more fundamental vision of art as being more like disinterested play, as in Kant and Külpe, then perhaps Cai and Paulsen held some views in common. In particular, Cai believed not that art reflected the unity of a people but that it could bring about such unity. In that sense, art was not entirely disinterested, and aesthetics—learning the proper judgment of the beautiful and sublime—was enormously powerful.

During his three years at Leipzig, Cai studied with leading neo-Kantians, who reflected the dominant German academic philosophy although they formed a large and amorphous rather than clearly defined school of thought.[119] Perhaps Cai was more loyal to Kant than some of the critical and revisionist neo-Kantians. Having said that, Cai's optimistic epistemology, which assumed that at least some knowledge of the noumenal was possible, was as revisionist as that of any neo-Kantian. Cai at least continued to root his thought in the distinction between the thing-in-itself and phenomena, while those neo-Kantians who self-consciously modeled epistemology and even ontology on the exact sciences could not accept anything that lay outside of space and time.

Although Cai took Wilhelm Wundt's courses on psychology as well as philosophy at Leipzig, Cai seems to have had little interest in psychology, at least outside of its bearing on ethics, in later years. Wundt (1832–1920) was by today's standards a polymath competent in philosophy as well as physiology; he was one of the founders of the field of psychology and developed the first experimental laboratory for psychology at Leipzig. Wundt even designed a set of experiments to test the Kantian notion of the universality of beauty. He showed that people were aroused by complexity—but not too much complexity. Very simple stimuli are perceived as boring, while excessively complex stimuli induce anxiety; there is thus a middle range that produces the greatest pleasure. Wundt also wrote on a topic of direct interest to Cai, who took other courses on the subject as well: the history of civilization. Wundt's *Elements of Folk Psychology* was not published until 1912, but Wundt was developing his synthesis of the "psychological history of the development of mankind" during the years Cai was in Leipzig.[120] Wundt's approach was evolutionary, tracing the historical stages of mental development of peoples, from lower ("primitive") to higher ("cultural"); via a totemic age, an age of heroes and gods (from tribe to state), an age of national state and religion, and onward to the future development of humanity. Wundt treated the gods and religion in naturalistic terms; he even wrote a paean to globalization avant la lettre. He postulated that parallel to the mental drive to spread a world religion came also the expansion of national states.

> Corresponding to this expansion, we find these reciprocal influences of cultural peoples in economic life, as well as in custom, art, and science, which give to human society its composite character, representing a combination of national with universally human elements. . . . How immense is the chasm between the secret barter of primitive man who steals out of the primeval forest by night and lays down his captured game to exchange it, unseen by his neighbors, for implements and objects of adornment, and the coming of an age when fleets traverse the seas, and eventually ships course through the air, uniting the peoples of all parts of the world into one great commercial community![121]

This utopian, though secular, vision of the future accorded with Cai's instincts. Cai's notion of ending the distinction between self and other was not mystical but stemmed from a world that was abolishing many "boundaries," to use Kang Youwei's terminology. Did Wundt also believe in this kind of progress? In other words, does it follow that a truly global community can arise to transcend family, tribe, nation, and sect? In his *Elements*, Wundt did speak of "the development of humanity," that is, "a universally human culture" and "the *whole* of mankind."[122] In a word, we appear to be headed in this direction but are not there yet. But contrary to Cai, Wundt explicitly says we can never fully arrive there. Citing Herder's "education of humanity," Wundt believed this ideal has been clarified but cannot be "completely" realized, if only because the ideal is itself "subject to growth," that is, historical. Thus, the evolution of larger social units—states and the world religions of Christianity, Islam, and Buddhism—seem to have for Wundt a dual significance.[123] He notes both their expansionism and the growing strength of their particular, self-conscious features. If there is a future "age of humanity," it will retain in some form earlier social collectivities. Human nature itself would have to evolve before the world of humanity could emerge.

Religion was key to Wundt's analysis of contemporary and future society. By "human nature" he meant the collective consciousness of humanity, which world empire—the spread of institutions of law, administration, and commerce—might begin to alter, but for which world culture, world religions, and world history were equally necessary. That religion lay at the root of the kind of changes that Wundt was analyzing seems a fair inference, though Wundt did not explicitly draw this conclusion. But he described historical world empires and world cultures as theocratic—the world empire being legitimated by theocratic claims and the world culture backed by a world Church at least through the Renaissance. Finally, Wundt noted that world religions effectively provided the motive force for the creation of a "common mental heritage for mankind," having already destroyed earlier national religions.[124] Now, what will the future bring? Here, Wundt, without quite saying so, seemed to suggest that religious feeling in any traditional sense of the term was dissipating and in its place we could find new knowledge of historical laws of humanity's education and self-development. Looking both to Herder and to Hegel, Wundt did not deny the (Christian) role of an immanent God, but he seemed to find God increasingly irrelevant, at least for analytical purposes.

Cai Yuanpei was quicker to do away with religion. He believed that aesthetics could replace religion, as we have seen, and, further, that this would provide a great leap forward in ethical behavior as people realized their essential, shared human identity. Wundt saw a somewhat similar endpoint, but only through a psychological reading of Hegel's philosophy of history. That is, as history continued to unfold, ever more universalistic values emerged. Cai was perhaps not interested in trying to think in historical terms.

Conclusion

The notion that art and aesthetics have didactic value can loosely be traced back to Plato and Confucius alike. In ancient China, almost supernatural effects were attributed to "rites and music," and in the long Confucian tradition art was seen as public and communal, not private.[125]

Aesthetic theory acknowledged the importance of pleasure and play, but said nothing about transcendence through art. The category "aesthetics" (*meixue*) was introduced to China via the Japanese, like so many fields of learning, at the beginning of the twentieth century. It was relatively new to Europe as well, beginning to be used in its modern sense in the early eighteenth century. Of course, this does not mean that the intellectual drive to understand and discuss art only emerged in the eighteenth century, merely that the need to conceptualize it as a discipline emerged then.

The revolutionary function of art is often associated with the avant-garde, and major avant-garde movements have been politically inspired to one degree or another.[126] Could more conventionally beautiful or sublime art also make revolution? Transform the world? Schiller's view that the way to Freedom lay through Beauty might give rise to a political reading that Schiller himself did not mean. Or it may be that the European aesthetic tradition through Kant was tied to bourgeois sensibility that steered between freedom and order.[127] In the view of Terry Eagleton, modern aesthetics emerged partly as a response to the problem of political absolutism. This may or may not be an adequate description of the role aesthetics was to play in nineteenth-century Europe, but it is clear that Schiller, at least, highlighted (if only sporadically) the parallels between aesthetics and politics and their mutual imbrications.[128] However, the question is not whether or how art and politics, or art and morality, are related—as had been consistently recognized in the Confucian view of aesthetics—but whether aesthetics could be emancipatory.

Cai Yuanpei: scholar, revolutionary, educator, bureaucrat, anarchist. Cai's view of the power of aesthetics might be interpreted apolitically or conservatively, if the purpose of extinguishing the distinction between self and other was to produce a kind of harmonious hive existence devoid of any individuation. But assuming this is not what Cai meant, he was proposing a pedagogical project that had something in common both with a radical Buddhist challenge to the illusion of the individual and with a Kantian concept of the rational being making judgments on grounds that were ultimately universal.

It may be that some of Cai's attraction to Kantianism reflected a degree of familiarity that stemmed from the Asian sources of much of the philosophy produced in Germany in the eighteenth and nineteenth centuries.[129] It may also be that Cai radically misunderstood Kant, who, after all, never discussed the noumenal in terms of erasing the distinction between self and other. But Cai was of course making use of Kant for his own purposes and as read through Schiller.

As pedagogy, Cai's aesthetics represented the final stage of the socialization of the child. Aesthetic understanding did not obliterate citizenship—the penultimate stage of socialization—but supplemented it and even supported it through subject identification with all humans. As well, Cai remained interested in secular institutions and foresaw their perfection through aesthetics. Surrounded by beauty, citizens would further develop their characters. When Cai spoke of aesthetics replacing religion, he had in mind both its psychological function in meeting spiritual needs and its ethical function in guiding interpersonal relations.

Cai was not alone in advocating the importance of aesthetics education in the late Qing period. The self-taught philosopher and education writer Wang Guowei, also making extensive use of the Kantian tradition (though especially Schopenhauer), was equally convinced that moral education depended not on rote dogma but a kind of transformative learning.[130] If religion was no longer able to perform one of its traditional roles, to regulate desire, then modern people had to turn to aesthetics. "Now, there is one thing that can raise one above the struggle for gain, and lead one to forget the distinction between self and the world. In this state, one is without hope or fear; one is no longer a desiring ego, but only a knowing self," Wang wrote. "This one thing is, of course, art. The art object at once describes the suffering of life and provides us a way of escaping it. It enables us, enshackled and ensnared as we are in the world, to leave behind the struggle with desire and obtain some measure of peace. This is the aim of art."[131] Wang's own desire—for escape from suffering—was at odds with Cai's fundamental vision, which was more one of empathy.

Cai's vision of beautiful world full of people with beautiful minds was simultaneously a metaphysical vision and a secular vision. As a metaphysical concept, aesthetics could help people transcend the mundane. But Cai's continuous involvement with education and politics illustrates that this utopian impulse helped fuel his radicalism. Cai's tone was moderate but his commitment to fundamental social transformation was firm.[132] Though Cai is generally considered a liberal, or at least a founder of Chinese liberalism, his utopianism has been noted by Chaohua Wang in her biography of Cai, even while he maintained a "non-confrontational attitude toward the existing social order."[133] In his study of Chinese Communist aesthetic theory, Kang Liu further notes the "utopian dimension" of Cai's aesthetics.[134]

Yet for all its metaphysical mysteries, Cai's utopianism was perfectly secular. He celebrated the accomplishments of science and modern social organization, all part of the "phenomenal world." He simply added art or aesthetic experience as a route to the noumenal, which helps awaken people to the falsity of the distinction between self and others. Unlike Kang Youwei, Cai did not end up by abandoning the secular. But he saw that through aesthetics people could become awakened to the essential unity of the cosmos. Cai read evolution as proving that the duty of humanity is to promote the ethics of the group and not the individual self; to promote the future and not merely the present; and to promote the joy of the spirit and not merely the satisfactions of the body. Again rejecting social Darwinism, Cai denied that evolution promotes only the strong individual and the strong species. Whether we read Cai as a neo-Kantian, a Bergsonian, or a Buddhist or Confucian of sorts, the question here is not the influences on his thought but what his thought accomplished. Cai found a new philosophical language to replace the humaneness/ren of Kang Youwei and Tan Sitong, but nonetheless constructed a similar basis for utopia on the common human condition and even the common condition of all things. For Cai, eventually the transformative, subjective experience of beauty led to the transformation of the very nature of society.

Cai, like thousands of intellectuals trying to strengthen China as the Qing collapsed and the Republic was trying to be born, was a patriot who sought to modernize his country. But his ideas, whether or not systematically expressed, were among the most truly cosmopolitan that a global citizen could create.

4

Democracy and the Community

Chen Duxiu

Chen Duxiu never wrote a full-fledged utopia, but many of his writings linked liberation and democracy in a way that can be called utopian. His political vision of participatory democracy for China in the 1910s was transformed into a vision of the "dictatorship of the proletariat" as he helped organize and lead the Chinese Communist Party in the 1920s, but he began to synthesize Marxism and liberal democracy in the 1930s. Chen's political visions revealed a utopian impulse not because his approach was totalistic but because it attempted to reconcile the tensions between individual and state. Ultimately, Chen sought to reconcile the particular and the universal. His approach also revealed a utopian impluse because it was based on slash-and-burn rejection of Chinese traditional culture and even what Chen sometimes called national character. Chen's totalistic rejection of traditional culture in the 1910s stemmed from a despair that rhetorically targeted not outside imperialism or capitalism but China's own cultural backwardness. Over the course of the 1920s, his diagnosis became more sophisticated, relying on an analysis that placed China in a system of global capitalism. In the 1930s, borrowing to an extent from Trotsky, Chen conceived of "permanent revolution" that was simultaneously anti-imperialist, anticapitalist, and socialist and democratic.

Chen was largely critical of nationalism, but there is no doubt of his fundamental support for rebuilding China specifically, for the rights of national self-determination in general, and for all forms of anti-imperialism.

He sought to reconcile universal values ("civilization") and the values of group identity (or "patriotism").[1] In the course of universal human progress, the nation, for Chen, remained an essential unit or locus of efforts at improvement. Nonetheless, Chen never doubted that social truths—ultimately, moral truths—applied to all humanity. His teleological faith in progress was eventually to inform his understanding of revolution as necessarily a worldwide phenomenon. Chen's views on many issues certainly changed dramatically over the course of his tumultuous life as a student, anti-Qing revolutionary, journalist, scholar, philologist, academic administrator, prisoner, anticapitalist and anti-imperialist revolutionary, political leader, political prisoner, and political pariah. Toward the end of his life, Chen wrote that he regarded himself largely as a political activist and thus as a failure.[2] But as an intellectual/polemicist pioneer, his influence was enormous, though it may have led people in directions he did not anticipate. Chen's turn to Marxism and his personal commitment to Communist Party discipline in the 1920s rested partly on a repudiation of his earlier liberalism. His promotion of individual liberty and egalitarian political participation was now forgotten. He now put his faith in class struggle, the vanguard Party, and the dictatorship of the proletariat. Nonetheless, this was not Chen's final political turn. When due weight is given Chen's writings of the 1930s, it turns out that his foray into Leninism-Stalinism led him to a more historically mature view of democracy. The historian Gregor Benton is right to argue that Chen's turn to Trotskyism in the early 1930s was fueled in part by a deep commitment to democratic thinking.[3] Chen was able to use the Trotskyist interpretations of permanent revolution and class struggle to construct a liberal view of "proletarian democracy." The impulse that lay behind Chen's shifting positions was utopian.[4]

Utopian Liberalism

In 1915, at the age of thirty-six, Chen Duxiu founded a new journal in Shanghai. It was called *Youth*. This moment was later taken as the beginning of the "New Culture movement." At that moment the president, Yuan Shikai, was on the verge of establishing a new imperial dynasty with himself as emperor (in reality, Yuan was a fairly weak military dictator who was trying to gain greater authority by promising to rule as a constitutional monarch). Energized rather than dispirited by the rise of reaction, Chen responded with passionate calls for cultural renewal. Echoing and magnifying some of the revolutionary criticisms of Chinese culture heard in the last years of the Qing, Chen called for the complete destruction of the old ways of life. This was essential if China were to survive and progress. He soon renamed his journal *New Youth*—the new and the young representing his still amorphous political position. The *New Youth*'s advocacy of "science and democracy" was resounding but not always concrete. Still, during these politically chaotic and increasingly violent first years of the Republic Chen staked out his view of democracy.

Democracy represented, for Chen, the abolition of boundaries. It was more than a set of political institutions. Although he, unlike Kang Youwei or Cai Yuanpei, did not regard boundaries as a metaphysical problem or ontological illusion, he certainly saw the boundaries separating people as a practical obstacle to progress. If fully carried out, democracy would erase the boundaries between ruler and ruled, men and women, and rich and poor. In other words, democracy and equality were two sides of the same coin. Furthermore, Chen saw this coin as the product of liberation—he meant the emancipation of the individual from such ties as those of the clan, and the emancipation of groups suffering oppression, such as women. If nowhere else, Chen's utopian impulse lay in this instinct to reconcile all good: individual-group; liberty-equality; order-democracy. He never lamented any aspect of the past that might be swept away in forms of progress that were necessary but, for some, painful. He shows none of the nostalgia of a Kang Youwei, a Cai Yuanpei, or even a Hu Shi.

In 1915, Chen defined progress simply as the development of civilization. His teleological approach paid no attention to byways, detours, or dead ends.[5] Civilization, then, was a universal process operating across the globe, though at different rates in different places. While Chen did not specifically define it in this way, what he meant by civilization was political: how humans organized themselves into communities.[6] Thus, the first stage of civilization, found in all ancient societies, referred to relatively peaceful societies whose order was fostered by religion, enforced by laws and institutions, and legitimated by a theocratic ideology. The social system in this stage of civilization was hierarchical and stagnant: everyone knew their place and seldom challenged it. However, Chen said, truly modern civilization developed in the West and was now spreading to the rest of the world. What was modern civilization? For

Chen, it essentially consisted of three elements: rights, evolution, and socialism. The modern social system was based on democracy, which meant all persons were equal before the law. Chen acknowledged that inequalities remained in the West in regard to wealth; and, as long as the system of private property remained in place, capitalist oppression would continue. He thus posited the need to complete the "political revolution" with a "social revolution."[7] Europe's socialist movement has not (yet) succeeded in its goals, but governments have at least become aware of the problem of poverty and taken measures to ameliorate it.

In Chen's view, Darwinism fostered the mental liberation of Europe by freeing people from the prison of theocratic superstition. People understood that they were not created by gods but were responsible for their own fate. Chen attacked religion—and Confucianism—for supporting despots, but he also acknowledged religion's role in encouraging goodness in the past development of society, or of civilization at a primitive stage. And here it is further worth noting that he seems to have regarded evolution as providing the modern equivalent of religion: some sort of common knowledge, this time genuine knowledge.

The principles of the French Revolution—liberty, equality, and fraternity—Chen saw as natural desires, underlying the drive toward "civilization" or progress. What suggests Chen's vision was a utopian one and not merely a teleological version of progress is partly his tone. Chen's famous "Warning to Youth" essay of 1915 found something like utopia in the future, but partly in the present as well. This utopia of the present, then, was not "here" but "over there"—albeit a fictional projection of Chen's imagination.

> It is said that modern European history is "the history of liberation": the destruction of monarchy represents political liberation; the rejection of religious authority represents religious liberation; the rise of socialist thought representes economic liberation; and political rights for women represents liberation from male authority.
>
> "Liberation" means gaining freedom from the yoke of slaves in order to become fully human based on autonomy and freedom. We have hands and feet and so can plan how to feed and warm ourselves; we have mouths and tongues and so can make our preferences clear; we have the capacity for thought and so can exalt what we believe in. And we abso-

lutely do not allow other people to represent us and equally should not make ourselves masters by enslaving others. On the basis of recognizing our character as independent and autonomous, all our actions, rights, and beliefs are based on our own knowledge and ability, and absolutely cannot be based on blindly following others.[8]

Of course, this was a political program disguised as historical analysis. As we have seen, Chen regarded political liberation even in Europe as woefully incomplete, because it left capitalist oppression and exploitation in place. But what is striking about this passage, aside from its heroic tone, is the faith that liberation can be based on the natural dsires and attributes of individuals.

Chen attributed Yuan Shikai's monarchical movement to the evil effects of Confucianism. Chen loathed what he saw as the support that Confucian morality and cosmology inevitably gave monarchism due to their preachment of natural hierarchies, or anti-egalitarianism.[9] But these attacks were twinned with a utopian vision of democracy that was, for Chen, the precise opposite of Confucianism. He feared that the Chinese people were trapped in a Confucian swamp of delusion.[10] But he simultaneously believed they had the capacity to free themselves. What society would look like once they did so, Chen said, was essentially a congeries of small participatory democracies. The direct participation of all individuals in public life was the core of Chen's utopian vision.

Chen believed that the modern nation was in some basic sense democratic by definition—autocracies could not be modern states. Nor could they be effective ones. Thus, both a general law of civilizational progress and the iron workings of social Darwinism demanded that China take a democratic turn. Chen noted, "The state refers to that which is formed by the people assembling together, unifying within and resisting from without to protect the benefits of the whole people, and resisting rule as private possession."[11] Autocracies were "false states" that sacrificed the good of the people for the sake of an individual monarch. This kind of prose merely echoed the writings of Liang Qichao from the previous decade. But Chen went farther when he demanded that the Chinese people take *direct* charge of their own affairs. It was through political participation that they would achieve their own liberation, or as Chen put it in 1916, "enlightenment."[12] This notion stemmed directly from Chen's analysis of the failure of the Republic.

Whether "constitutional political order" and "citizen politics" can be practiced depends entirely on one basic condition: that a majority of the people are able to consciously understand their active agency as masters in regard to politics. Active agency as masters stems from the people themselves establishing a government, themselves establishing laws and obeying them, and themselves determining rights and respecting them. If agency in a constitutional order lies in the government and not the people, then not only is the constitution merely empty words that can never be enforced, but also the people will not take its guarantees of liberty seriously and will not protect it with their lives. In this way the spirit of constitutional order is completely lost. Thus if the constitutional order does not arise from the self-consciousness of the majority of the people and through their own actions, but rather they only hope for good government or the governance of wise men, then their depravity and ugliness is the same as when slaves look for a little kindliness from their master, or when the vulgar masses look for the virtuous governance of the sagely kings and wise ministers."[13]

Chen continued to look to Europe for models of republican government, but his point for the Chinese people was that they themselves needed to take action. He further sketched out these ideas in several essays published in 1918 and 1919. By this time, the Republic had descended further into warlordism, but the defeat of "German militarism" and the success of the Bolshevik Revolution created an optimistic moment for Chinese progressives.

Although some of the New Youth circle rejected political activism for the sake of promoting cultural reform on the grounds that China's political problems would never be solved until basic cultural predispositions had been reformed, Chen had only opposed cooperation with warlord governments. He defended the realm of "politics" as a site of legitimate work—that is, of discussion and action.[14] In delineating what should be rejected and outlining what should be adopted, his utopian impulse was on full display.

First, Chen rejected the politics of military force. Acutely, Chen noted that the failures of attempts to restore monarchy had proved that military force alone could not form a modern state. Chen then leapt to the conclusion that military force would play no role in state formation. He noted that if the Republic had failed, so had autocracy and monarchism. Chen called on both the northern and southeastern factions—meaning the major warlords and Sun Yat-sen's fledgling Guomindang equally—to abjure their militarism and follow the law. How or why they would do so, Chen did not say.

Second, Chen thought that no single faction of China's many military and political groups could unite the country. Showing himself to be a student of politics in the usual sense after all, Chen pointed out that the factions could not even unite themselves. Their efforts to unify China were having the effect of dividing it instead, and—here Chen was echoing an old trope—inviting the foreigners to come in. But all Chen could advise was that the factions learn how to share power.

Third, Chen said that the Chinese themselves had to decide between conservatism and reform. This point amounted to an expression of Chen's utopian democratic views. It was phrased, however, as a challenge. If the Chinese people chose conservatism, then they could follow the old Chinese ways and not waste money in sending students abroad, building schools, and studying Western Learning. But if they wanted reform, then they should entirely adopt new Western methods and not worry about "national essence" or "national sentiment" and other nonsense. That is, Chen continued, if the choice was for a constitutional republic, the people should respect the spirit of democracy, rule by law, and treat all citizens equally, and they should reject the politics of sovereigns, divine spirits, sage-kings, and all such ilk. But if they believed in rule by divine right, then they were correct to ignore republican constitutionalism and even science. Chen demanded that the people choose, and not try to mix constitutionalism and Confucianism. Chen suggested that constitutionalism was "scientific," while he somewhat sneakily associated Confucianism with ghosts and spirits, magic spells and potions, fortune telling, and the like, as well as, with greater justification, repeating his charge that Confucians justified monarchism.

Chen, Dewey, Democracy

Chen's real interest was now, as he said, political. The clearest expression of his utopian view of participatory democracy perhaps came in his 1919 essay "The Basis of Democratic Practice." Chen's thinking here was clearly provoked by John Dewey's highly popular lecture tour in China, which lasted almost two years from 1919 to 1921.[15] The American philosopher spoke to academic and student audiences, of which Chen was a recognized leader. In his brief experiment with Deweyan political theory, Chen was inspired to a utopian interpretation of democracy precisely because he did not regard it as the ultimate goal.[16] The ultimate goal was the improvement of "social life," a project not timeless in the sense that a static perfection would be reached, but timeless in the sense it was a never-ending project. Thus, Chen stated, politics, economics, and morality are tools in the never-ending improvement of social life. Chen did not define the notion of social life, and so the outlines of his utopianism remained murky, but he clearly was thinking of something like happiness, even while Chinese understanding of the Benthamite-Millsian utilitarianism this calls to mind remained critical. While claiming that the "social question" was now paramount, Chen actually devoted most of this essay to political issues.[17] However, it is also true that democratic politics and democratic economics were indivisible for Chen. Chen had come to this conclusion a few years previously, but he was now happy to cite Dewey's thought: Dewey showed that in the West, the concept of democracy had evolved from the political sphere to other spheres as well.

Chen cited four aspects of democracy as preached by Dewey. First, the political: a constitution to define powers and representative institutions to express the will of the people. Second, rights: in particular freedoms of speech, publication, belief, and residence. Third, the social: egalitarianism, seen in the destruction of hierarchical classes and anti-egalitarian thought and in the recognition of the dignity of all. And fourth, the economic: the eradication of the distinctions between rich and poor. Having followed Dewey thus far, Chen granted the usefulness of the distinction between the socioeconomic sphere and the political sphere. The fundamental economic problem had to be solved first, he said. Whether this was an unconscious reflection of Confucius's words on the subject or reflection of his new Marxist reading, Chen did not here follow his own advice. Rather, he noted that all fair-minded persons should agree with Dewey's socioeconomic perspective on democracy, which he claimed was essentially socialist; and he further noted that Chinese were preoccupied with political questions, which he found understandable given the failures of the Republic. Chen then proceeded to write as if indeed getting political forms right would lead to solving the economic problem. In my reading, this was not so much a contradiction in Chen's thought—moving target though it was at the time—as it reflected Chen's utopian faith that the proper practice of democracy and the solutions to economic problems were two sides of the same coin.

Overall, Dewey both confirmed and deepened Chen's thinking on democracy. In other words, Chen was not merely citing Dewey as an authority to support views he already held, nor was he merely echoing Dewey. Chen displayed little interest in Dewey's theories on education, including the links between schooling and democracy that became extremely influential in Chinese educational circles. Nor was Chen much interested in Dewey's explanations of pragmatism or experimentalism, which Hu Shi advocated, as we will see in the next chapter. Rather, Chen found much in common with Dewey's highly participatory vision of democracy.

In particular, one of Dewey's first lectures in China, at Peking University, introduced a broad definition of democracy that covered the political, civil, economic, and social spheres.[18] Dewey further emphasized that all countries had to develop democracy based on their own conditions—British, French, and American versions of democracy have all developed through different paths and with distinct characteristics. In America's case, the distrust of government rooted in the colonial period was now evolving into recognition of the need for government to take on a bigger role promoting equality under conditions of the laissez-faire economy. Again, Chen took to heart the need to think about how democracy would emerge out of Chinese culture and conditions, though he did not do so in very original ways. Finally, Dewey attacked statism—the view that government could be the highest good—and in effect suggested that democracy was the best means of combatting statism and assuring that government worked for the good of the people. This view was already extremely congenial to Chen and essentially reemerged in his 1930s attacks on Stalinist bureaucratism.

In his extensive series of lectures on "Social and Political Philosophy" given in Beijing, Dewey made the case that ideas about society should be rooted in concrete situations and not airy theory, whether conservative or radical.[19] This was to link the experimental and particularistic methods of the philosophy of pragmatism to the cause of reform. Dewey's explicit opposition to Marxism and revolutionism may have appealed more to his interpreter, Hu Shi, than to Chen. But Chen did agree with Dewey's rejection of grand theories based on binaries—such as the people versus the government, the individual versus society, and the like—in favor of communication and gradual consensus building among individuals and interest groups. Dewey claimed that it was democracy that best guaranteed social and political stability, fostering the unity of a social organism.

Dewey's own views on democracy were fairly utopian; that is, as he suggested in an essay composed on his way to Asia in 1918, nature as described by modern science was in accord with the democratic objectives of human beings.[20] This was virtually a metaphysical case for democracy, or at least a claim that metaphysics must fail to construct a case against democracy. Dewey suggested that although traditional philosophy had sought for absolutes and was intertwined with feudal thought, there was a link between the rise of modern experimental science and democracy. That democracy could be tested against the laws of nature did not depend on qualities unique to democracy (Dewey's half-facetious alternatives for testing were Presbyterianism and free verse), but the implication was that democracy was a successful experiment of considerably broader scope. "Liberty," Dewey said, pointed to a "universe in which there is real uncertainty and contingency," never complete and always in the making, and hence a universe that was, to a degree, open to human will.

> Now whatever the idea of equality means for democracy, it means, I take it, that the world is not to be construed as a fixed order of species, grades or degrees. It means that every existence deserving of the name of existence has something unique and irreplaceable about it, that it does not exist to illustrate a principle to realize a universal or to embody a kind or class. As philosophy it denies the basic principle of atomistic individual as truly as that of rigid feudalism.[21]

Three decades earlier, in one of his first writings on democracy, Dewey had concluded that "democracy is an ethical idea, the idea of a personality [to be developed freely by all persons to their potential], with truly infinite capacities, incorporate with every man. Democracy and the one, the ultimate ethical ideal of humanity, are to my mind synonyms."[22] All good government allows all members of society to obtain their most complete development possible through their proper place in society, but only democracy allows them to find their own places in society. "The end is not mere assertion of the individual will as individual; it is not disregard of law, of the universal; it is complete realization of the law, namely of the unified spirit of the community. . . . and individualism of freedom, of responsibility, of initiative to and for the ethical ideal, not an individualism of lawlessness." Regarding people as innately social, and society as an "organism" that possesses a common will, Dewey did not deny the existence of "struggle and opposition and hostility" but insisted that democracy was more than majority rule. As members of the organism, citizens are wholly sovereign. The organic metaphor, for Dewey, represented the reciprocal relations of its parts, and not some kind of hierarchy of head and hands. He thus denied the "delegation theory" of government, insisting that democracies could not be divided into governors and governed but, precisely insofar as they were organic, were unified.

Scholars have noted the influence of Hegel on Dewey's early thought as well as Dewey's lingering Christianity.[23] There are also echoes of Rousseau's general will in Dewey's organismic interpretation of democracy, and probably coincidental reverberations with Mencius, who also believed in humanity's inherent sociability. As for Rousseau, Dewey firmly rejected the notion of the social contract, which he found not only ahistorical but also philosophically mistaken insofar as it regarded persons as essentially atomistic individuals. Nonetheless, Rousseau had found a friendly audience in China since the turn of the century, and Dewey's vision of democracy as based on communication and consensus was rather like Chinese understanding of Rousseau's social contract and general will as based on equality.

Just before his prolonged visit to China, Dewey gave a series of lectures in Japan that became a major work, *Reconstruction in Philosophy*.[24] In general, Dewey wanted to show why pragmatism was immensely superior to previous philosophies. Here, however, I focus on Dewey's comments on democracy. Not surprisingly, Dewey linked democracy to modernity—"the new science and its industrial applications," urbanization, and financial capital—all ultimately "emancipating the individual from bonds of class and custom and . . . producing a political organization which depends less upon superior authority and more upon voluntary choice . . . contrivances of men and women to realize their own desires."[25] Dewey now concluded with an explicit refutation of the organic theory of society. As long as the organic theory of society was used to support the "established order," it could not stand. Dewey further refuted Hegel for, intentionally or not, enshrining "bureaucratic absolutism."[26] The fundamental philosophical problem, according to Dewey, lay in the "logic of rigid universals" that failed to take into account specific conditions. He highlighted the existence of conflicts—such as individual-state, capital-labor, male-female—that could not be swept away in a tide of generalization. Coming at Hegel head-on, Dewey suggested that the territorial national state, though today the culmination of integrative forces since at least the eighteenth century, was not a "supreme end in itself" but merely "an instrumentality for promoting and protecting other and more voluntary forms of association."[27] The rise of states has in fact allowed individuals freed from the restrictions of old classes and customs to voluntarily combine themselves into new associations. In this sense, individualism and free forms of cooperation are two faces of the same phenomenon.

To define democracy, Dewey described the conditions of what he termed pluralism: a field of social activity restricted neither to the state nor the individual, as in traditional theory, but which therefore "demands a modification of hierarchical and monistic theory."[28] Dewey did not in fact have much to say about conflict, but seemed to assume that goods will be enhanced as they are mutually communicated and shared precisely through numerous associations and organizations. And social experimentation is intrinsic to the process through which society develops so that all its members fulfill their capacities. Democracy in this sense is social, not political.

> The best guarantee of collective efficiency and power is liberation and the use of the diversity of individual capacities in initiative, planning, foresight, vigor and endurance. Personality must be educated. . . . Full education comes only when there is a responsible share on the part of each person, in proportion to capacity, in shaping the aims and policies of the social groups to which he belongs. This fact fixes the significance of democracy. . . . It is but a name for the fact that human nature is developed only when its elements take part in directing things which are common, things for the sake of which men and women form groups—families, industrial companies, governments, churches, scientific associations and so on.[29]

In the lectures he gave in Beijing in 1919, Dewey spoke about the conditions, nature, and limits of democracy. He eventually reached the point where he could offer a strong critique of authoritarianism—of social and cultural authoritarianism as well as political authoritarianism—on the grounds it obstructed rather than developed "the common life" (*gongtong shenghuo*), that is, "a life of free communication, social intercourse, mutual empathy, and the exchange of all sorts of valuable things."[30] It was this social good, not democracy as such, that represented the highest value for humanity, in Dewey's view, but democracy better than any other political system fostered all those traits associated with the common life. Furthermore, it is authoritarian societies that are more prone to disintegration, because they depend on force rather than consent—which results from the free exchange of ideas and building of consensus that define democratic societies. Some of these notions were long familiar to Chinese intellectuals, but Dewey offered an unusually clear explanation of how individual freedom and social cohesion depended on one another.

In another lecture, Dewey suggested that China might build on its indigenous traditions of guilds to foster a kind of locally based "industrial democracy."[31] This would be socialism with relatively small government involvement, which Dewey also saw developing through the young Russian Revolution. Perhaps, he tentatively suggested, guild socialism offered a way for China to develop its resources while making "these common-interest groups the central units of political organization." Dewey's tentativeness was principled. He deprecated overly general attacks on existing institutions on the one hand, and "doctrinaire solutions to problems in general on the other." The rise of moral and religious as well as political individualism has encouraged challenges to old verities and a new emphasis on observation, experience, and experiment. Essentially, then, Dewey's vision of democracy made the social and political spheres indivisible.[32]

Democracy as a process of building consensus; society as an organism composed of free and equal parts or members; skepticism, at least, of "delegation"; the perhaps crucial nature of communication: these Deweyan themes might have been deliberately designed to appeal to Chen Duxiu. Agreeing with Dewey on some kind of generic socialism, as well as the importance of basic rights, Chen could offer only partial support for constitutionalism and representative institutions. He feared that reliance on "constitutional limits of powers" and "representative institutions to express the people's will" leaves some liberty rights (*ziyouquan*)—necessary to people's livelihoods—in the hands of the few. True democracy, according to Chen, means that the constitution is directly determined by the people, and that they use the constitution to establish limits on powers and use republican institutions to carry out the people's will in accord with the constitution, "in other words, destroying the distinction between ruler and ruled as the people themselves are simultaneously both rulers and ruled."[33] Engaging in a perilous balancing act, Chen emphasized that he was not opposed to constitutionalism—parliaments, cabinets, good government, infrastructure, provincial and county self-government—but that all of these political forms needed to be built on the foundation of true democracy in order to develop properly.[34] Democracy (*minzhi*)—"direct and real self-governance and associations of the people"—had to be built from the bottom up. The alternative was bureaucratic rule (*guanzhi*), which might be competent but could never be democratic.

Chen's faith in the possibility and even practicability of this vision was rooted in his analysis of Chinese and world conditions. Conditions could scarcely be worse. In Chen's analysis, in spite of the revolution, China was at heart still an imperial bureaucratic state. It was flailing around since the revolution, and the revolutionaries themselves had not thought through the question of how to build a new state. Above all, perhaps, neither the militarists nor the politicians, including the Guomindang, understood the nature of democracy. They believed in the power of government instead. Chen linked their delusions not only to their hunger for power but to the very problem of even good political leadership cited above. In a word, Chen implied that even the best constitutions cannot create democracy, but that only democratic practices might create constitutionalism. The answer lies not in government.

Notwithstanding China's political conditions, Chen found several grounds for optimism. First, China was still at the beginning of the road to republicanism and had only started to deal with its problems. Second, China's local self-governing traditions could provide a basis for democratization. Here, Chen was echoing arguments made by anarchists and ignoring for the moment all the ways in which local organizations were hierarchical and patriarchal. What he emphasized was their disconnect from the central government, which traditionally left local communities largely alone. While communities had to pay their taxes and roughly obey the law, they were able to establish their own village and clan temple organizations, charitable institutions (such as orphanages, nursing homes, clinics, and firefighting), schools, professional associations and guilds, and so forth. And third, precisely because China had failed to build up industry and commerce, it lacked capitalist and militarist classes like those of the Europe. Furthermore, China's cultural tradition had produced egalitarian ideals, such as Xu Xing's notion of aristocrats and peasants "farming together" and Confucius's demand that no one be poor, as well as recurring discussions of land redistribution.[35] "For all these reasons I believe that in the future political democracy and socioeconomic democracy will develop greatly in China."[36]

The notion that China could develop socialism because it lacked big capitalists had become something of a shared premise of political discourse since the turn of the century. That Chen would adopt this view was a sign of his intellectual desperation in the face of worsening political conditions. Looking beyond China, Chen again found something of a model in the West, though he continued to distinguish between the West's successful political democracy and its failure thus far to institute socioeconomic democracy. Still, his implication was that China had much to learn from the West. Chen cited "occupational associations" (*tongye lianhe*) as the key to the development of democracy there. Chen explained that "occupational associations" referred neither to guilds in the traditional sense, nor to modern trade unions, but rather were locally based organizations that included both bosses and workers, though not big capitalists.[37] Chen's example was that of shop workers where the shop owner himself engaged in the same basic tasks as his employees. Such associations were the basis of grassroots local self-government. Whether Chen's notion of local organizations was an accurate reflection of European history, it reflected his sense of the potential sources of change in contemporary China.[38] In the case of America, in Chen's reading of Dewey, immigrants' villages became the basis of towns, which became the basis of states, which even eventually formed a nation-state, albeit in a federal form that maintained local self-government. In China, then, occupational associations could perform this grassroots role.

Like so many writers of various political persuasions, Chen turned to the organic metaphor of the state: a life form composed neither of a single massive structure nor of scattered sand, but rather countless cells unified into a functioning whole. Whereas typical proponents of the organic state envisioned a commanding head and more or less servile limbs, Chen envisioned a state whose foundation lay in purely voluntary cooperation among the cells of local self-governing groups. "What is this foundation? It is the people's direct and practical self-governing and associating" (*renmin zhijie de shiji de zizhi yu lianhe*).

Chen was writing at least two decades into a policy debate over local self-government (*difang zizhi*) going back to the late Qing period.

The term had often referred to new techniques of central administration, and it had become associated with a discourse on the autocratic ways of "local despots" rather than to anything recognizable as democracy. Chen thus tried to redefine the term in ways parallel to his notion of occupational associations. The point was that *all persons* were to become involved in public questions directly, and not through representatives. Chen's reasoning might have been that representation allows for the cooptation of powers by either central forces or local power holders. He insisted that democracy would not be built by people following rules set by some distant government, but by procedures established by local self-government, properly understood, and by occupational associations. The facts on the ground will create the laws, which flow from social reality and never create that reality. Given the disorder of conditions in China today, Chen said, it was more imperative than ever for Chinese to take control of their own circumstances.

But how? Chen proposed what amounted to five principles. These reflected his utopian impulse applied to the horrors of the day. For example, Chen urged that people cut off all ties to the three pests of militarists, officials, and politicians. Chen had, of course, been saying as much since the beginning of the New Culture movement. Now, at the height of the May Fourth movement, he saw hope in persons who could follow the demands of their consciences, awaken the people, and plan a unified march toward democracy. Chen attributed political agency not to individual leaders or a vanguard party but to grassroots organizations. Chen's utopianism can be seen in how he imagined those associations.[39]

First, he urged that associations be kept small. "Self-government" (*zizhi*) should begin with villages and township; in cities, with neighborhoods; in unions, with particular sets of workers. Writing in the wake of the May Fourth movement with its plethora of organizations, Chen was able to point to many groups formed on a voluntary basis, if also examples of groups that had become too hierarchical to function democratically. Second—this point followed from the first and in my view lies at the heart of the impulse that informed Chen's utopianism—decision-making powers (*yijuequan*) must be in the hands of all members. All adult men and women are to meet together and directly participate in the governance of their associations. This would avoid, in Chen's view, the problems of minority rule and corruption. And it would nourish the organizational abilities of the people, encourage thinking about the public good, and foster involvement in public affairs. Citing

Dewey approvingly, Chen claimed that one point of democracy was to educate people: so they have to be involved; and once involved, they learn how to support the political sphere. Chen particularly emphasized the importance of involving women, who more than men, he said, are harmonious, careful, and empathetic. Third, heads of the various associations were to be elected by all the members, regardless of education, property or gender, and they were to serve limited terms. In fact, Chen wanted all meetings to be chaired only provisionally. And fourth, each group should focus on its members' needs. Thus local self-government organizations, in Chen's vision of democracy, would attend to education (schools, reading rooms), elections, roads, public hygiene, and in rural areas take charge of managing grain storage, water, and pests, and the like. Occupational associations would attend to education (night schools, reading rooms, popular lectures), credit unions, public hygiene, simple insurance (illness, old age, unemployment, and the like), consumer unions, employment contacts, leisure, and so forth.

Writing at the height of the May Fourth movement, Chen supported its anti-imperialism but wanted organizations to maintain their immediate focus. Once associations grew large enough to require representation rather than direct participation, Chen said, they became vulnerable to outside takeovers. Possibly Chen had in mind the compromise-inclined Shanghai Chamber of Commerce. At any rate, Chen believed that small-scale associations could meet the real political and economic needs of the Republic. Indeed, he argued as an aside, their very smallness protected them from the baleful attentions of politicians and officials; they did not threaten social revolution.

Chen's utopian impulses thus flowered in his vision of democratic participation, his belief that healthy human associations could form inside the larger corpse of a dead society, and his faith that their governance would lead to "making habits" that would eventually ensure that political and economic organizations of a larger scale would not fall under the domination of minorities.

Chen's vision of small, free, and democratic associations as the keystone of political order brought him close to an anarchist position. However, as noted above, Chen could not and did not reject the nation-state in principle or practice. The closest he came was perhaps, in 1918, when he equated the state with other "idols" of superstitious worship. Ignorant people allow themselves to be cheated by gods and monarchs, and Chen was happy to see that the Chinese and Russian revolutions had destroyed their monarchs.[40] States also cheat people, he said. Domestically, they protect aristocrats and the wealthy from internal disorder, while externally, they invade smaller countries. Chen cited the European war to argue that states were useless in preserving the peace, although he also thought people had the right to defend themselves. When in the early 1920s he began attacking anarchism explicitly, Chen admitted that all past and present states were exploitative but argued that the state nonetheless could be used to eliminate exploitation.[41] That is, under working-class control, they would become a source of "new power" used for good instead of evil. Indeed, as a newly minted Marxist, Chen argued that the state was the only source of power strong enough to abolish the system of private property and wage labor.

Marxism and Proletarian Dictatorship

Initially, very few established Chinese intellectuals were particularly impressed by Marxism, though the vast majority considered themselves socialists of one kind or another. Many took a sympathetic interest in the Russian Revolution. Having celebrated the Allied victory in World War I, in which China had participated after 1917 by sending workers to fill British and French factory and transport jobs, they found the Versailles Peace Treaty a sharply disillusioning disappointment. The Allied victory had, indeed, been more than celebrated in China: leading intellectuals thought it presaged the end of militarism, imperialism, and racism. The Versailles Treaty, as we have seen, provoked the May Fourth protest movement, and the Chinese government was forced to refuse to sign the treaty. The intellectual and political trends of the 1920s grew out of disillusionment, then, but led to optimism and activism rather than cynicism and quietism. A handful of intellectuals and students turned toward the Russian Revolution and Lenin for lessons on how to break out of China's civil wars and foreign oppression.[42] In 1919 Lenin had founded the Third International ("Comintern"), and its representatives traveled to China to find support and helped build the Chinese Communist Party (CCP) over the course of 1920 and 1921. As for Chen Duxiu, as the historian Feng Chongyi points out, by 1920 Chen was skeptical of parliamentary democracy, attracted to the notion of direct democracy, and interpreted "liberty" less as a set of rights and more as the "positive liberty" of achieving individual enlightenment and moral responsibility.[43]

In fact, such views were quite deep-rooted in radical circles from the late Qing onward. But in Chen's case the attractions of Marxism were more positive than negative. His intellectual and activist turn was not a reaction against (say, against liberalism), or at least not purely so, but a move toward (toward a genuinely new political order in the foreseeable future). Marxism—at least through the lens of the Russian Revolution, as well as Lenin's Bolshevism and the effective party organization promised by democratic centralism—offered a new way of thinking about political action. And as Hung-Yok Ip has shown, for Chen and a few others, Marxism seemed to offer a way of achieving democracy.[44]

Chen's new ideological militancy was a return to revolution, and his turn to the "laboring classes" undoubtedly signaled a major new factor in his political analysis.[45] If anything, Chen's thinking was even more shaped by the utopian impulse than before. His attempt to mount a principled defense of power (force, coercion, *qiangquan*) continued to be based on twinned despair over the conditions of China and limitless hope in political action. With a handful of other leading intellectuals and Comintern advisers, he helped organize the Chinese Communist Party in 1921 and became its first leader. He was now ready to condescend to traditional "idealistic socialism" as ineffective.[46] All the various forms of socialism, including Marxism, shared the same basic goal, Chen suggested. But Marxist socialism offered scientific methods to change patterns of production and consumption on the basis of a true understanding of socioeconomic conditions. Chen thus distinguished between the idealistic, subjective, and utopian (or "fantastical," *kongxiang*) on the one hand, and the scientific and objective on the other. We may question whether Chen's understanding of Marx at this point was less utopian than his earlier views—there seem in Chen's vision to be no real obstacles to the transference of the forces of production to public ownership, nor to increasing productivity once public organs were in charge of the economy, nor to distributing surplus value (profits) more fairly to the actual workers. Nonetheless, for Chen the key term to understand social relations had shifted from "equality" to "production and distribution."

The point for Chen was that when capitalism was properly understood, the way to overthrow it became clear. Notably, Chen equated capitalism with anarchism, that is, a lawless and unregulated regime. Citing Marx, Chen proclaimed that while capitalism looked impregnable, it was creating the means of its own destruction through the accumulation of surplus value. That is to say, capital accumulation and investment leads to overproduction, which leads to economic panic and social crisis. The market is flooded with goods that the vast majority of the population, the workers, cannot absorb, then production stops, prices drop, unemployment soars, and capitalism collapses. In good Leninist fashion, Chen explained the failure of capitalism to collapse on schedule thus far as due to the move of surplus value (capital) into new colonial markets: war and imperialism. This brought capitalism and militarism into close association, the way to break the latter lying in the destruction of the former. Chen took for granted that socialism would replace a deceased capitalism, but he did not explain the exact mechanisms through which this replacement would be effected. He did, in his discussion of various types of socialism, emphasize the importance of the seizure of political power (which Chen thought syndicalism and of course anarchism neglected). He was suspicious of calls for the liberty of individuals and small groups. Furthermore, he remained deeply skeptical of parliamentary systems, now on two grounds.[47] First, because class struggle left no room for any cooperation with the bourgeoisie that participation in parliamentary politics would imply. And second, because parliaments were inherently controlled by the bourgeoisie for their own benefit; even if small reforms might be placed on the political agenda, the bourgeoisie would never allow its own instrument to be turned against it. Coming to the question of proletarian dictatorship versus democracy, Chen encapsulated the differences between the German Social Democratic Party and the Russian Communist Party in a dialog:

> The German SDP asked the Russian CP: "Since the property-owning class are also citizens, how can you simply insist that the proletariat carry out class dictatorship?"
>
> The Russians replied: "How can you not advocate that all the people join the proletariat?"
>
> The German SDP then asked: "Doesn't any class dictatorship contradict democracy?"
>
> The Russians replied: "Isn't the real meaning of the democracy you talk about simply the class dictatorship of the property-owners?"[48]

For the point was the seizure of power. Citing Marx, Chen said that only then could all capital and all forces of production be moved from the hands of the bourgeoisie to those of the state, that is, the organized force of the proletariat. Especially in China, the politicians of the propertied class were so corrupt and incompetent that only revolutionary steps, not democratic steps, could break the system.

By the next year Chen was ready with a Marxist explanation of how revolution followed the laws of historical materialism and the class struggle. At least by implication, he argued that as capitalism developed through new modes of economic production, and since the proletariat developed along with the capitalist class and was of course vastly more numerous, it stood to inherit those productive forces when capitalism collapsed—collapsed not least due to class struggle led by the proletariat.[49] The struggle between proletarian and capitalist classes is necessarily, Chen said, a struggle for political power, and so he concluded his essay with extensive quotes from the *Communist Manifesto*, *The Civil War in France*, and *The Critique of the Gotha Program* to illustrate the need for proletarian dictatorship during the transition from capitalism to socialism.[50] While harshly critical of anarchism, Chen suggested that even anarchism and communism shared a final goal: from each according to their ability, to each according to their need.[51] Proletarian dictatorship would be especially difficult to carry out in China, Chen said, because the Chinese disliked leaders and following orders, but it was the only way to achieve a "great organizational and fighting force." And the task of the Communist Party was to lead the proletariat as its vanguard. For Chen, then, Marxism obviated the need for democracy as either means or goal; he evidently envisioned that proletarian dictatorship would give way to an anarchist paradise.

Much of Chen's ideological work emerged in debates with China's anarchists, as well as the putatively utopian socialists, as Arif Dirlik has shown.[52] The stickiest question was the role of the state, which of course anarchists abhorred, and in particular the concept of proletarian dictatorship. Chen understood that the state was a source of coercion (*qiangquan*) and capitalist exploitation.[53] But he could not condemn coercion as such. In fact, if used for the sake of the weak and in the cause of justice, then coercion was a scientific solution. Facing powerful capitalists, workers had no choice but to seize the organs of the state in order to dismantle the systems of private property and wage labor.

Herein lies class struggle, which alone the bourgeoisie fears. Chen not only spoke of the necessity of force in suppressing the bourgeoisie in the wake of the revolution, but condemned "superstitious belief in the omnipotence of liberty." But to insist on the necessity of the state was not in itself to justify proletarian dictatorship except as a revolutionary necessity, and Chen cited *The Communist Manifesto* to promise that as new forms of production eliminated all classes, then the special powers of the proletariat would also disappear. But there could be no real democracy before that happy day. This was to deny democracy as a topic of interest for the foreseeable future. Indeed, at least once Chen went so far as to dismiss democracy as "a weapon previously used by the bourgeoisie to overthrow the feudal system, and today being used to trick the common people in order to hold onto power."[54] Whatever its positive historical function had been, Chen said, democracy no longer represented the "whole popular will" (*quan minyi*). It could not, since in a world divided between capitalists and workers, there simply could be no such thing. If one possible implication of this view was that once everyone became workers, then democracy could be implemented, Chen's point was not that. Rather, he emphasized that democracy could only represent the interests of the bourgeoisie.

Trotskyism, Revolution, a National Assembly

In the early 1920s, then, Chen rejected anarchism as a fantasy and a trap for the unenlightened. He dismissed liberal democracy as a form of false consciousness meant to disguise the violence of the bourgeoisie. And he simply had very little to say about any kind of democratic order. However, starting in the late 1920s, democracy gradually assumed an ever greater role in his political theory. Chiang Kai-shek moved to crush the communist movement in 1927—just four years after the Guomindang and the CCP entered into a de facto alliance called the United Front. By the end of 1928 the GMD had "reunified" China or at least taken control of the central provinces. Some 90 percent of Communist Party members had been executed. Not surprisingly, the CCP's leader, Chen Duxiu, was held to blame. Ironically, while policies supported by Chen contributed to the debacle, he had been dubious of the United Front from the beginning. It was disastrous Comintern instructions that were mainly responsible for leading the CCP to its destruction—save for a few hundred exiles in Moscow, a pitiful number of survivors hiding in China's cities, and remnants that fled to the most remote parts of the countryside where, eventually, the party would revive.[55] Into 1930 or so, in the face of Trotsky's criticism, the Comintern, which was under the control of Stalin, insisted that the revolution was on the verge of success even after Chiang's attacks in April 1927. Chinese Communists were ordered to unite with the so-called anti-Chiang "left GMD," which soon turned on them as well. Then, in 1930, small bands of Communists were ordered to attack major cities such as Guangzhou, Nanchang, Wuhan, and Changsha in order to create an impression of revolutionary momentum. All these moves were disastrous for the Communists; not surprisingly, they also engaged in internecine slaughter.

Meanwhile, Chen himself had gone underground in Shanghai, where he began reading Trotskyist writings in 1929.[56] Refusing any direct cooperation with the CCP, he was expelled from the party in late 1929. In 1931 he helped establish a Left Opposition group with ties to Trotsky, though the small number of Chinese Trotskyists remained divided among themselves. Between 1928 and his arrest by the Nationalists in 1932, Chen rethought Marxist doctrine. He began to combine his belief in revolutionary class struggle with his belief in democracy. After his release from prison in 1937, though ill, spied on, and isolated, in the few political writings Chen managed to produce before his death in 1942, he explored the concept of "proletarian democracy." This was eventually to lead him away from Trotskyism as understood at the time.[57]

At the end of the 1920s, then, Chen faced the need to explain how the Communists' plans had failed so utterly and what now needed to be done. First, he read the situation as a major defeat. Even as the Comintern was insisting that a revolutionary "high tide" was gathering, Chen considered why what he called the "second revolution" had been so thoroughly routed and what revolutionaries could do when most of the roads forward seemed blocked. The "first revolution"—that of 1911—had of course also failed in Chen's analysis and, as we have seen, he ultimately blamed traditional culture and looked to a new Chinese culture as cure. Now, at the end of the 1920s, he could no longer simply focus on cultural questions, and he looked to a new political movement as cure.

To examine the question of when Chen became a "Trotskyist" and what kind of Trotskyist he became quickly leads to large swamps of sticky ideological quicksand from which escape is difficult. To call for a "dictatorship of the proletariat" versus a "dictatorship of the proletariat and the poor peasantry" versus a "dictatorship of the proletariat at the head of the poor peasantry" versus a "democratic dictatorship of the workers and the peasants" might or might not correspond to factional infighting, party policy of the day, or, just perhaps, a larger vision of revolution. It suffices for my purposes to say that in 1931 and 1932 Chen regarded himself and was generally regarded as a Trotskyist.[58] After Chen's release from prison, while still obviously close to Trotskism in many ways, the label seems less and less useful and was eventually abjured by Chen himself.

The fissiparous Trotskyists came together with Chen, under Trotsky's personal prompting, in the spring of 1931 as the Left Opposition Faction of the CCP Left Opposition, or simply Left Opposition. Looking back, its platform blamed the Communists' defeat on their own decision in 1923 to join with the Guomindang and then on the Stalinist "opportunism" and "putchism" (i.e., failure to fight when fighting was possible, failure to hunker down when hunkering down was necessary, and premature formation of soviets) between 1927 and 1930.[59] The Trotskyists charged that the Comintern had failed to recognize the true nature of the Guomindang; that is, as a party of a bourgeoisie that was inextricably linked to "feudal forces" (the agrarian landed classes) and especially to international capital. Imperialism in China could not drive the bourgeoisie to cooperate with progressive classes, as the Comintern hoped, but rather served to sharpen class struggle; the bourgeoisie would always cooperate with imperialist forces rather than risk social change. The United Front had thus left the workers without their own party, and the CCP had focused on attracting unreliable petty bourgeois intellectuals instead of recruiting workers to rouse the "oppressed poor of cities and villages." As history, this account is dubious in several places. Certainly, much of the decimation of the party between 1927 and 1930 can be laid at the door of Comintern policy and Stalin's personal interventions, but it is difficult to imagine how the party would have grown as it did in the mid-1920s without the United Front, and it is difficult to imagine how any policies could have actually defeated the GMD at any point after the dissolution of the United Front. The "second revolution" of 1925–27 that brought the GMD to power—or in the GMD's terms, the "national revolution"—had revolutionary overtones but was never going to be a social revolution. But the point here is that the Trotskyists rightly insisted that they faced a counterrevolutionary period of unknown length, not a revolutionary upsurge.

Looking forward, the Left Opposition platform saw a period of "preparation" coming, during which the proletariat would recover its earlier confidence and power.[60] The Trotskyists, like the CCP, could not analyze the Guomindang and "warlords" except in terms of class; that is, they could not conceive of these groups as state-based or proto-state-based groups independent of any classes that might support them. But the Trotskyists did understand that the bourgeoisie would eventually become dissatisfied with the Guomindang's military dictatorship. Their platform noted at least implicit tensions between the militarists and the bourgeoisie, and between the Chinese bourgeoisie and foreign imperialism, as well as, of course, between the workers and the bourgeoisie. While stressing that the bourgeoisie would not move against the government until the workers' and peasants' movements were entirely crushed, the platform implied that the Communists could use the bourgeoisie's penchant for democracy, however limited that democracy, to pursue their own claims. In what might seem to be a contradiction to persons who have not mastered the dialectic, for Trotskyists as much as for Stalinists the bourgeoisie is simultaneously a historically objective friend and enemy. What the Trotskyists insisted against the Comintern, was that the Chinese Communists should be advocating democracy and that the proletariat, as it matured, should use the democratic movement to seize power when the time was right. The point was, contrary to Stalin's views, that there need be no phase or "stage" of bourgeois democratic rule: the "third revolution" would carry right through to overthrow the system of private property.

This was a plan, not a utopian vision, though it may have been unrealistically hopeful. It reflected Chen's basic position at the time, but in essays that Chen wrote himself over the next few years the fire of democracy grows increasingly brighter. Chen never returned to the liberal-democratic position he held in the 1910s, but the utopian impulse behind his view of democracy in the 1930s is revealed in his use of the concept as the fundamental basis of political action and organization.

Chen first fastened on to the Trotskyist notion of a broad-based movement for an all-powerful national assembly to be elected by universal suffrage. At this stage, Chen wanted to use democracy as a means of garnering support—it was not the ultimate goal of the revolution. More clearly than in the platform's hints, Chen did not think the Guomindang was the representative of the bourgeoisie so much as simply the mask of a military dictatorship. He noted that the Guomindang relied on imperialism and military forces, and was itself an assemblage of warlords.[61] China's economic growth was real, but was insufficient to throw off the obstacles imposed by imperialism, and the bourgeoisie was too weak to unify the domestic market. If this analysis was not enough to turn Chen into a Trotskyist, given his initial opposition to the United Front, Trotsky's critique of the alliance was no doubt satisfying. More broadly, Trotsky's analysis of what had gone wrong in China and his forthright acknowledgment that the communist movement was in a "trough" seemed considerably more to the point than the Comintern's faith in revolutionary momentum. No doubt, as well, it helped that Trotsky blamed Stalin rather than Chen for the catastrophe in China. Finally, it should be noted, Chen associated Trotskyism with calls for democracy in China and in the party.[62]

The chief aim of the concept of permanent revolution as Trotsky first developed it was to explain how, contrary to Marx, revolution could occur in a backward country such as Russia. Trotsky's answer was the "permanent revolution."[63] While in classical Marxist theory the bourgeoisie destroyed feudal forces and augmented capitalist institutions, thereby creating the conditions amenable to the rise of the proletariat, the route to revolution in colonized and semicolonized countries would have to be different since the native bourgeoisies were tied to imperialist forces. At the same time, however, that meant feudal forces (large estate owners, if any) were also tied to the imperialists, or, to use today's terminology, global capitalism. Although it seemed that backward countries were "feudal"—after all, the vast majority of their people remained peasants—in fact they were already fundamentally capitalist, according to Trotsky: that is, they were inextricably tied into global capitalist networks. Revolution would stem from workers leading peasants to overthrow their oppressors, meaning both native bourgeoisie and foreign imperialists. This movement would combine the revolutionary tasks of building democracy and socialism, as well as that of national liberation. "Democracy" for Trotsky largely referred to the "democratic dictatorship of the proletariat and peasantry." That is, a government formed by a solid majority of workers.[64] The government then becomes an organ to further "revolutionize the masses" and thereby widen its basis. For Trotsky that meant working-class leadership of the peasants and suppression of the bourgeoisie. He concluded, "With regard to countries with a belated bourgeois development, especially the colonial and semi-colonial countries, the theory of the permanent revolution signifies that the complete and genuine solution of their tasks of achieving *democracy and national emancipation* is conceivable only through the dictatorship of the proletariat as the leader of the subjugated nation, above all of its peasant masses. . . . The democratic revolution grows over directly into the socialist revolution and thereby becomes a *permanent* revolution."[65] Which all must be led by the vanguard party.

What was permanent about the permanent revolution? First, the term referred to the rapidity or even simultaneity of revolutionary tasks rather than distinct stages: the bourgeois class was to overthrow the monarchy, build representative institutions, and reform and rationalize agriculture; while, very quickly, the proletariat was to overthrow and suppress the bourgeoisie, set up self-governing organizations, nationalize industry, and so forth—the proletariat would carry out these tasks (with support of the peasantry) in one vast movement. It was thus always necessary for the proletariat to maintain their autonomous organization, even if they entered into alliances with others. "The permanent revolution, in the sense which Marx attached to this concept, means a revolution which makes no compromise with any single form of class rule, which does not stop at the democratic stage, which goes over to socialist measures and to war against reaction from without; that is, a revolution whose every successive stage is rooted in the preceding one and which can end only in complete liquidation."[66] (This was the theoretical basis for Trotsky's criticism of the United Front of the GMD and CCP.)

Second, permanent revolution highlighted the international character of socialist revolution. Trotsky doubted that any socialist system limited to one nation could succeed. It was definitely impossible that a colonized nation could carry out all the tasks of revolution until the forces of imperialism were defeated around the world. But furthermore, Trotsky insisted that generally speaking the world economy "is fully ripe for the socialist revolution."[67]

Third, permanent revolution described the continuation of revolutionary change even after the proletariat had seized power. "For an indefinitely long time and in constant internal struggle, all social relations undergo transformation. Society keeps on changing its skin. Each stage of transformation stems directly from the preceding. This process necessarily retains a political character, that is, it develops through collisions between various groups in the society which is in transformation."[68] Socialism would still take time to build, needing the higher productivity that had only so far been achieved by the advanced capitalist countries. Under the dictatorship of the proletariat this process can occur through continued class struggle. One lesson that Chinese Trotskyists (and Mao Zedong, though no Trotskyist, as well) took from the so-called second revolution was that both workers and peasants were prepared to pursue their own revolutionary aims—land confiscation and control of factories—beyond even steps that the party approved of.

Although the Chinese Left Opposition derived a strategy from Trotskyism, Trotsky's discussion of the permanent revolution was anything but a formula. Perhaps one of the appealing features of Trotsky was, indeed, his sharp awareness of the unique qualities of every historical period and every potential site of revolution. Russia in 1905 was not much like France in 1789 or Germany in 1848. Chinese reading Trotsky at the end of the 1920s could infer that much of his specific analysis of his own backward nation applied to China, but that they must analyze China's precise conditions on their own terms. "Marxism is above all a method of analysis—not analysis of texts, but analysis of social relations."[69]

The question of when Trotsky believed exactly what about the Chinese Revolution has been much debated among historians and partisans.[70] Here it suffices to note that a number of Chinese students in Moscow had been attracted to Trotsky's ideas, limited as was their access to them at the time, as early as 1923. Prominent Chinese members of the two-year-old party had consistently opposed the First United Front starting that year. Trotsky was also a critic of the alliance, or at least insistent that the CCP keep its organizational independence. Caught up in his losing struggle for power with Stalin, he was sensitive to the threat posed by the Guomindang in 1926 and quick to realize the extent of the Communists' losses in 1927 and 1928. The theoretical problems at stake included the class nature of the Guomindang and of the revolutionary forces. Essentially, Trotsky considered that the GMD represented both big and petty bourgeois elements of Chinese society, but was increasingly under the control of the former. He did not believe any "national bourgeoisie" was capable of anti-imperialist action or reform. This was contrary to the Comintern view, which distinguished between national bourgeoisie, which were supposedly independent of the foreigners and could be brought to support the revolution, and "comprador bourgeoisie," which simply represented the interests of foreign capital. For Trotsky, given China's status as an "oppressed semicolonial country," the bourgeoisie *as a whole* was tied to imperialist forces.[71] In 1927 Trotsky had felt that the Chinese Revolution was a bourgeois-national revolution but, "in conditions of the imperialist decay of capitalism," it was a revolution capable of bringing an alliance of workers and peasants to power.[72] That is, as the principle of the permanent revolution stated, revolutionary momentum would prove unstoppable, as long as the revolutionaries themselves did not falter. They would create a democratic political system, albeit a transitional one. There was to be no "bourgeois stage" as Stalin taught; rather, the tasks of the bourgeois democratic revolution would be led by the proletariat. By the end of the year, however, this dream had turned into nightmare.

In October 1928 Trotsky urged the Left Opposition to advocate a "constituent" or "national" assembly.[73] His reasoning was based on the premise that not only had the revolution been defeated but China was entering into a period of "bourgeois stabilization." The implication was that since some kind of national assembly was in the cards, it behooved the Communists to use the opportunity to raise their voices and associate themselves with general demands—even bourgeois demands—for popular representation. Yet a truly representative national assembly scarcely seemed likely: "In the process of agitation for this slogan, it will obviously be necessary to explain to the masses that it is doubtful if such an assembly will be convened, and even if it were, it would be powerless so long as the material power remains in the hands of the Guomindang generals."[74] *But*, "From this flows the possibility of broaching in a new manner the slogan of the arming of the workers and the peasants," or at least in effect Communists might be able to reemerge into the political sphere. Their discussion of a national assembly could metaphorically arm the workers and peasants against the "influence of petty-bourgeois democracy."

A national assembly for Trotsky was neither necessary nor sufficient for the third revolutionary stage to form; it was not even particularly likely, but it was the right struggle at the right time: between two revolutions though not itself revolutionary. By focusing on demands for the eight-hour day, confiscation of the land, and national independence, such a struggle would at least further the "democratic stage of the revolution" regardless of the attitude of the bourgeoisie. And: "If the Chinese proletariat is obliged to live a few more years (even if it were only another year) under the regime of the Guomindang, could the Chinese Communist Party abandon the struggle for the extension of legal possibilities of all sorts, for the freedom of press, of assembly, or organization, to strike, etc.?" As Trotsky again insisted at the end of the year, given the impossibility of establishing soviets, it was still possible to mobilize "the broadest possible layers of the workers to participate actively in the political life of the period we are in."[75] In 1930 he seemed to take more seriously the possibility that a national assembly with Communist participation might really happen, in which case the Communists would have a public platform to build the party and even encourage the creation of soviets. The polemical point was that soviets and a national assembly were not contradictory goals under the right circumstances, even while soviets remained a further stage of development away. (The scattered rural forces of Communists, including a group led by Mao Zedong, began to establish soviets—that is, territories under their control—in several remote areas by 1931, but these remained extremely small.)

Chinese Trotskyists were initially skeptical of such a bourgeois-sounding slogan as that for a national assembly, but accepted it as a tactic, not a strategy. They saw it as a means of maintaining some kind of contact with the masses until the revolution could build up a new head of steam.[76] In 1930 Chen emerged from silence, insisting that China was not in a revolutionary situation but in a "trough" between the failed second revolution and the third revolution to come.[77] He foresaw that the urban petty bourgeoisie and intellectuals would grow increasingly dissatisfied with Guomindang rule. Under these circumstances, Chen said, Communists should not be thinking about armed uprisings and soviets, but rather they should rally around calls for a national assembly that would appeal to elements of the bourgeoisie. Thinking about the coming third revolution, or how to engage in revolutionary activities in the currently unpromising situation, Chen pointed to the fundamental contradictions of capitalism: the unrest of workers and peasants, and the growing disillusionment of the petty bourgeoisie and intellectuals with the Guomindang. Calls for a national assembly to have supreme power and to be elected by universal secret ballot, Chen said, were appealing to these groups. Even the bourgeoisie itself, he thought, was beginning to turn against the Guomindang, or at least favored a bit more democracy. Fundamentally, Chen was thinking in terms of how to hasten the revolutionary movement, and he was still using orthodox (Stalinist) notions of stages of revolutionary development that had to go through a bourgeois phase. Nonetheless, his thinking about democracy reveals a utopian impulse that he was to develop throughout the decade. As early as 1930 he noted:

> Of course democracy does not transcend classes, and what is normally called democracy is in fact only bourgeois democracy. This kind of democracy was previously used as a tool

by the bourgeoisie to oppose the feudal aristocracy and trick the working class; but when social class relations were transformed, then as the feudal forces collapsed and the working class entered upon the political stage, the ruling bourgeois class immediately recognized that the cutting edge of this tool could slice themselves, and the hurriedly put it away, and once again took out from the trash barrels the old religion, ritual dogmas, and morality that had been previously used to oppose democracy. While it remains under the control of the bourgeoisie and has not yet seized political power, the proletariat should use this sharp tool of the bourgeoisie without any niceties to deal with the bourgeoisie, to sweep away obstacles to the proletariat's entrance on to the political stage, and to bring about the conditions for their own class liberation. . . . But the democracy that the masses demand from the ruling class: this is substantive and not in name only; we must stop the bourgeoisie from cheating us with fake democracy and the petty bourgeoisie's compromises; thus we must struggle for a national assembly chosen by equal and direct and secret balloting. We must propose as our indivisible four slogans: the national assembly; the eight-hour day; land confiscation; and national independence. . . . The endpoint of bourgeois democracy becomes the starting point of proletarian democracy, which is to say the starting point of the preservation of the political power of soviets and a government of rights and liberties acquired by the majority of the popular, the laboring masses.[78]

Chen acknowledged that the future would see armed uprisings and soviets while the present was a time of propaganda; in effect, this was to consider "democracy" a means and not an end.[79] The movement for a national assembly could draw the working class back into politics, expose the "political bankruptcy of the upper classes," and ultimately demonstrate the need for armed uprising. "Democracy is not our basic goal." In a 1931 essay Chen insisted that while the slogan of democracy could rally people in a counterrevolutionary period, the future dictatorship of the proletariat had to be built on the foundations of mass organizations such as labor unions, poor peasants' associations, and strike committees.[80] It would not be built through a national assembly, at least not directly.

Only revolutionary struggle would "dry up the springs of the bourgeois class democracy."

Nonetheless, Chen understood bourgeois democracy to play a progressive role in history. Chen further distinguished between a kind of true or even—protestations notwithstanding—a transcendent democracy from bourgeois democracy. In 1932, while again claiming that democracy cannot transcend classes since it is historically shaped by class struggle, he nonetheless stated that bourgeois democracy of the modern period was a higher form than that of the Middle Ages.[81] This implied a view of democracy as evolving through time: a historical subject in its own right. Indeed, Chen traced democracy from the popular assemblies of prestate clan societies to the rise of the bourgeois class of the modern period. Saying that bourgeois democracy was narrower than proletarian democracy, Chan was saying that proletarian democracy will broaden bourgeois democracy as bourgeois democracy had broadened what came before it, and hence that if democracy did not precisely transcend class, it evolves progressively along with the rise of first the bourgeoisie and then the proletariat. Chen was to further develop this idea after his release from prison in 1936. A note of teleological utopianism crept in: "Democracy is the banner under which in every age, ever since man first developed political organization, right down until the withering away of politics (in Greece, in Rome, and from the modern period into the future), the majority class opposes the privileges of the minority."[82]

Meanwhile, in 1931 and 1932 Chen had insisted that, evil as the Guomindang's form of democracy was, a fight for even bourgeois democracy offered a way forward. On the one hand, Chen noted that, unlike China, Western bourgeois democracies at least had the forms of universal suffrage for representative organs, as well as freedoms of association (including political parties), publishing, and religion.[83] On the other hand:

> The fundamental meaning of democracy is that the majority of the people manage national political affairs. Not only is this not democracy when a simple minority monopolize power, but even in the bourgeois countries of Europe and America—although they seem to have considerable freedoms of association, publishing, speech, and religion, although formally they have universal suffrage for the election of representative organs, and although there has been great progress since the

> political system of the Middle Ages—they are still incomplete and fake democracies. Democracies that are limited to the narrow framework of capitalism really can only benefit the minority of the wealthy class.[84]

This is because as long as the bourgeoisie controls the state organs of the army, police, courts, and prisons, the majority of people—workers and peasants—can never get real power. Elections are manipulated by money and propaganda, bribery, employer pressures, and so forth. Freedoms of assembly and the press are meaningless when ordinary people do not have the resources to pursue them. Chen believed that the Chinese bourgeoisie was completely "backward" and in thrall to the imperialist powers, while the petty bourgeoisie, students, and intellectuals were tending somewhat leftward.[85] The bourgeoisie was even more afraid of Western-style "fake democracy" than it was of socialism, if only because the former was a little closer to realization. They were happy to have a military dictatorship to suppress workers. Chen thought the petty bourgeoisie was becoming restless because it had failed to benefit from Chiang Kai-shek's counterrevolution. However, it was not really allied to the majority of Chinese—workers and peasants—and so was largely limited to the notions of formal bourgeois democracy.

For all his disdain for bourgeois democracy, Chen also thought that democracy and revolution were inextricably linked. Perhaps more significant, in light of the utopian impulse that energized Chen's rethinking about democracy, was his suggestion that it was "advantageous for the working class' struggle for self-liberation."[86] Or: " 'True' democracy will never come about through peaceful means, but can only be realized when the workers-poor peasants-laboring masses with their blood overthrow the class that is oppressing them and build soviet political institutions that combine legislative and executive powers. . . . In a certain sense, we communists are basically the most sincere and thorough-going democrats."[87] Chen insisted that a democratic movement would both garner widespread support and bring the working class back into political life. In this struggle the working class would in a sense create itself as a political being. In 1931, Chen described what they should be fighting for: *not* what the Guomindang had on offer but a national assembly that would represent the "whole people" and not incidentally fight for the "elimination of all of the special privileges and interests of the imperialists in China."[88] Chen had moved on from thinking of propaganda for a national assembly as a means to envisioning a national assembly as a goal.

> The national assembly that all the oppressed masses of China want is not that of the Guomindang, nor that run entirely by the upper classes, but a national assembly that represents all the people of the nation through direct universal suf-frage. Not one that that embraces the military tutelage of the Guomindang, but a national assembly that fights for representative government of the whole people. Not one that aids the various factions of the Guomindang to divide up the loot but a national assembly that protects the interests of the workers and peasants and all oppressed masses. Not one that bangs the drums for the imperialists to raise up the position of the compradors but a national assembly that categorically proclaims the elimination of all of the special privileges and interests of the imperialists in China.[89]

The key to Chen's thinking at this point lay in his understanding of the concept of "permanent revolution" or even better, in Chinese, "uninterrupted revolution" (buduan de geming). Chen traced the concept to Marx and Engels via Lenin and Trotsky, while condemning Stalin for promoting the concepts of revolutionary stages and socialism in one country.[90] Chen understood the notion of permanent revolution in the case of China as a strategy for moving from the present counterrevolu-tionary conditions to a high tide of revolution, and then quickly on to building socialism under the rule of the proletariat.[91]

In the wake of the Japanese invasion of Manchuria of September 1931, Chen consistently supported Chinese resistance against Japanese aggression. He pointed out that the Japanese occupation of Manchuria cost China not only sovereignty over a particular territory, but resources such as coal and timber, markets, routes for migrants, and so forth.[92] And worse, if the Western imperialists followed Japan's example and carved out their own territories in China, China would move from semicolonial status to outright colonization. It would then become a "lost country" (wangguo). In that case, the big shots of the Guomindang would become the tools of imperialists like the Indian princes, and the sufferings of a lost country would be visited upon the laboring masses.[93]

While Chen never believed that nationalism was a direct route to social revolution, he saw that nationalist movements had a natural connection to democratic movements.[94] We might put it this way: since foreign imperialists and Chinese capitalists worked hand in glove, the struggle for national independence and the struggle for the liberation of workers and peasants was much the same struggle. The Guomindang was betraying the country just as it had betrayed the working class, Chen said.[95] Chen analyzed the Guomindang's inability to unify the nation in terms of imperialist pressures on China.[96] From the late Qing, Chen pointed out, different parts of China had fallen under foreign influence, each with its separate economic core that became the basis of the war-lordism of the Republic. The 1911 Revolution sought neither to oppose imperialism nor to liberate the workers, which helps explain why it failed to fulfill its promise to complete the bourgeois revolution. The chance to unify the nation through revolution in 1927 was lost with the Guomindang's counterrevolution, which in turn stemmed from the fundamental weakness of the Chinese bourgeoisie, which ultimately stemmed from the pressures put on it by the imperialist powers. Guomindang leaders may have thought they did not need support from the workers and peasants, but their inability to unify China was proving them wrong.

Many Chinese blamed the Guomindang for not offering stiffer resistance to the Japanese, and Chen optimistically noted in 1932 that Chinese economic conditions were leading to a rise of national conscious-ness among the "laboring masses"—even peasant armies were offering local resistance to the Japanese.[97] Therefore, the rise in popular national consciousness could be linked to calls for greater democracy, an uprising against the Guomindang and the Japanese could lead to revolution, and the proletariat could seize power from the bourgeoisie. Again, this was a highly optimistic strategy, not actual utopianism. It was also betrayed by events, once Japan invaded China proper in 1937.

Trotsky's views on conditions at this time were broadly similar. Trotsky thought the growing Japanese presence was radicalizing urban petty bourgeoisie (intellectuals), but that the Chiang Kai-shek govern-ment was more Bonapartist than fascist.[98] That is, that the Guomindang was entirely militarized, lacking any social base, while the Italian and German fascists were backed by the counterrevolutionary petty bour-geoisie. Indeed, Trotsky noted, calls in China for a constituent assembly had never been so widespread nor public opinion so directly critical of the Guomindang. And he continued to envision an immediate political program that linked calls for the independence of China, land to the poor peasants, and an elected assembly.

Class Struggle and Proletarian Democracy

From 1936 to his death in 1942, Chen was rethinking the role of democracy in the revolution in ways that took him beyond permanent revolution. In particular, he began to see democracy as fundamental to social progress. Japan's invasion of Manchuria in 1931 and its invasion of China proper in 1937 forced Chen to think about the relationship between communist revolution, democracy, and national resistance. At the theoretical level, the existence of fascism prompted him to insist strenuously on the distinction between fascist dictatorship and bourgeois democracy. Opposed to younger Trotskyists who saw no difference or thought that fascism might even prove a better foundation for prole-tarian revolution, Chen furiously argued that bourgeois democracy, for all its faults and limitations, was infinitely superior in itself and also gave revolutionaries greater scope for activism. Ultimately, Chen was heading toward the view that democracy transcended classes, at least in the sense that there was a kind of ideal democracy—we might call this the logic of democracy—that was not reducible to class democracy (whether bourgeois or proletarian). Chen was not ready to say this as of 1936. But in his essay on "The Proletariat and Democracy" Chen insisted that democracy "developed in tandem with history" and formed various historical stages.[99] The roots of democracy are ancient, and if it has not constantly improved or progressed as history unfolded, it has served as a "motive force" for progress. The bourgeois revolution's "task" is to replace the minority rule of kings and nobles with that of the majority through elected assemblies. This task remains unfulfilled, but today, at least, revolutionary forces throughout the world are pushing it to completion. Indeed, completion of this "bourgeois democratic revolution" will lead to the socialist revolution.

Chen's thinking thus far remained within the bounds of the Trotskyist concept of permanent revolution. He continued to deny that the bourgeoisie was capable of supporting "true universal suffrage" or liberating the peasantry, and he implied that the bourgeoisie—at least in the case of China—would not move beyond counterrevolution. Thus, it was up to other classes to take up the "democratic task of the bourgeois type."[100] Engaging in comparative analysis, Chen implied that only in England had the bourgeoisie, leading the peasantry, actually carried out a democratic revolution, albeit one of course limited to formal rather than substantive democracy. In France, the petty bourgeoisie led the workers in a similar move, and in Russia the proletariat led the peasants. In Russia, Chen found the prototypical case of permanent revolution, whereby the proletariat in carrying out the bourgeois democratic revolution could immediately move on to socialist revolution. Thus permanent revolution, for Chen, referred to the ability of the proletariat to seize power in the course of the democratic revolution, at least in the case of backward countries.[101] The democratic revolution inescapably turns into the socialist revolution.

But as socialism is being achieved, there is no turning back—and here Chen moved beyond Trotsky:

> The moment we seize power is precisely the start of the era in which we carry out our democratic platform, not its termination. We need to say that at that time we cannot limit ourselves to a democratic platform, while we still cannot say it can be discarded. *The platform and slogan of democracy that we use is our goal, not a mere method.* Democracy is the antidote for the poison of bureaucratism. It is not inescapably incompatible with socialism. After the proletariat gets power, it will not discard democracy but rather expand it. In replacing bourgeois democracy with proletarian democracy, it will extend the narrow democracy of the bourgeoisie to the masses, who are the large majority of the nation and who have been exploited and oppressed. Thus is quantity transformed into quality, and parliament into soviet, and as well the government of the majority of the people will continue to expand to become the government of the whole people.[102]

Chen now put greater emphasis on the compatibility of socialism and democracy in ways that would have been foreign to Lenin and Trotsky. To some extent this may have simply been a reaction to what Chen saw as excessive Chinese Communist skepticism of democracy. He wanted to remind the Communists that bourgeois democracy was not the only form of democracy. Indeed, the implication was that as new, more broadly based classes developed historically, they broadened the scope of democracy. From this teleological perch, Chen had little to say about conservative and fascist criticisms of democracy.[103] But his view of democracy was, at the least, tied to a historical teleology wherein the proletariat will become the force that restores "true democracy." Thus, Chen again denied the "stage theory" of orthodox Stalinism and now even came close to denying the notion of the political realm as mere superstructure resting on the basis of economics. Chen essentially equated class struggle and "democratic struggle." In other words, he believed in what he called the "dialectical" view: that class struggle constructed the concrete institutions of democracy. He said that those who were criticizing the very idea of a national assembly were engaged in a form of idealism: a "national assembly" was simply a site of public discussion. And to associate some institution with a given class is "metaphysical" or "textbookish" thinking.

This was to say that something called a national assembly might be a useless bourgeois institution, but it might also be a truly democratic institution in a socialist society. "The essence of democracy lies in the management of the common concerns of the people by a majority or by the whole people, and the opposition of the majority to the control by a minority: this is democratic struggle, and outside of this there is only stinking analysis based on mystical idealism."[104] The question was, what made the "majority," and of course Chen answered this question through the prisms of class and history.

> The bourgeoisie had greater numbers than the landed aristo-
> crats, and so they opposed the aristocrats through democratic
> struggle. Now the proletariat and all the laboring people have
> greater numbers than the bourgeoisie, and so they will over-
> throw bourgeois class rule through democratic struggle. When
> newly arisen classes have won all their political struggles, even
> when they take all power into their own hands, they cannot
> find basic solutions to all their economic struggles. Therefore,
> we have reason to say that every great political struggle is a
> class struggle, and the final struggle of every great class struggle
> is a political struggle. What is every struggle of the majority
> of those who have been oppressed to overthrow the ruling
> classes if not a democratic struggle?[105]

As for proletarian democracy, Chen said it will be "dictatorial" toward the bourgeoisie but consisted fundamentally of a process of broadening and extending political participation. So far, so Leninist. But by 1940, Chen had broadened his definition of democracy to include specific liberties. He now insisted that the "concrete content" of proletarian democracy was the same as that of bourgeois democracy. " 'Proletarian democracy' is no empty phrase": all citizens have the freedoms to assemble, form associations, speak, publish, and go on strike.[106] In letters to younger Trotskyists in 1940, Chen further explicated the "true content of democracy," which included, in effect, checks on the powers of any government as well as freedoms inherent in the people.[107] Democracy includes but is not limited to elected legislatures. Chen listed: no organ has the right to arrest people outside of the court system; there can be no taxes levied without political participation; the government may not levy taxes without legislative approval; opposition parties have the freedom to organize, speak, and publish; workers have the right to strike; peasants have the right to till the land; there must be freedom of thought and religion; "and so forth." Chen's tendency to regard democracy as a transcendent force throughout history was thus sharpened. The freedoms he listed above, he said, represent the demands of the masses and what they have struggled to achieve—at least in the (limited) form of bourgeois democracy—over seven centuries. Democracy is the banner under which all majority classes have fought against the privileges of minorities, from ancient societies through every age.

Though not entirely new, one feature of Chen's last writings was his antipathy for the Soviet Union. While Trotsky had famously called the Soviet Union a "degenerate workers' state," Chen denied it was a workers' state at all: it was a bureaucratic dictatorship: "brutal, corrupt, hypocritical, fraudulent, rotten, degenerate, and incapable for engendering any form of socialism."[108] Chen's emphasis on the freedom to form opposition parties perhaps stemmed from his understanding of events in the Soviet Union as much as his experience of Chinese conditions. In any case, his horror of Stalinism led Chen to utterly oppose the formula of "proletarian dictatorship," and he predicted that without democracy to "act as an antitoxin" to bureaucratism, any new revolution would fail. It is correct to oppose bourgeois democracy, but not correct to oppose democracy. Chen tirelessly repeated these points in letters to skeptical Trotskyist comrades. One such letter seemed to trace the lack of mass democracy in Russia all the way back to Lenin.[109] Lenin, Chen said, understood that democracy could prevent bureaucratism but had failed to act on that understanding, while Trotsky had supported democracy only after he had been cashiered. Chen condemned the Soviet Union's false use of the slogans "proletarian democracy" and "mass democracy"—while continuing to insist the true proletarian democracy represented the broadening of bourgeois democracy. For Chen, then, democracy was an unending project.

Meanwhile, Chen continued to vehemently support efforts to resist imperialism, particularly the Japanese invasion. On the eve of that invasion, he had already claimed that the national struggle was part of the democratic struggle, a point other Trotskyists did not necessarily believe.[110] This view led Chen to support the Guomindang (and the new Guomindang-CCP alliance) after Japan's invasion of China proper in 1937. In the meanwhile, like many non-Communists, he heartily condemned the Guomindang's failure to offer resistance to Japan. He attributed this to the influence of the bourgeoisie, which invariably wished to cooperate with imperialism and actually feared nationalism. Thus, China will only throw off the imperialists when the "worker and peasant laboring masses" rise up to do so, and "thus the struggles for class liberation and for national liberation are inseparable."[111] As war came in 1937 and China under Chiang Kai-shek, again backed by the CCP, joined the Allies against the Axis powers, several Chinese Trotskyists condemned both sides as equally imperialist. Not Chen. If the Trotskyists claimed to follow Lenin's condemnation of both sides in World War I, Chen replied that Lenin did not know fascism.[112] Chen distinguished "bourgeois democratic imperialism," an alliance between the financial oligarchy and the middle classes, from fascism, an alliance among the financial oligarchy, the lumpenproletariat, and the radical right wing of the petty bourgeoisie.[113] The former offered limited toleration of the proletariat's political activities; the latter, none.

Trotsky himself, in the wake of the Japanese invasion of China proper in 1937, fully supported Chinese resistance, called it a "just war," and predicted the defeat of Japan.[114] Now that Chiang Kai-shek was fighting the Japanese, revolutionaries must support his forces while maintaining their independence. Revolutionaries who wish to put anti-Chiang struggle first are missing the point: "China is a semicolonial country which Japan is transforming, under our very eyes, into a colonial country. Japan's struggle is imperialist and reactionary. China's struggle is emancipatory and progressive."[115]

Trotsky displayed some optimism that the coming world war would result in revolution, and not merely in China. Chen Duxiu's reading of global conditions was much more pessimistic. He did not see how the war would lead either to national liberation or to a worldwide socialist revolution.[116] Nonetheless, Chen firmly supported the Allies. In essence, he argued that Britain and America might be corrupt bourgeois democracies and imperialist powers, but at least they were democracies of a sort. If the Axis powers won the war, even the very limited democratic freedoms of bourgeois societies would be lost. In terms of China's position, it would be reduced from its semicolonial status to an outright colony.[117] A return to prewar Anglo-American imperialism offered a better starting point for democratic and socialist revolutions than a world plunged into fascist darkness. Furthermore, even if there was a large degree of hypocrisy in the Allies' claim to be fighting for freedom and democracy, that was still a healthier slogan than any that the fascists could provide.[118] Ultimately, for Chen, this was a war being fought for democracy, not for nationalism.[119] Of course, he thought no better of the police state of Stalinist Russia than of the fascist nations, though he continued to blame "capitalist imperialism" as the ultimate cause of the oppression of nations.[120] In one essay in the last year of his life, Chen threw off some of his earlier pessimism and broached the possibility that national liberation movements in tandem with socialist revolutions in the advanced countries could succeed in breaking the power of the bourgeoisie. Not without the workers' unity across national boundaries, however. Although this essay did not touch on democracy, a utopian impulse was exhibited in the link Chen drew between international socialist revolution and national liberation:

> The only way forward is to unite with the oppressed laborers and the oppressed and backwards nations of the world to overthrow every trace of imperialism and replace the old world of the international capitalism marked by commodity exchange with the new world of international socialism marked by mutual aid in the division of labor.[121]

Conclusion

The Trotskyist Zheng Chaolin remarked that Chen "had a wealth of political experience and acute political antennae, but he was short of the skills in basic and systematic theoretical analysis."[122] I would rather say Chen was an enthusiastic but unskilled politician while he was an insightful if unsystematic political theorist. He came of political age at a time when Chinese thinkers were snatching at Western ideas in transla- tion and incorporating them into programs of change. The translations may have been imperfect and subject to misunderstanding even when accurate, and the approach to Western ideas may have been decontex- tualized and so subject to misunderstanding—but so what? It was the creative appropriation of a mix of ideas used to wage "brush-wars," build solidarity, and seek truth that mattered. Chen's obvious use of Dewey, Marx/Lenin, and Trotsky was central to his evolving views; perhaps as important but less obvious are the roles of Mencius, Bergson, and even Kant. Even that old feudal, Kang Youwei.

In the end, Chen developed a theory of Marxist revolutionary democracy that was simultaneously rooted in class struggle and the long historical development of democracy—popular power—over centuries. Chen never said that "class struggle is the motor of democracy" but, at the end of his life, he might have. Disillusioned by real existing Marxism both in China and in Russia, but maintaining the understanding of his- torical materialism he had gained in the 1920s, Chen finally synthesized the concepts of class struggle and democracy.[123] Indeed, by the end of his life, Chen was ready to criticize even Lenin and Trotsky on the grounds that they were insufficiently committed to democratic principles.

Chen also had a deep understanding of the complex relationship between Chinese nationalism and class struggle. He early on noted that the Guomindang was less a representative of the bourgeois class than a military organization, and he feared the CCP was becoming another one. The conclusion Chen drew was that while all Chinese should unite against the Japanese, the intellectual vanguard should still work to prepare the proletariat for its moment. Chen essentially remained attached to the Trotskyist understanding that China was not a truly "feudal" society, because the rural economy was thoroughly dominated by urban capitalism: "feudal exploitation" there was, but it benefited no landed manorial class. In this view, capitalist relations were dominant in China: the backward rural economy was in thrall to urban capitalism and the urban bourgeoisie benefited from what were at ground level feudal structures of exploitation. Chinese Trotskyists, including Chen, did not, as is sometimes charged, ignore the countryside, but they did conclude that China was ready for a workers' revolution.

At the same time that Chen maintained this view of the Chinese social structure, he was treating democracy as both a product of historical forces and also as a "motive force" of history. He believed that democracy could only be practiced through historically determined institutions, and he remained a historical materialist in that sense. He foresaw that through class struggle the proletariat would rise to form a more perfect set of democratic institutions than had ever existed before. It is in this sense that democracy was a transcendental force in Chen's eyes, unfolding through history. And this was liberal democracy insofar as Chen's "proletarian democracy" would still guarantee the freedoms that bourgeois democracy had developed in a limited way.

Chen's views on democracy matured over his lifetime of political involvement and analysis. Matured how? And were his views of democracy coherent? In 1940, Chen wrote: "Science, modern democracy, and socialism are the three most brilliant inventions of modern society."[124] That sounds little different from the "democracy and science" that he was promoting in 1915, when he wrote, "Human rights, the theory of evolution, and socialism are the three main features of modern civilization."[125] As his Trotskyist comrades noted disapprovingly, it seemed Chen had returned at the end of his life to his New Culture positions. Hu Shi also thought so, and orthodox Chinese Marxists had long regarded Chen as a lost cause, even as a traitor.[126] However, Chen's sometime follower Wang Fanxi was closer to the truth: "Chen Duxiu's last four articles, written shortly before he died in 1942, are socialist and internationalist in content; in essence, they are still Trotskyist. So it is wrong to say that Chen Duxiu went over to Trotskyism by mistake and later reawakened to bourgeois democracy."[127]

In my judgment, Chen was no longer a Trotskyist by the end of the 1930s, because he had come to regard the views of both Trotsky and Lenin on democracy as fatally flawed. But neither had he simply returned to his liberalism of the 1910s. In his turn to Marxism in the 1920s, Chen abandoned his faith in participatory democracy seen as based on small, local groups, which was not far from the quasi-anarchist position widely shared in the 1910s. As well, in the 1910s Chen linked democracy to ethics—and autocracy to a decadent moral system.[128] By the 1930s he was thinking in materialist, not idealist terms. This does not, however, mean that Chen's democratic impulse was any less a utopian impulse that formed the keystone of his political philosophy.

In the early 1920s Chen did not write about democracy. But by the 1930s, he had reconceptualized democracy as inextricably linked to class consciousness. Chen's new understanding of democracy was based on class struggle. Like his understanding of twenty-five years previously, Chen's new understanding of democracy was populist and majoritarian, but Chen no longer assumed that people would simply come together in free associations. Political participation was part of his new conceptualization of democracy, for class consciousness was certainly found in local sites, but it was also situated nationally and internationally. In the 1910s, Chen's utopian impulses flowered in his vision of democratic participation, his belief that healthy human associations could take form inside the larger corpse of a dead society, and his faith that their processes would lead to "making habits" that would eventually ensure that political and economic organizations of a larger scale would not fall under the domination of minorities. Later, Chen focused on the "bourgeoisie" as the most dangerous of such minorities. In the 1910s, Chen thought—along with many intellectuals of the day—that China could avoid class struggle. In the 1930s, he believed in class struggle and that class struggle would make China into a socialist state, as well as remake the world. But, by the end of the 1930s, almost alone, he increasingly insisted that class struggle itself must be based on democratic practices. The goal of class struggle was the fulfillment of a democracy that included but was not limited to everything meant by "bourgeois democracy."

5

Experimentalism, Process, and Progress

Hu Shi

Hu Shi's view of the future was deeply informed by utopian impulses. This is not to say that he was a committed utopian thinker. Hu's moderation, antiradicalism, liberalism, and elitism prevented him from consistently promoting any particular view of the perfect world, much less emphasizing a need for a totalistic break with the present. Though a strong believer in progress, Hu also understood that precisely because progress was unending—and basically gradual—any attempt to describe a perfect world would only be describing a passing moment.[1] Hu's famous 1917 essay on "Problems and Isms" was an attack on the incipient Marxism of Li Dazhao and Chen Duxiu, which he framed as a call to study specific social issues rather than engage in grand theory, but it also amounted to an attack on utopianism. His equally famous 1919 essay on "Pragmatism" emphasized science's uncertainty principle: the experimental method more or less guaranteed progress but there could be no epistemological certainty.[2] Nonetheless, Hu's thinking revealed a strong utopian impulse: faith that humanity could master nature, that morality could be based on science, and that some kind of democratic socialism would prevail. This was more than a vague kind of optimism or idealism, and, without a clear sense of the end of history, it cannot be called teleological thinking. It is best called a kind of processual utopianism insofar as Hu treated the process of achievement—progress ever upward, improvement never-ending—in utopian terms rather than imagining what final triumph would look like.

Above all, Hu believed in a cosmopolitan modernity based on science.[3] Other goods, such as democracy and spiritual development, flowed from this. Hu repeatedly claimed that spiritual life depended on material civilization, but he was little interested in the spiritual life itself, at least as far as spirituality is usually conceived. What Hu Shi promised was material progress that would give people the capacity to develop their own spiritual lives if they wished. More exciting to Hu were the ways that modern science had liberated humanity from the oppression of nature and was giving people the capacity to develop better forms of social organization. For the present, this was democracy, but whether democracy was inevitable or society's ultimate form, Hu left ambiguous.

Hu insisted that Western civilization had produced not only material wealth but also a superior spiritual life. It is as if Hu had seen utopia—in the West (the United States in particular)—and it worked. The revival of Confucianism and talk of "Eastern spirituality" that had arisen by the early 1920s made Hu bilious, and he glorified Western accomplishments partly to goad his countrymen. Some of his enthusiasm was rhetorical overkill, as Hu himself was aware. His tone when writing in English was milder than when writing in Chinese. Audience mattered; he was trying to break through what he saw as Chinese complacency, and was considerably less worried about Western racism.[4] Hu did not change his fundamental argument depending on his audience, but writing in Chinese he harped on the backwardness of "daily life" and expressed his fury that talk about "Eastern spirituality" acted to justify the indignities heaped on the poor. In Hu's historical vision, the traditional West was much like the East today: the East had yet to leave behind social and economic structures that the West had abandoned. It was due to the breakthrough of the scientific method that the West was able to create a modern world that the East should emulate. Contrary to his conservative intellectual enemies, for Hu the key distinction was not East versus West. Civilizational values were mutable, and such distinction was at best temporary. Rather, what mattered was the distinction between tradition and modernity, or, in other words, between religious superstition and science. The utopian impulse at the root of Hu's view of science formed the basis of his social and political reformism.

Science and Civilization

In his essay "Our Attitudes toward Modern Western Civilization," published in 1926, Hu demolished the argument that the West was materialist while the East was spiritual.[5] He was no happier with Westerners disillusioned in the wake of World War I than with Chinese who made this argument.[6] Material progress made people better off—obviously—and the destruction of a war fought with advanced technology had not cancelled out this basic fact of modernity. But Hu did not merely base a defense of material civilization on a utilitarian calculation of prosperity; rather, he denied that the material-spiritual dichotomy made any sense in the first place. *All* civilizations are *both* material and spiritual. By the material, Hu meant ways of controlling natural forces; by the spiritual, he meant the intelligence, sentiments, and ideals of a people.[7] Hu was thus implying that the ultimate source of civilization was spiritual: human intelligence invented the material ways to deal with the environment. In this sense, a motorcycle and a poem are equally expressions of human intelligence. For Hu, then, to confuse material achievements with a neglect of spiritual needs was to make a categorical mistake. And if material achievements in some sense rest on the life of the spirit, the opposite is also true: the spiritual depends on the material.

> We deeply believe that spiritual civilization is necessarily built on material foundations. In supporting people's material pleasures and in increasing the material convenience and ease of life, we are headed in the direction of liberating human capacities and freeing human spirit and intelligence from the tasks of mere survival, and finally allowing for the satisfaction of spiritual needs.[8]

Going cold and hungry was tragic, but pretending there was no problem because we are achieving holiness was even worse. Hu accused the advocates of Eastern spiritual civilization of kidding themselves and of failing to respect "basic human desires" (*jiben de yuwang*).[9] In raising the concept of human desire, Hu was referring to a controversial issue in the Neo-Confucian tradition that stretched back to debates of the eleventh century. Hu had no use for the predominately negative, or at least skeptical, attitudes toward desire among the leading Neo-Confucian thinkers as seen, for example, in the slogan of "no desire" (*wuyu*) of Zhou Dunyi (1017–1073). In fact, the Neo-Confucian tradition was not an ascetic one, and certainly some thinkers in the tradition believed in the rightness of something like Hu's "basic human desires."[10] Yet overall, in the orthodox view—and in imperial ideology as reinforced through the civil service exams that lasted right into the twentieth century—desires were to be tightly controlled. A critique of this view thus had radical political implications. To control desire was to assert political control. Chen Duxiu's vehement condemnations of Confucianism was based on this relationship.

Hu did not draw out the political implications of Confucian ways of regulating desire, but he condemned the failure of Chinese leaders to find ways to increase human happiness. Instead, Hu claimed, they were hypnotizing the people with slogans such as "delighting in Heaven," "contentment with Heaven's will," "knowing sufficiency," and "contentment with poverty," and other phrases drawn arbitrarily from the *Mencius*, *Xunzi*, and other classical texts. Hu had little more use for the classics than did Chen, though his criticisms were both less vehement and yet ran deeper. Their shared target, of course, was not the ancient philosophers but the cultural attitudes of the present day. Hu's fear was that delegitimizing material desires would lead to a "lazy society" whose members were too crippled to pursue either material or spiritual development. When people lie to themselves about the virtues of poverty, they act contrary to nature.

Rather, Hu said, it was necessary to regard poverty and disease as evils—fixable evils. For Hu, then, the West was not materialist in the crass sense of the word but idealistic and even spiritual precisely because of its strong material foundations.[11] Hu praised the Western view that the goal of life is happiness and therefore that poverty and illness were evils. The result was an emphasis on economic production and commerce that provided people with medicines, sanitation, transportation, exquisite art, and an orderly society. True, Hu admitted, the result included powerful weapons of murder and a system of aggression and expropriation, but Hu's attention remained firmly placed on the good achieved by material civilization. And the evil perpetuated by the rejection of materialism. An example Hu turned to in other essays was that of the rickshaw puller versus the automobile. How can a civilization that uses people as beasts of burden be considered more spiritual than the one that uses machines?[12] Here, Hu launched into a rhapsody to the automobile: cars were efficient, letting farmers get their eggs and milk to market; cars provided mind-body training, keeping limbs and senses nimble; cars symbolized equality, as carpenters and professors both drove; and cars make possible a better use of leisure time. Highlighting the West's contrast with China, Hu claimed that while people in America drove to work, and even children were driven to school, in China officials were carried to their offices by other men.[13]

What it all came down to, Hu concluded, was machines. While every American has twenty-five or thirty mechanical slaves (*jixie nuli*) the Chinese have just one, if that.[14] "Our workers are menial laborers; their workers are masters of mechanical slaves." More poetically: "Other people have flown over the seas, while we still crawl upon the earth. People have flown from Paris to Beijing in just 63 hours, while it takes us 104 days to get from Gansu to Beijing (or 2,500 hours)!" Again, attempting to measure the power of machines, Hu stated that in China it took four men to carry a palanquin, while three pullers would share the rental of a rickshaw to keep it on the road all day.

The notion of the mechanical slave had been popularized by the early nineteenth century. Machines seemingly replaced people and did their work. Or it could be said machines made human labor more efficient. The polymath inventor and reformer Charles Babbage remarked, "The advantages which are derived from machinery and manufactures seem to arise principally from three sources: *The addition which they make to human power.—The economy they produce of human time.—The conversion of substances apparently common and worthless into valuable products*."[15] Like Hu Shi nearly a century later, Babbage delighted in precise figures and examples of the labor savings made by machines (in Babbage's case based on extensive experimentation). Although critical of certain aspects of British society and its scientific establishment, Babbage had confidence in the continual advance of machinery, made possible ultimately by the progress of science. Yet industrialization (though the term was not yet invented) was sharply criticized by Thomas Carlyle, John Ruskin, and their ilk, as well as many of the workers whose livelihoods were lost or lives displaced.[16] It was often said—in a debate that has lasted till today—that mechanization dehumanized people themselves, making them more like machines. The term *robot* appeared in English in 1923, in a translation of Karel Čapek's play *R.U.R.* ("Rossum's Universal Robots"). Čapek or his brother invented the term *robotnik* (forced worker) based on the Czech word *robota* (servitude).

The global implications of industrialization were clear from the beginning. Babbage, for one, celebrated the success of British manufactures in India and China. Debates over the advantages and disadvantages of machines also moved abroad. Chinese leaders of the late Qing period often resisted proposals to build railways, telegraph lines, and modern factories, though these were making their way into China by the 1890s. All this inevitably led to a new definition of civilization. World War I suggested to some in the West as well as China that modern industrial society had its dark side, but improving technology remained a civilizing project headed up, so to speak, by Britain, the United States, Germany, and France. And pursued by Japan and Russia, which were late modernizers of particular interest to Chinese observers.[17]

According to Hu Shi, based on its technological achievements, modern Western civilization was immeasurably better equipped to meet humanity's spiritual needs than was the so-called wisdom of the East. Western civilization was both idealistic and spiritual. And if by implication China was neither, at least not to the same degree, Hu's target was not Oriental culture as such but the "*old* Eastern civilization."[18] This was to turn the East-West binary into the old-new binary. In a sense, Hu Shi was a utilitarian pursuing the greatest happiness for the greatest number of people. As a student of John Dewey and a self-proclaimed follower of pragmatism, Hu spoke of "experimentalism," but he did not believe in experimentation for its own sake.

The American philosopher John Dewey was not particularly worried about the East-West question. He was, however, a strong defender of material civilization and the American technological drive. An escapee from an intensely religious upbringing, Dewey noted the frequently heard lament that "the development of the material civilization leads to the corruption of morality and blocks the development of spiritual civilization" and insisted that the advocates of this view "fail to realize that while such 'materials' are aspects of material civilization, they truly provide the basis for spiritual civilization. It is because material civilization can bring all social relations ever closer that it not only refers to material aspects but also provides the basis for a spiritual and moral life."[19] This aside came in a lecture that Dewey gave in China on economics and the notion of the division of labor, which Dewey treated as a feature of society's organic nature. In one of his final lectures in the series on "Social Philosophy and Political Philosophy" in 1919, Dewey brought together his central concerns—economics, politics, and "knowledge and thought"—to, in effect, define what he meant by spiritual civilization.[20]

> First, the life of knowledge, thought, and the spirit can raise the value of social life. Second, the life of knowledge, thought, and the spirit may be considered the basis of social life. In regard to the first point, human beings are not animals, only interested in eating, drinking, and sex. It is necessary to

include knowledge, thought, and the spirit in the lives of human beings to transform them and bring their [animal] appetites into accord with civilized standards and not merely live by satisfying their appetites.[21]

If Chen Duxiu's early ideas on democracy paralleled those of Dewey in some ways, as seen in the previous chapter, Hu Shi represented himself as Dewey's scientific apostle in China. Hu had earned his PhD under John Dewey in 1917 with a dissertation titled *The Development of the Logical Method in Ancient China.* Notwithstanding Hu's reputation as a Westernizer, he devoted his scholarship to the history of Chinese thought and literature. But his political models came from the modern West. It was largely due to Hu's efforts that Dewey's trip to Japan was extended into a lecture tour across China's major cities lasting two years from 1919 to 1921. Hu wanted Dewey to speak on social and political issues, as well as on his views on how to conduct philosophy or, in simpler terms, how to think. Of course, Dewey also gave a series of lectures on the philosophy and practice of education.

Dewey thus spoke on a wide variety of issues during his sojourn in China, including yet another lecture series on "Experimental Logic," and he referred repeatedly to the role of science in thinking about social issues. As Barry Keenan has pointed out, to his Chinese audiences Dewey emphasized the historical role of science in improving morality.[22] In Dewey's words, the "influence of scientific progress on morality led to new hopes, new beliefs, and the enlargement of the scope of morality."[23] Furthermore, Dewey emphasized that the difference between West and East can be explained simply by the earlier development of modern science in the West. Material progress was important, but the "scientific attitude" even more so. One implication was that the West was morally as well as materially advanced over the East, although Dewey was perhaps too polite to say so. He did, however, suggest that Oriental people, while appreciating the material achievements of the West, had failed to understand the mode of thinking that made those achievements possible, and in particular the mode of thinking that kept those achievements—many of them dangerous—under control. In the wake of Word War I, as we have seen, the dangers of science were on the minds of intellectuals everywhere. So Dewey stressed that new ways of thinking and new morality were needed to accompany such new forms of material civilization as railroads, telegraphs, and automobiles. Dewey pointed to Japan as a society that seemed to be progressing materially more rapidly than it was progressing morally. No doubt, whether his audiences fully understood his larger point or not, they appreciated Dewey's criticism of Japan.

Dewey was *not* saying that material progress led to moral or spiritual improvement, as Hu Shi seemed to be saying. Rather, Dewey claimed that both sets of changes stemmed from a common cause: the progress of science and the changes in "methods of thinking" associated with the modern world. Dewey did not dismiss the dangers of scientific progress. Though he did not speak to the issues raised by the mass violence of World War I, he did acknowledge the evils of capitalism. But Dewey's point was that regardless of the dangers of scientific progress, it had given people confidence in their ability to shape their shared future. Failure, he implied, was possible, but surely, armed with new hopes and courage, people will engage in a successful, purposive construction of a new society. "Where did these new hopes and courage come from? Simply a new form of belief in the wisdom of humanity. Under the influence of science, we now understand that the wisdom of humanity can destroy the ignorance, mistakes, and disorder of the past."[24] In beginning to conquer Nature, or at least free themselves from its uncontrollable depredations, humanity was beginning to free itself from old traditions and take an active role in shaping their future.

In his first lectures, Dewey suggested that "social and political philosophy" could help us steer a course between excessive idealism and excessive materialism in understanding and shaping social phenomena. The rise of science as eventually applied to social questions broke with an unconscious acceptance of existing institutions and practices—things were the way they were because that is the way that they were—to give humanity a sense of making conscious choices. Dewey's original typescript upon which the lectures were based is clearer on this point.[25] He remarked, "After theory had once arisen [e.g., in ancient Greece], life does not go on just the same. Men do not breathe and eat because of their knowledge of anatomy and physiology. These acts still depend upon deeper forces. But they may eat and breathe somewhat differently, especially in emergencies, because of their knowledge."[26] There is something radical, Dewey suggested, about the very process of thinking, which disrupts unconscious attitudes: "Thinking means the introduction of a novel and insofar incalculable factor—a deviation or departure, and an invention. The hidebound conservative is justified in the uneasiness which he shows at attempts to formulate and justify rationally even his own beliefs. The appeal to reason that is implied is unsettling."[27]

Dewey was equally critical of radicals and conservatives, who, in their theorizing, are prone to overgeneralize. They are incapable equally of instituting total change or of resisting all change, because they ignore the specific facts on the ground and the dialectical relationship between facts and theory. Dewey also ruthlessly criticized the so-called social sciences for mistaking particular cases for scientific laws. A critic of Eurocentrism avant la lettre, in his original typescript Dewey nonetheless praised nineteenth-century economics, political science, history, and the like for their "scientific spirit" or "scientific method."[28] The entire point of social philosophy, then, as opposed to the social sciences, was to follow the latter in attempting to derive laws from facts, but to keep in mind that such laws were always provisional hypotheses subject to experimental verification. Social philosophy is neither purely speculative like classical philosophy, nor entirely objective like the goal of the social sciences, according to Dewey, but capable of providing direction to the solution of concrete problems. If there is a general difference between Dewey's notes for his first two lectures and the published versions, it is one of tone. Dewey's need to justify the use of theory comes across a little stronger in the former, while his emphasis on the graduated "step by step" nature of reform is a little stronger—but not an interpellation—in the latter.

Dewey highlighted a "new honesty" that stemmed from scientific approaches and understanding of Nature. Until recently, without modern science, not much truth was even possible, and social harmony was often valued above the truth. Not incidentally, Dewey was again attacking old customs and "superstition." But perhaps more to the point, Dewey saw no reason not to apply the scientific method to social questions by isolating problems and bringing out the facts through public discussion.[29] The "new honesty" thus frees people from their selfish interests and partial perspectives.

Rightly or wrongly, Dewey and other Pragmatists have been accused of the sin of "scientism"—the belief that the scientific method can solve all problems capable of solution and that nonscientific viewpoints are invalid.[30] Hu Shi was more prone to scientism than was Dewey. But if Dewey did not directly tell Chinese audiences that science could solve all their problems, he did tell them that scientific approaches were the proper way to analyze social and ethical problems. The utopian impulse behind this vision is clear: ultimately, no problem is insoluble, even if solutions are tentative, temporary, and gradual. In his two lectures in China on William James, Dewey emphasized that "knowledge" for James stemmed from the interaction between environment (stimulus) and organism (response), and functioned to determine appropriate responses.[31] Perhaps of more immediate interest in an otherwise quite abstract lecture was Dewey's emphasis on the role of will—the active pursuit of knowledge—and his attack on pure skepticism. For truth emerges from the test of predictions, which, when accurate and useful, are true: experimentalism rather than absolute truth. Dewey's examples implied this was a matter of daily life, not laboratory science, but was also a new approach that the new scientific age would ratify. Thus, in another lecture Dewey simply reduced the scientific method to experimentation (shiyan) or, "a method for uniting the functions of the mind and the phenomena of nature through human action."[32] For example, performing various actions on a metal to determine if it is gold. Dewey was not, of course, speaking of random actions but forming plans (testing hypotheses) in a process that leads ever on through cycles of new facts, new hypotheses, and new tests. He insisted that the experimental method was both conservative and progressive: if traditional theories turn out to be worthwhile, they should be conserved, but by and large the experimental method led to change.[33] "There is no true knowledge without action."[34]

The scientific approach that Dewey described in these talks was largely based on his essay of 1900, "Some Stages of Logical Thought," his 1903 chapters in Studies in Logical Theory, and his 1910 work How We Think, a two-hundred-page monograph that was both a guide for teachers and a description of the thought processes, particularly but not only of children.[35] As Joachim Kurtz points out, Hu Shi was especially attracted to Dewey's understanding of the importance of experience in logical thought, emphasizing the importance of "Some Stages of Logical Thought" for his own ideas.[36] For Hu, it was doubtless key that, as David Hildebrand noted of Dewey's epistemology, it was directly linked to his meliorism, the belief that "life should be understood as improvable, primarily through intelligent, human effort."[37]

Above all, for Dewey, it is doubt that gives rise to knowledge, which in turn may be destabilized by further doubt. Dewey admitted the importance to any society of "set ideas"—that is, unquestioned beliefs taken to be true, which Dewey also found similar to Hegel's Verstand (understanding) and which, if sometimes resulting in dogmatic conservatism, are also necessary for any effective action.[38] At the same time, a historical-cultural shift has led from societies dominated by set ideas in this sense to those that experienced the rise of scientific thinking. For Dewey, this was a fundamental transformation of subjectivity, though he did not use this vocabulary. In Dewey's words: "At the outset, fixity is taken as the rightful possession of the ideas themselves; it belongs to them and is their 'essence.' As the scientific spirit develops, we see that it is we who lend fixity to the ideas, and that this loan is for a purpose to which the meaning of the ideas is accommodated." Through self-consciousness, people distance themselves from reality: "We *take* the idea as if it were fixed," thus enabling action but keeping, as it were, our options open. In other words, ideas (descriptions of reality) are never entirely set but always tentative propositions subject to doubt. Historically, Dewey thought, the accumulation of "ideas" as well as new circumstances led to the need to think though which ideas really work. Looking to the Greeks, Dewey said:

> We have assemblies meeting to discuss and dispute, and finally, upon the basis of the considerations thus brought to view, to decide. . . . Discussion is thus an apt name for this attitude of thought [i.e., logic]. It is bringing various beliefs together; shaking one against another and tearing down their rigidity. It is conversation of thoughts; it is dialogue—the mother of dialectic in more than the etymological sense. No process is more recurrent in history than the transfer of operations carried on between different persons into the arena of the individual's own consciousness. The discussion which at first took place by bringing ideas from different persons into contact, by introducing them into the forum of competition, and by subjecting them to critical comparison and selective decision, finally became a habit of the individual with himself.[39]

This is as much a description of democracy as it is a theory of epistemology, as Dewey was certainly aware. Challenges to old ideas certainly produce doubt while the dialectic prevents them from becoming mere solipsism. Dewey seems to have assumed that the syllogism, which the Greeks used to decide how evidence in court cases should be assessed, provided a kind of "reasoning or proof," though this Aristotelian logic ultimately remained a matter of consensus rather than absolute truth.[40] It seems that for Dewey intellectual progress consisted largely of enlargement of the function of doubt, which is to say the sphere of investigation. The model here is that of the laboratory, not designed to answer a simple question but to pursue open and ongoing inquiry. Dewey praises inference precisely because it does not pretend to be proof; rather, it opens up new ideas that are subject to empirical testing and modification. Equally, Dewey celebrated the modern world's attention to detail and to the practical. Together, these approaches result in judgment based on free inquiry that "effects the growth of experience."[41]

In *How We Think*, Dewey discussed many kinds of "thought" but was really interested in intentional, rational reasoning. He also wanted to show that if thinking in this sense was not entirely a "natural" process—people needed training—it was nonetheless based on psychological tendencies that are themselves natural, such as following one's curiosity, drawing inferences, and even experimenting. A "complete act of thought," Dewey said, involved a double movement: first from partial data to a "suggested comprehensive (or inclusive) entire situation," and then back from this whole (a meaning or idea) to the "particular facts" to connect them together and to link up to new facts: induction (toward hypothesis) followed by deduction (back to facts).[42] In turn, "systematic" or "critical" thinking seems to rest for Dewey on bringing greater consciousness to this double movement, and a recognition that hypotheses require testing. Although Dewey peppered this book with mundane examples of how to think, he clearly based the ideal of systematic and critical thinking on the experimental sciences.[43]

Dewey proposed that thinking proceeded through five stages, although this scheme was not necessarily prescriptive or followed in all cases.[44] As a kind of ideal type, then, first one encounters a "felt difficulty"—some problem whether of fact, analysis, or simply making a decision. Second, one defines "its location and definition," a process that grows naturally out of the first stage. Third, one finds a "suggestion of possible solution," that is, coming up with various tentative explanations or hypotheses. Fourth, one engages in "development by reasoning," or considering in abstract or logical terms what explanation makes the most sense. And fifth, perhaps most critically of all, one continues "further observation and experiment leading to its acceptance or rejection," allowing a right conclusion to be reached. As Alan Ryan points out, Dewey's scheme did not distinguish between the thinking required to make decisions and that required to determine facts.[45] Yet Dewey was writing here as an educator, and he sought to modify the Herbartian approach to teaching. Thus, the vagueness of the fourth step left a great deal to thinking beyond the "facts": the main goal was not the acquisition of information, though that was important, but rather learning how to solve problems.

In the wake of Dewey's lecture tour of China, Hu Shi claimed that in the entire history of Chinese-Western contacts, no foreign scholar had influenced Chinese intellectual circles to the extent that Dewey had.[46] For Hu, Dewey was important both for his ideas of educational reform and for his "philosophical methods." That is, Hu said, while Dewey did not have the answers to China's problems, if Chinese used his "philosophical method," they could solve their own problems. Deweyan pragmatism or experimentalism rested on attending to concrete facts, remembering that all explanations are hypotheses subject to testing, and that only testing produces truth. (Like Dewey himself, his Chinese followers tended to avoid the label *pragmatism*, preferring empiricism and experimentalism, though the Chinese also avoided Dewey's use of *instrumentalism*, which perhaps in Chinese sounded too close to utilitarianism.) For Hu, the epistemology of pragmatism did not rest on abstract logic but was a practice. Though Hu did not use the terms *conservative* and *revolutionary*, pragmatism for him was simultaneously both: conservative in that experimentation and proofs proceeded step by step and "true progress" could not be hurried, and revolutionary in that it utterly freed people from the dicta of their ancestors. Hu emphasized that science did not teach unalterable laws like the old "Heavenly principles" but rather operated through hypotheses. Hypotheses won assent when they worked to explain natural phenomena, but they were subject to change, that is, improvement. This improvement was simply the gradual extension of understanding.[47] Improvement comes about when superior explanations (humanly constructed scientific laws) are devised to explain known or newly discovered phenomena. Hu did not rule out the possibility of the existence of absolutely true scientific laws, only the possibility that people could achieve certain knowledge of them. Scientific laws were proved, always ultimately as hypotheses, as long as they could be applied in practice.

At least as a goad to China, Hu held up modern Western science. "The first characteristic of the spirit of modern Western civilization is science, and the basic spirit of science is the search for truth."[48] It is truth that sets us free: free of thoughtless habits, superstitions, and prejudices; free of the fetters of the environment and the fear of natural forces. Free "to become fully human in a dignified manner." Hu claimed that the

West had not only succeeded in creating mastery over nature, but met the needs of emotion and imagination through its literature and art. And furthermore, that the West was at least well along the road to establish a new religio-morality. If the West had not abandoned all traditional views, it was abandoning those views that rested on superstition. The scientific search for "human happiness" led inevitably to superior ways of finding spiritual happiness. "To completely use the intelligence and wisdom of humans in this way, seeking truth to liberate human intelligence, to subjugate Nature to benefit humanity, to remake the material environment, to reform social and political systems, to plan for the greatest happiness for the greatest number—this kind of civilization should be able to satisfy the spiritual needs of humanity; this kind of civilization is spiritual civilization, a truly idealistic civilization and not a materialistic civilization."[49] In fact, Hu implied, the only reason why people could not create a "human paradise" was that the search for knowledge and improvement was endless—but the search itself was pleasurable. Paradise was a project. In a certain sense, then, Hu was saying that utopia was impossible to create but the search for utopia was itself a kind of utopia, a processual utopia. "Every single effort produces its own satisfaction, and progressing steadily through this endless series of efforts gives wonderful joy to those who are contributing their efforts [to the improvement of the human condition]."

At heart, the uncertainty principle that Hu drew from pragmatism, rightly or wrongly, was an attack on metaphysics. What prevented a world without absolute truths from descending into epistemological chaos, for Hu, was an appreciation for the concrete and specific to time and place; in other words, what was adaptive to the environment in Darwinian terms.

Humanization and Socialization

In holding the West up to China as a model to be followed spiritually as well as materially, Hu inevitably turned the West into the future that worked. Utopia was not a vague future prospect, but now, albeit over there. This was, of course, not utopia as anything like a perfect society. Hu's utopian impulse lay in his faith in the means by which improvement could be achieved. These were means that were universal, available to all, and not restricted to any one culture. Hu never attributed any kind of essential superiority to the West, but rather assumed that the

East had simply fallen behind. In other words, there was a single path to modern civilization. Hu claimed that in ancient times people sought emotional comfort through ghosts and spirits, heavens and hells.[50] In his understanding, traditional religion focused on individual salvation and individual moral training, at a time when any efforts to put universal values into practice were stymied for a lack of means. Religion thus not only failed to improve material life, it even failed to carry out moral reforms—for eight hundred years Neo-Confucians ignored the inhumane crime of footbinding. For all the talk of "equal land distribution" heard in many dynasties of the past, no reforms actually occurred. Hu charged that while the desire to seek knowledge was a universal human attribute, Oriental civilization—its old civilization—had blocked this natural desire. As a matter of historical fact, then, the breakthrough came in the West.

How did this happen? For Hu, the European explorers of the fifteenth and sixteenth century may have been pirates, thieves, and slavemongers, but the merchants who followed them opened up new lands, inspired the human imagination, and created new wealth. The industrial revolution that followed created new forces of production.

> In the course of two to three centuries, material enjoyment gradually increased and humanity's empathy gradually enlarged. This enlarged empathy became the basis of a new religion and morality. As the self sought liberty, the self also considered the liberty of others, so not only did liberty mean not transgressing the liberty of others, but also progressed to the point of seeking liberty for the greatest number of people. The benefits enjoyed by the self became the benefits to be enjoyed by [all] people, and so the philosophers of utilitarianism advocated the standard of the "greatest happiness for the greatest number" for human society.[51]

The notion of universal empathy shows that Hu's utopian impulses went beyond the merely technological, though he traced an increase of empathy to the increase of material goods that allows people to help others and let themselves feel others' pain.

Hu linked sociopolitical systems to material progress as well. He claimed that the "religious creed" of the eighteenth century had already evolved into that of "liberty, equality, and fraternity." And after the mid-nineteenth century, into socialism. Thus, the West's "spiritual civilization," which, if hardly perfect, nonetheless had opened up political participation, fostered the emancipation of women, and formalized equality and liberties under the law. The move toward socialism in the nineteenth century, Hu said, had come about as a reaction to the evils of individ-ualism and the cruelties of capitalism. "Men of vision realized that the capitalist system of free competition could not achieve the goals of true 'liberty,' equality, and fraternity.' "[52] If modern Western civilization was initially built on basis of the right to pursue individual happiness and the sacrality of property rights, a new knowledge of property as partly social in nature had already led Westerners to institute political reforms such as income and inheritance taxes. Hu foresaw that the labor movement would sweep the world, having already led to the worker-peasant class dictatorship of the Soviet Union and, elsewhere, at least to further reforms: factory inspections, hygiene, protections for child workers and women workers, minimum wages, regulation of working hours and bonuses, workers' insurance, unemployment insurance, progressive income taxes, and so forth. "This is the new religion and morality of socialization."[53]

By "socialization" (*shehuihua*), Hu meant something more than social-ist policies. He was pointing to a new kind of spiritual existence—one closely related to his notion of "humanization" (*renhua*). Until recently, Hu thought, humanity had been subject to Nature's whims, unable to discover its secrets or resist its ferocity.[54] People understandably lacked confidence in their own powers and sought to placate natural forces. But today people have conquered Nature. People fly high in the air, dive deep in the seas, see distant constellations and tiny microbes. Humanity is now "master of the world."[55] It was not science alone that fueled Hu's utopian impulse. It was that he further sought to turn science into a new religion. At the very least, Hu said, religious ideas had to be in accord with rational judgment and evidence. Thus is religion "humanized."

> Today we do not fantasize about heavens and paradises, but we should think about creating a "kingdom of joy" on earth. We do not fantasize about eternal life but we should build strong and vigorous people on earth. . . . We may not lightly believe in the omnipotence of the Lord, but we believe that the scientific method is omnipotent, and that the future of humanity is limitless. We may not believe that the soul is indestructible, but we believe that human dignity (*renge*) is sacred and that human rights are sacred.[56]

Scientific thinking could meet the moral and spiritual needs of humanity. Even if people continued to practice their "old religions," Hu said, "modern civilization naturally possesses its new religion and new morality."[57] Again, these were not features unique to Western civilization, but a part of a modernity that was fundamentally universal: not restricted to any one culture. The essence of that modernity for Hu was, of course, science. Indeed, loosely following principles of social Darwinism, Hu implied that this modernity was irresistible; at the least, old superstitions would gradually diminish in the face of new knowledge. The existence of God and the immortality of the soul are now subject to doubt. The new religion, then, is marked by its turn to rationality (lizhihua). The increase in humanity's knowledge and power has gradually increased its belief in itself and therefore, Hu said, diminished the need to believe in supernatural forces. It is this mastery of nature that leads to the humanization (renhua) of new religious attitudes. As well, it is the rise of fellow feeling among people (made possible by material abundance) that leads to the unprecedented socialization (shehuihua) of morality. For Hu, then, new religious feeling revolved around rationality, humanization, and socialization.

In thinking about the origins of religion and humanity's early belief systems, Hu repeatedly indulged in a kind of psychological reductionism. People's needs for emotional comfort led them to spirits, gods, heavens, hells, and other irrational and unprovable beliefs. Hu perhaps respected the human need to explain the world, but he dripped with contempt for the persistence of old explanations. Nevertheless, Hu believed in belief, so to speak. He was convinced that rationality and the comfort of belief were not irreconcilable, only that belief had to be the kind that could withstand rational criticism and be subject to proof. By now, with its marvelous conquest of nature, humanity could believe in itself.[58]

For Hu, the process of "humanization" in effect referred to replacing the gods with humanity. The self-confidence justifiably engendered by the successes of science opens up new worlds, new possibilities, the imagination, and empathy. Unlike other utopian thinkers, Hu did not base his prediction of utopia directly on the human capacity for empathy. Rather, he traced the roots and efficacy of empathy to the material abundance of modern civilization. Empathy, then, was the natural result of the "socialization" that marked modern morality. This socialization not only manifested itself in the rise of socialism but in older concrete policies of equality before the law, universal education, women's rights, and the like. At the same time, Hu believed that socialization in this sense was the basis for the individual's own search for happiness.[59] Socialization in no way implied the negation of individuality.

Hu's views resonated with the movements for humanism and ethical culture in Britain and the United States at the time. It is interesting that the then-prominent philosopher and former professor at Hu's own undergraduate university of Cornell, F. C. S. Schiller, became a proponent of the philosophy of humanism. Schiller, who regarded himself as a follower of Jamesian Pragmatism and held a favorable opinion of Dewey, emphasized the link between truth and experience, and attempted to forge a middle way, as it were, between excessive positivism on the one hand and excessive metaphysical speculation on the other.[60] Or, as Schiller also put it, a third alternative to realism and idealism.[61] If pragmatism referred largely to an epistemology of experience, humanism was the spirit of pragmatism. Schiller defined humanism as "merely the perception that the philosophic problem concerns human beings striving to comprehend a world of human experience by the resources of human minds. . . . For if man may not presume his own nature in his reasonings about his experience, wherewith, pray, shall he reason? What prospect has he of comprehending a radically alien universe?"[62] Hu Shi was less inclined to question and more to affirm, and readier than Schiller to regard humanism as a kind of religion. Schiller did, however, refer to it in terms of the "free indulgence in all human power, the liberty of moving, of improving, of making, of manipulating," which was to say humanism was a way of life.[63]

Hu had originally sketched out his view of religion in 1919 by rubbishing notions of the individual soul or spirit but maintaining that society was "immortal."[64] Using a traditional terminology of the small self (individual, *xiaowo*) and great self (group, *dawo*), Hu offered a vision in which individuals without exception influenced everyone around them and everyone who came after them, just as they were influenced by their contemporaries and predecessors. No one is ever isolated, but for good or evil all persons contribute to the ongoing existence of the great self. Hu stopped short of a mystical vision that might include all life or all things in his vision of immortality, as we found in the thinking of Kang Youwei and even Cai Yuanpei. But clearly Hu shared the widespread predilection for thinking in terms of collectivities. In Hu's case, as with other utopian thinkers, the fully legitimate collectivity was humanity as a whole. That said, however, his famous 1918 article on "Ibsenism" highlighted the role of the individual in leading social reforms and formed an important chapter in the New Culture critique of tradition for suppressing the individual.[65]

Furthermore, Hu's attacks on religion hardened with the Confucian revival of the 1920s. In his preface to the collection of writings on the "science versus philosophy of life" debate, Hu reached an uncomfortable position.[66] He did not deny that science had contributed to the disasters of World War I, but he claimed that Chinese were simply in no position to criticize science. "What we need to remember is that science in Europe has already reached an unassailable position, and cannot be harmed by the attacks of third-rate metaphysicians. . . . However, the situation is different in China, where, at this time, the benefits of science have not yet been realized, still less the disasters brought by science."[67] The Chinese "philosophy of life," Hu rather unfairly taunted, consisted of the ideals of becoming wealthy through official careers, relying on Heaven, and begging favors from the gods. Hu claimed that science *could* construct a real philosophy a life, one that would be universally recognized.[68] In effect, this is that Hu set out to do in the late 1920s.

John Dewey was equally critical of religion, but he was not so optimistic about the control people could assert over outside forces. In his extended essay of 1934, *A Common Faith*, Dewey sought to describe a "humanistic religion" that was devoid of any supernatural elements but still open to the "sense of a connection of man, in the way of both dependence and support, with the enveloping world that the imagination feels is a universe."[69] Dewey stipulated that science—or "observation, experiment, record and controlled reflection"—was necessary to establish the truths on which religious experience must rest.[70] This was to assert the existence of a certain "genuinely religious" aspect of experience that was freed from superstition and any kind of dogma and yet entirely real. In other words, not a traditional religion at all but a kind of consciousness that sometimes results from various experiences: "aesthetic, scientific, moral, political," as well as "companionship and friendship."[71] This was perhaps to imply that religious experience was synthesized from more immediate experiences, such as the sense of transcendence that aesthetic appreciation could produce (as Cai Yuanpei emphasized), rather than a kind of direct experience of the divine in its own right, but Dewey was not entirely clear on this point. Dewey did define religious faith "as the unification of the self through allegiance to inclusive ideal ends, which imagination presents to us and to which the human will responds as worthy of controlling our desires and choices."[72] Dewey thus equated the religious attitude with the "harmonizing of the self," which was in turn an adaptive process dependent on the imagination, without which no one could conceive of the "whole self" based on necessarily partial observations.[73] Furthermore, the integrated self can never be conceived in isolation but only as part of that further product of the imagination, the universe in its totality.

Thomas Alexander suggests that this complicated and controversial text can be read best by understanding "the 'religious' as a dimension of experience, one that is revealed through an attitude of existence rather than as a quality of experience."[74] Dewey's faith lay in human potentiality, situated in environments that produce culture, not in transcendent forces. Dewey's targets included orthodox religious believers and institutions on the one hand, and "aggressive" and "militant" atheism on the other. If I understand Dewey's point, there could be no religious claims to knowledge, nor to any special realm immune to scientific investigation. He disdained all creeds. He denied that science was a body of knowledge; rather, it was a method of tested inquiry, open and public, achieving truth by undermining old beliefs and findings. Ideals for Dewey originate in imagination but are real, as seen in "their undeniable power in action." He acknowledged "God" in "the unity of all ideal ends arousing us to desire and actions," but not as a Being apart from the self.[75] And: "The unity signifies not a single Being, but the unity of loyalty and effort evoked by the fact that many ends are one in the power of their ideal, or imaginative, quality to stir and hold us." By freeing religiosity from any external source, Dewey found it in ideals, or values, that were rooted entirely in nature—in human action. "It is this *active* relation between ideal and actual to which I would give the name 'God.' "[76] That is, for Dewey, God lies neither in the actual world as it exists nor in wild utopian fantasies, but in the various forces bringing about the ideal. As an attitude, in Alexander's reading, "common faith" expresses an orientation to existence as a whole that inspires a kind of commitment to social good. Later in this essay, Dewey remarked, "There is such a thing as passionate intelligence, as ardor in behalf of light shining into the murky places of social existence, and as zeal for its refreshing and purifying effect."[77] In effect, Dewey claimed that intelligence combined with natural human passions for justice and security *was* a religious vision.

The terms Dewey used were derived from the notion of unity found in mystical religious experiences, while Dewey insisted that the union of ideal and action was entirely natural. This union had to be called God, or at least understood as religious, because in celebrating humans in nature, piety is appropriate. Both atheism and supernaturalism tended to treat humans in isolation, in a hostile world, Dewey charged. "A religious attitude, however, needs the sense of a connection of man, in the way of both dependence and support, with the enveloping world that the imagination feels is a universe. Use of the words 'God' or 'divine' to convey the union of actual with ideal may protect man from a sense of isolation and from consequent despair or defiance."[78] Dewey's phrasing here seems strange even as it is poetic: one might expect him to assert that our natural sense of the "enveloping world" gives rise to religiosity rather than seeking to meet the needs of a religious attitude that he has not shown exists or should exist. It is ultimately not clear why God or any kind of religious attitude are needed except for a psychological comfort that other means might provide.[79] But there is no doubt of the optimism of Dewey's vision, and even of the utopian impulse behind it—Dewey's too is a processual utopianism—even if we accept Dewey's equation of utopianism with fantasy as opposed to practical ideals. Freed from its supernatural foundations, religiosity becomes the realm of choosing the right ideals. Without recourse to supernatural intervention, it is possible to imagine the "radical intervention of intelligence in the conduct of human life."[80]

Democracy

The utopian impulse at the base of Hu Shi's thought is seen most clearly in his belief that through science a world of material abundance leads to an ever more perfect society—that is, the ongoing processes of "socialization" and "humanization" described above. He derived a faith in human dignity and human rights from these processes. But his utopian impulse is also seen in the steadfastness of his work for the gradual promotion of democratic institutions. Hu did not deny the problems of functioning democracies, such as corruption and power mongering. Nonetheless, Hu not only believed that progress toward democracy was historically inevitable (or at least probable), but also that democracy served as a kind of single-root solution to China's problems. Here is the heart of the utopian aspect of Hu's democratic thought, devoid of radicalism as it was: democracy was experimentism in social action. As Pan Guangzhe has shown, Hu's personal experience of political campaigns and elections during his university years in the United States from 1910 to 1917 shaped his favorable views of democracy.[81] Hu was aware of the flaws of democracy in practice but nonetheless concluded that the American system was an appropriate basis for thinking about democracy in China.

"Do democratic political systems have the effect of producing good citizens?"[82] Hu Shi regarded this as a key question in any study of politics, and an especially urgent question for China. On one level, to move beyond Hu's own terms, this is a chicken-and-egg question: Which comes first, the good citizens to construct democracy or the democratic system that makes good citizens? Any view that postulated that the Chinese were not "ready" for democracy assumed that good citizens had to be in place before democracy could be practiced. Admitting that democratic institutions on their own could scarcely create good citizens, but also recognizing that it was always nondemocratic systems that produced democracy, Hu insisted that democratization could not wait for perfect citizens. He perhaps envisioned a kind of dialectical process in terms of the interactions between society and the state. Hu first argued that institutional reforms did in fact produce better forms of political life, even though political corruption could never be eliminated entirely. Furthermore, "We cannot make people good but institutional reform can make people fear to lightly do evil."[83] As the ancient Chinese Legalists knew, according to Hu, institutions were important, and in his words, institutional reform was necessary for political renewal. One of Hu's examples was the voting system that evolved from public to private ballot, which eliminated numerous abuses. He also argued that direct elections minimized vote buying and cited (though not by name) the set of election reforms proposed by the Progressive Movement in America in the early twentieth century.

Hu's discussion of election law, including the contemporary Chinese case, is a good example of his cautious and moderate approach to politics. No doubt this instinctive caution lies behind his general opposition to radicalism and revolution. Hu's pragmatist philosophy, as described above, was of the step-by-step variety. As well, however, it is worth noting Hu's respect for the 1911 Revolution: unlike other intellectuals of the day, he did not consider it a failure but rather a beginning, the basis on which a democratic politics could be build. Hu's view of the nature of politics was thus radical in its way, based on the legitimacy of revolution. In terms of legal regime, he simply felt that while no set of laws can entirely stop bad people from breaking them, good laws can maximize the abilities of good people to enforce them. And looking abroad, Hu concluded that the experience of democratic nations showed that such institutions did indeed train better citizens.[84]

So, how do democratic systems come about? Hu pointed out that they might evolve in a single society, such as Britain, or may be adopted by other societies. In all cases, democracy emerges as a kind of reaction to corruption, and creates the good citizens we see today. Democracy was not created by those good citizens, for they did not initially exist. Speaking to China's conditions, Hu urged the country not wait until "the level of the people is sufficiently high" to adopt democratic institutions: in that case, the institutions would never come. Rather, since other countries now offer models for China to follow, the institutions can be adopted and will then function to educate citizens. As Chinese have learned how build electricity grids and how to form corporations, so the political realm, while more complicated, is at root simply another form of organizational life. Again, Hu turned to America for a more or less utopian example: "In all those countries that have undergone long training in democratic institutions, civic knowledge and morality is higher than in other countries." The citizens of democratic countries "were simply born under republican institutions, grew up in the air of democracy, received training of institutions, and so naturally the knowledge acquired by many citizens of democratic countries is higher than that of people who learn about politics from books in university."[85] Hu cited his personal interviews with lower-class American voters in 1912 and 1916, whom he determined to be quite knowledgeable about what they were voting for, even though they lacked theoretical knowledge of politics.

But what did this have to do with China? Hu's ideas here were not very specific and perhaps could not be. He adopted the notion of education in democracy as a kind of metaphor for institutional change. Education required practice, Hu said, and practice required commitment. Students who skipped classes would of course fail to learn—hence, the failures of the Republic of China. Civic knowledge was key, not civic morality, nor fine theory. Hu was firm on one point: "Civic knowledge is an element of civic morality; and the spread of civic knowledge is a key condition for the cultivation of civic morality." In other words, merely armed with knowledge, citizens could act to check governmental abuses and bring about further progress. This progress in turn assured that popular supervision would tend to eliminate corruption—for Hu, this was the simple essence of civic morality.

There is, arguably, a tension in Hu's thought: he seems to be admitting that the "level of the people" in China is not sufficiently high, which is why education is necessary. This might imply first education, then democracy. But ever the Deweyan experimentalist, Hu's point was that education as he was using the term was only found in practice. It is democracy that provides a "universal educational system" that allows those with the qualifications of citizenship to participate. Hu was saying that through participation, and as the system limits the opportunities for corruption as well, "good citizens" in effect produce themselves.

Insofar as Hu's approach toward democracy attempted to build it out of existing institutions rather than overthrow them, it might be described as moderate or conservative. Yet insofar as his approach rested on the total dismissal of any notion of tutelage, it constituted a radical challenge to mainstream views. "Political tutelage" (*xunzheng*) formed the very basis of the Guomindang regime and the official ideology of the Nanjing government since 1928. Sun Yat-sen had proposed a three-stage theory of revolution in the lead-up to the 1911 Revolution: military government, political tutelage, and finally democracy. The rise of dictatorship and warlordism in the wake of the revolution—and the lessons of the Bolshevik revolution in Russia—had confirmed his conviction that China needed vanguard leadership to move from its backward state to functioning republican institutions. At the same time, the new Guomindang's party-state under Chiang Kai-shek derived part of its legitimacy from the promise of democracy. In theory, democracy could begin to function locally as the cultural level of the populace was raised and then gradually expand. In practice, the Guomindang did little to bring this about. For Hu Shi, then, the failure of the Guomindang was explained not only by its own autocratic tendencies but also its theoretical incoherence. Instead of Sun Yat-sen's vague promises of democracy some day, Hu argued for combining democracy and education in democracy into a single package. This might not obviate the need for teachers—a role Hu Shi might think of filling himself—but did declare coercion to be illegitimate.

Hu Shi did *not* believe in the perfectibility of society, nor did he believe in the perfectibility of humanity. The promise of progress was real, but if pushed, Hu might have said he believed in Zeno's paradox: the goal came ever closer but was never reached. If it was a goal at all. If we think in terms of the question of the chicken or the egg again, beginning with the proposition that all societies have institutions and laws, and recognizing the dialectic that people make institutions but institutions also make people, the key really lies in institutional reform. It is impossible for a flawed people to remake all their institutions over-night, but it is possible to make "step by step" reforms, which in turn improve civic habits, and on that basis further reforms can be made, and so on in a virtuous cycle.

Hu Shi's views of democracy and Dewey's were not identical, but they did have a great deal in common. Several of Dewey's writings and speeches on democracy were discussed in the preceding chapter; in this chapter it remains to discuss his views of the roots of democracy, or what constitutes democratic culture. Obviously, the two men lived in dramatically difference political cultures. Yet key to both Dewey and Hu Shi were the links between epistemology and democracy, and between education and democracy.[86] An epistemology that emphasized experience and experimentalism need not necessarily impel its practitioners to democracy, but it subverts claims to any kind of final authority, includ-ing political authoritarianism. As Dewey put it in one of his talks in China, "The most pressing social problem in the world today is that of replacing the authority of tradition with the authority of science. What do we mean by authority? Basically we mean any thought or belief that influences human behavior."[87] This rather intellectualist-sounding pas-sage—beliefs shape behavior—is in fact built on the assumptions that experiences shape belief and that individuals are always members of social groups that, in turn, are largely determined by shared interests. At the same time, Dewey emphasized that progress was possible because people had the capacity to manage both their material environment and their inner lives. Authority is universal and inescapable, but its nature and methods can be changed. That is, changed to scientific authority that judges existing institutions based on facts and observation rather than supernatural fantasies, on open processes rather than esoteric secrets. Like Hu Shi, Dewey denied that the scientific attitude was any kind of crude materialism, but asserted that it would promote the spiritual life.[88]

The differences between Hu Shi and Dewey seem largely those of emphasis and context. Hu was the greater supporter of more scientistic approaches and of individualism, and he was more explicitly antipolitical (in the specific sense of personal involvement in political movements or in official administration). Dewey was more sensitive to the intimate bonds of communities and even respectful of religion, as long as it is broadly understood, as we have seen above. But it should be remembered that

Hu also spoke of the immortality of the social body and the promise of spiritual development. As for individualism, the somewhat different tones adopted by the two men are least partially explained by the different contexts wherein Dewey faced a strongly individualistic society while Hu faced a strongly communitarian society, as the two men thought.[89] Granted, Dewey's views of individualism were considerably more complicated than this. While Dewey was repeatedly critical of classic liberalism with its emphasis on the rights of property, and made little use of the language of rights, he spoke much on freedom.[90] This had to be a real freedom, however, not based on legal formalities and institutions that mask inequalities.[91] Put crudely, Dewey could advocate greater communalism without fearing a loss of individualism, while Hu could advocate the values of individualism without fearing that the Chinese sense of family and the communal would disappear (though other intellectuals strongly disagreed with Hu on this point).

Both Hu Shi and Dewey fundamentally believed in gradual social reform rather than revolution. Again, there may have been a difference in tone as Dewey was from time to time more sympathetic to the cause of revolution, but Hu also expressed great interest in the "experiment" of the Soviet Union, as we will see below. During his lecture tour in China, Dewey strongly promoted the reformist line. In *Democracy and Education*, Dewey had put it this way: "We cannot set up, out of our heads, something we regard as an ideal society. We must base our conception upon societies which actually exist, in order to have any assurance that our ideal is a practicable one. . . . The problem is to extract the desirable traits of forms of community life which actually exist, and employ them to criticize undesirable features and suggest improvement."[92]

The key difference between Dewey and Hu is that while Dewey saw democracy as part of his larger goal to promote "associated living" based on the cooperation of social groups, for many Chinese intellectuals, including Hu, democracy was a goal that still needed to be achieved, a goal that was as radical in its social and cultural implications as in its political meaning. Dewey published *Democracy and Education* in 1916, just three years before his trip to Asia. This work combined Dewey's interests in education defined as both formal schooling and lifelong learning in psychology, in philosophy, and in social progress.[93] It also formed the basis of many of his lectures in China. Much of the book is devoted to educational psychology, and one theme is the role of education in creating citizens who are open to new learning and to communication and inquiry. In other words, education continues across a lifetime and is intrinsic to any true democratic order. "A democracy is more than a form of government; it is primarily a mode of associated living, of conjoint communicated experience."[94] Forces in the modern world such as industrialization, communications technology, and increasing levels of commerce, travel, and migration, Dewey thought, were breaking down barriers of class, race, and national territory. The modern world was marked by both greater individualization and "a broader community of interest," that is, social groups from the family to the nation are becoming less closed. Space, Dewey grandly declared, was being annihilated. The greater degree of interaction between social groups means that their members must be "educated to personal initiative and adaptability. Otherwise, they will be overwhelmed by the changes in which they are caught and whose significance or connections they do not perceive."[95]

Dewey did not envision the abolition of "societies" in the name of common humanity, but he did think education could foster equality within societies and more harmonious relations among them. Historically, Dewey said, the state's need to educate its citizens and the democratic idea of public schools both emerged in the nineteenth century. He emphasized that the goal of education at that time was to produce not "the 'man'" but a citizen.[96] Disciplinary training took precedence, and, based on the theory of the organic nature of the state, the old eighteenth-century ideal of personal development was reconceptualized as a state function. That is, Dewey remarked with disapproving reference to Germany, personal development was seen to occur only by being absorbed into statist institutions instead of aiming for a cosmopolitan humanism. For Dewey, nationalism was a problem to be overcome, the difficulty being that education had to be in the hands of the state. As well, the contemporary nation was based on class exploitation. Therefore, Dewey wanted education to be reshaped to carry out two goals. First, everyone must be "equipped to be the masters of their own economic and social careers." And second, "the fuller, freer, and more fruitful association and intercourse of all human beings with one another must be instilled as a working disposition of mind."

Dewey did not seem very confident these goals could be fully reached, but they represented an ideal to head toward. His vision of a democratic society was at root quite simple: a society where all contribute to the common good and where all have the opportunity to develop their capacities.[97] And such a society is dynamic and progressive, growing through the play of the gifts of all its individuals.[98] Breaking down the barriers among individuals and between societies creates not greater homogeneity but a vaster set of variations and even "transformation." Dewey simultaneously struck a utopian note and implicitly referred to a processual utopia, foreseeing

> a society in which every person shall be occupied in some-
> thing which makes the lives of others better worth living,
> and which accordingly makes the ties which bind persons
> together more perceptible—which breaks down the barriers of
> distance between them. It denotes a state of affairs in which
> the interest of each in his work is uncoerced and intelligent:
> based upon its congeniality to his own aptitudes. It goes
> without saying that we are far from such a social state; in a
> literal and quantitative sense, we may never arrive at it. But
> in principle, the quality of social changes already accomplished
> lies in this direction.[99]

In one of his first lectures in China, Dewey began by pointing out that people are always members of groups formed on the basis of all kinds of relationships: family and kinship, class, nation, ideas, village, religion, sports, and so on and so forth.[100] There were scarcely any limits to the multiple groups to which people belonged. In looking at the nature of social conflict, Dewey denied that binary formulations such as individual versus society or people versus government made much sense, since in fact conflict emerged from the competing interests among groups. In his typescript for the lecture, Dewey offered an "ideal picture" of intergroup cooperation "in which there is an equal (proportionate) development of all these forms of associated life, where they interact freely with one another, and where the results of each one contribute to the richness and significance of every other. . . . where in short there is mutual stimulation and support and free passage of significant results from one to another."[101] However, this was merely a kind of thought experiment, used to highlight the historical reality of brutal conflict and not included in the published lecture. Dewey emphasized the dislocations caused by large-scale industry and the expansion of the state, which have led to "new frictions" and a world in "critical state."[102] Dewey's published lecture nonetheless concluded with a hopeful gesture. The competition between groups could be alleviated through concrete instances of the general truth that all groups are so intimately related that they share a common fate.

Dewey's theoretical point was that society is best understood in terms of the conflicting interests of social groups, although groups that are always multitudinous, overlapping, and shifting, and not reducible to any simple formula. It then follows that the last three to four centuries of political theory that framed society in terms of individual rights (laissez-faire) versus the entire social body (socialism) had been on the wrong track entirely. Dewey's "middle way" thus referred to a path that was neither completely conservative, which is to say theoretically committed to a vision of society as an organic whole while actually representing the interests of the dominant group (say, a feudal aristocracy), nor entirely radical, which is to say theoretically committed to individual rights vis-à-vis the state while actually representing the interests of the dominant group (say, capitalists).

Dewey thus combined what he called social philosophy with political theory. In his published lectures, Dewey succinctly noted the practical issue: conservative forces, basing their legitimacy on "traditional social theory," pretended that any calls for reform reflected merely aberrant, antisocial individuals rather than the legitimate interests of new social forces. For example: the rise of the women's movement and the labor movement since the Industrial Revolution. However, new social forces should also avoid the delusion that the conservatives' view of society represents the whole of society—it does not, and revolution that seeks to overthrow all existing institutions falls into the same trap. Rather, reformers should engage in rational "scientific" analysis of which institutions should be retained and which abolished or improved. As Dewey put it in his original typescript:

> This means an appeal to intelligence, not to bias and prejudice and vested interests, to inquiry to trace causes and consequences, to see what produced this or that institution or arrangement, *the historical method*, and also to trace consequences, to see how the arrangement works, what effects it produces—and the same for any proposed measure of reform, improvement. The practical difference is thus the substitution of the scientific method for the method of opinion, dogmatic assertion, bitter recriminations and disparaging name-calling, epithets of abuse. Method of analysis, of taking things in details and discriminating, instead of wholesale isms.[103]

Such "analysis" was part of Dewey's vision of democracy, for it should lead to dialog and a degree of mutual respect. Starting from the fact that we all live in association with other human beings, Dewey implied that social institutions faced a kind of tradeoff between efficiency, which may lead to loss of liberty and control by the few on the one hand, and the lack of central organization and planning, which is also problematic, on the other.[104] Accepting this tradeoff, for Dewey, then, democratic political systems were part of a larger project of "associated living" (or living in common, *gongtong shenghuo*), which he defined as progress toward "free communication, mutual contacts, the exchange of feelings, and the exchange of all sorts of valuable things."[105] This requires the maximum possible equality, since obviously in stratified authoritarian societies open communication is difficult if not impossible. And hence, democratic societies are actually more stable than dictatorships. Even if the latter temporarily appear stronger, they are prone to disintegration because, depending on force, they are not properly integrated. They block free communication and cooperation, prevent most people from developing their potential, and corrupt the rulers. In one of his typescripts, Dewey remarked that a specific advantage of parliaments is precisely that they foster "speech back and forth." This was the ideal way to discover "social laws, that is desirable regulations of conduct" because it "subjects ideas to criticism, improves them by selection and combination, leads to new thought and to inquiries."[106] And, Dewey later remarked, it is democracy that makes such communicative speech *possible*, while "education, companionship, the breakdown down of class and family walls and barriers make it *actual*."[107]

Dewey, too, thus sought to abolish boundaries. Democracy provided three benefits: relative social stability; ongoing education in civic life (and to some extent private life); and the basis for the communication and development of of ideas (without which, at best, societies will stagnate). In a published lecture, Dewey said:

> Dictatorships are never based on associated living and are never able to let all social segments to share their feelings and concerns. As for the basic principle of democracies (*pingmin zhengzhi*), that is simply that government is based on the consent of the governed. If every action taken by the government is based on the consent of the governed, if the governed feel that they are a full part of society, that the social will is their own will, and that in fulfilling their duties they enjoy their rights, then everyone will wish to

support the government. This is the most stable basis for a state. . . . Democracies are based on the desires of all, and although they may seem prone to volatility, experience shows they are actually stable. . . . This kind of society affords every member the opportunity for their free development, free communication, mutual aid, mutual interests, exchange of emotions, and the exchange of ideas and knowledge. The foundation of such societies is the free contributions of their members based on their abilities.[108]

The utopian impulse behind this description of democracy is striking. It is also worth noting again that Dewey never essentialized China or the West. He noted differences among various countries, in particular the United States, China, Germany, and Japan, but he was interested in how fundamental principles of politics, society, and economics applied to all, albeit in different ways. In his reading of history, Dewey emphasized the birth of individualism in the Industrial Revolution and capitalism. He thought of socialism as a correction to the "self-seeking" individualism of the West, and that it provided the egalitarianism needed for associated living. China, however, Dewey thought, might be able to achieve social equality without going through a period of individualism.[109] Noting that the goal was still to create conditions under which individuals were able to flourish, Dewey looked to China's traditional value of imperial benevolence and the role modern education could play in providing all people with equal capacities to flourish, and he finally concluded that China still had time to train the specialists needed to keep complex modern societies functioning (as opposed to the West's political individualism, which disdains professionalization).

Dictatorships, according to Dewey, distort the personality development of all their members, not just the oppressed. And if democracies do not *necessarily* provide what Dewey called associated living, at least they provided the conditions necessary for its possibility. Democracies can combine social integration with the full development of the individual personality. The greatest advantage held by democracies, Dewey believed, was their educational functions—the open discussions through which the individual's knowledge, ideas, and feelings are developed.[110]

The fundamental notion of democracy (*minzhi*) is precisely its great belief in education. This belief is simply the recognition that the large majority of ordinary people are all educable, the ignorant can be made knowledgeable, and the incapable capable—this is the basic notion behind democracy. Democracy *is* education: continuing and uninterrupted education. After leaving school and taking up positions in their democratic society, people continue training just as in schools. In this way everyone's individual views gradually extend to the whole society and even the whole world. Then this view of the common interests of the entire world is established, and the benefits [of democracy] will not be limited to a single society or country.[111]

Examining democratic institutions, Dewey stated that law should not merely express the "common will" (*gonggong yizhi*) of the people to preserve their "common life" (*gonggong shenghuo*). Equally important, "consciously derived legislation" (*you yishi de lifa*) replaces old customs and traditions.[112] That is to say, the law is derived from free and open discussions that build a degree of consensus. Again, Dewey emphasized that the individual and individual rights are important, but he did not begin with the premise of the presocial and prestate individual. Individuals are only the subjects of rights if they are members of their society and state.[113] Rights mean nothing as abstract statements; like duties, they only exist in practice.

Writing in 1939, Dewey stated his supra-political vision of democracy even more plainly.[114] Democracy was a task needing conscious effort; it required "the creation of personal attitudes in individual human beings" because it "is a way of life controlled by a working faith in the possibilities of human nature." Specifically, "The democratic faith in human equality is belief that every human being, independent of the quantity or range of his personal endowment, has the right to equal opportunity with every other person for development of whatever gifts he has. . . . It is belief in the capacity of every person to lead his own life free from coercion and imposition by others provided right conditions are supplied.[115] Looking to Nazism on his right and the Soviet Union on his left, Dewey again stressed the importance of communication: free gatherings of people to converse without abuse or intolerance. Race, color, wealth, and degree of culture were all irrelevant to the business of democracy. Not states, nor institutions, nor laws but actual lived consensus building, cooperation, and self-correction are the essence of democracy. Dewey believed that humans were educable and by nature social, not necessarily that human nature was good. In Deweyan terms, "Democracy is belief in the ability of human experience to generate the aims and methods by which further experience will grow in ordered richness."[116] Admitting this might be considered a utopian view, Dewey seemed to imply that since people had embarked on the course of democracy, with education, effort, and a willingness to be guided by experience, that course led ever upward. And he cited "need and desire" as those qualities that moved people beyond the current boundaries of knowledge and science. A radical utopian indeed.

Dewey was writing as a cosmopolitan, a philosopher whose ways of thinking used a scientific method applicable to all times and places, though recognizing that different circumstances would lead to different conclusions. He was also writing out of personal experiences in an America between the Civil War and World War I, as well as a cosmopolitan traveler. The great social forces fueling his political theorizing were the labor movement, secularization, the clash of nations, and racism. Hu Shi was also a cosmopolitan philosopher, but Hu's personal experiences revolved around the lived contrasts between China and America, imperialism, and a failed state. Through the 1930s, Hu Shi's criticism of the Guomindang revolved around what he saw as its self-indulgent cultural complacency.[117] China's problems required a fundamental "reconstruction of psychology"—a "new awakening" that would go beyond Sun Yat-sen's fatuous slogan that "to know is difficult while to act is easy"—a twist on Wang Yangming's famous formula that Sun believed justified his vanguard theory of party leadership.[118] For Hu, rather: "This kind of urgent new awakening is simply our recognition of our own mistakes. We need to acknowledge that we are inferior to others in a hundred ways, and not only materially inferior, not only in terms of machinery, but also inferior politically, socially, and morally." And Hu added, in an obvious retort to Guomindang rhetoric,

> Do not simply say that it is imperialism that is hurting us. This is how we lie to ourselves. . . . Even today we still follow superstitious slogan that we can overthrow imperialism. We still think that we can rule the country without learning or skills. We are still not willing to humble ourselves to learn the organization and methods by which other people enrich their countries. . . . Thus I say that today our first duty is to create a new kind of psychological state: we must acknowledge

our own mistakes, and we must wholeheartedly acknowledge
that we are completely inferior to others. . . . Second, we
must adopt an attitude of complete humility to learn from
others, and frankly speaking, we must not be afraid to imitate
them. . . . We need to learn how [other] people have used
railways, automobiles, telegraphs, airplanes, radio, to get blood
circulating, revive limbs, and unify the country. We need
to learn how people use education to eliminate ignorance,
enterprise to eliminate poverty, machines to conquer Nature,
and raise the capabilities and happiness of the people. We
need to learn how people use various avoidance-systems to
manage businesses and factories, and order national politics.[119]

China's true enemies, Hu insisted, were "poverty, disease, ignorance, corruption, and disorder."[120] He feared revolution would lead only to more
despotism. A kind of "revolution" can overthrow China's true enemies
through dedicated effort, but not a violent revolution. The right sort of
revolution was *"to make complete use of the scientific knowledge and methods
of the world,* and step by step to carry out a *conscious* set of reforms, and
under *conscious* leadership bit by bit to harvest the results of unceasing
reforms."[121] Even in his fearful moments, the utopian impulse permeated
Hu's thinking.

If this all seems rather vague, it was certainly hopeful. The failure
of democratic institutions to take root since the 1911 Revolution, for Hu,
was no sign of their weakness or inappropriateness. Rather, he implied
that the fault lay with the Chinese—apparently without discriminating
among political and military leaders, social and intellectual elites, and
the ignorant masses. Yet he believed the poltical will could be summoned
to construct new institutions "bit by bit." A pessimist might have concluded that there were no institutions in place to begin the process of
educating citizens who would then strengthen those institutions, and no
people able to found the new institutions to educate the citizens of the
future. In this light, Hu's faith that breakthrough somewhere was possible
almost seems utopian in itself. Hu relied on the notion that persons of
good will can make a difference, but of course he could also see realities
changing around him: the exhuberant growth of schools, journals, study
societies, China's participation in international organizations, and other
modern phenomena.

Hu's optimism also rested on his immunity to the sense of existential threat that haunted many of his contemporaries. This threat had motivated radical reformers in the late Qing and inspired the call, "Without reform our race will be exterminated." Hu had little fear of racial extinction, but he certainly agreed with the criticism of conservatism. He criticized Liang Shuming's 1921 *Eastern and Western Cultures and Their Philosophies* for its support of Orientalization (*dongfanghua*).[122] In Hu's reading, Liang's call for a revival of the Orient was based on the notion that Eastern thought was the only hope for humanity. Liang feared that if Eastern thought did not become a "world culture," then it would die. Eastern thought, Liang said, could not survive only in China, but in a sense must evolve through Western, Chinese, and ultimately Indian forms. Hu thought Liang was ignoring the fact that cultures are simply complex systems by which a people deal with their environment. A local culture may or may not become a world culture, but that has nothing to do with its survival.[123] Continuing his pluralistic approach, Hu pointed out that there were always a variety, but a limited variety, of responses to environmental conditions, and hence several distinct cultural patterns. Again, Hu argued that all cultures by definition had both material and spiritual aspects, and indeed that China was if anything more decadent, and not more orderly than the West. Hu urged Liang to open his eyes to concubinage, prostitution, and the vast literature celebrating alcohol and courtesans. In word, the world did not need "Eastern thought," at least not *tout court*. Then, returning to his natural home in the theory of linear progress, Hu pointed out that Europe had been an equally benighted place in the Dark Ages but that three centuries of progress in science and democracy allowed it to meet environmental challenges to lead the world. So,

> In the race to be first, although there can only be one man in first place, the people behind, although they cannot be first, can still gradually progress and ultimately get to the goal. In today's interconnected world, the environment and programs that had originally spurred on the Europeans now spur us on. *We cannot doubt the future of science and democracy in China and India.* Their backwardness is merely due to their lack of those environments and problems that forced and spured on [change], and not because of basic differences in their intuitions or sensations of life.[124]

Hu's gradualism here attenuates his more purely utopian impulses, but there is no doubt of his faith in happy outcomes.

Yet nonetheless, that Hu endlessly attacked those whom he saw as advocates of "Eastern spirituality" shows what a threat he thought they were. Deriding the "Oriental spiritual" and almost taking present-day America as utopia were two sides of the same coin. In America, Hu saw the successful implementation of the income tax, putting most of the burden on the rich, as a form of the "socialization" he believed in. He pointed to rising wages and spreading stock ownership as proof that the Marxist critique of capitalism was wrong. Even American blacks, Hu said, were becoming better off. In effect, Hu treated the United States as a kind of third road running between communism and capitalism, and perhaps even a processual utopia.

> Some self-proclaimed "prophets" constantly proclaim, "One day eventually America's material development will end, and when its material civilization is bankrupt, it will experience social revolution." But I can assert with complete confidence that America will never experience social revolution, because America is undergoing social revolution every day. This kind of revolution is progressive, moving forward daily, and so is an everyday revolution.[125]

Hu's utopian impulse was also seen to a limited degree in his support of the Soviet Union well into the 1920s. On the one hand, it might seem that Hu should disapprove of such an ideologically driven social experiment; on the other, precisely because he regarded it as an experiment, he looked forward to seeing the outcome.[126]

> I am an experimentalist and must express admiration for the large-scale political experiment of the Soviet Union. Now, experimentation and taking a little taste of something are not the same. Experimentation must follow a hypothetical plan (an ideal), and must come up with various methods to bring the plan to a practical conclusion. In the entire history of world politics, there has never been the experimental opportunity to bring a large-scale "utopian" (wutuobang) plan to fruition. If we look at Chinese history, we only find the "socialist state" experiments of Wang Mang and Wang Anshi;

we may admire the instance of the Wang Mang experiment. But their failures should inspire us to understand the value of the Soviet experiment of today.[127]

This did not mean Hu Shi had any patience with communists in China. Whatever achievements the Soviets might make, he charged that Chinese Communists either suffered from a superstitious belief in dictatorship or believed all of China's problems stemmed from foreigners. But Russian Communists he admired for their idealism and "seriousness of purpose." For, "they are here engaged in a great and unprecedented experiment; they have ideals, plans, and absolute confidence. These three qualities leave me deeply ashamed" (in that they are lacking among the Chinese).[128]

Hu claimed not to care about theory—whether capitalist or social-ist—and obviously had doubts about both capitalism and the Russians' "elimination of the propertied class at the hands of the dictatorship of the proletariat."[129] In a theoretical vein, Hu denied that liberalism was necessarily the philosophy of capitalism. Rather, the "new liberalism" or "liberal socialism" was the result of three centuries of "socialization." On the one hand, in a pluralistic vein, Hu denied that any system can be considered "universal"—it was up to people to decide what system they wanted to practice. But on the other hand, his general tone suggested that liberalism and socialization were in fact universal forms of social organization. The Chinese, Hu said, could not rely on superficial reforms. They could build democratic institutions if they could summon the will and commitment to do so at every level of society.

Conclusion

Hu revealed a rare moment of *depression* (he used the English term) in a letter to Xu Zhimo in 1926. "In the final analysis, in the nine years since I returned to China, what have I done? What have I accomplished? I have seen the country's politics getting worse day by day, and I have become truly depressed."[130] Hu accused himself and his friends of frivol-ity and laziness. Better the Russians' "seriousness of purpose" or even Mussolini's "live dangerously," or at least to commit to some kind of long-term plan like those being implemented in Germany or Japan. Hu was not tempted to turn to fascism or Stalinism, and, as we have seen, he was distinctly unimpressed by the Guomindang's efforts. Nonetheless, his flirtation with "long-term planning" revealed some disillusion with his reformist faith in "bit by bit" progress and is tied to the utopian impulse. "We could of course deny our own responsibility and attribute it to the evils of the earlier generation that have nothing to do with us. But even so, what about the results of our own actions?" Hu moaned. "Journals about the 'new literature and art' are everywhere, and superficial and pointless discussions of art and politics are everywhere: are these going to lead to new results?"

In some ways, the situation was to get worse, from Hu's point of view, with the rise to power in 1928 of a Guomindang that was committed to the "partyfication" of the schools. But Hu's essential optimism and commitment to reform based on existing institutions saw him through moments of depression. The relationship between pragmatism and political views that were infused with the utopian impulse is clear. Hu Shi's general optimism and his utopian impulses blended together in ways that make the distinction unusually difficult to sort out, but he did not simply have confidence that events would turn out well: he had faith in the ability of humans to make progress. Pragmatism consisted of an epistemology that led to democratic thought. In *How We Think*, Dewey remarked (as an aside): "Genuine freedom, in short, is intellectual; it rests in the trained *power of thought*, in ability to 'turn things over,' to look at matter deliberately, to judge whether the amount and kind of evidence requisite for decision is at hand, and, if not, to tell where and how to seek such evidence."[131] For the alternative of irrationality is "to foster enslavement." Freedom of thought necessitated free communication, the condition both for social continuity, as ideas and knowledge are passed from one generation to the next to be further advanced, and for democracy.[132]

As Jerome Grieder points out, Hu Shi was attracted to Dewey's version of pragmatism because he was searching for a "practical philosophy" and a universal one.[133] The experimental method promised not absolute truth but a way of finding usable, provisional truths that was as applicable in China as the West. And like Dewey, perhaps even more so, Hu saw democracy as a form of education. No matter how politically ignorant were the people, some degree of participation gives governments legitimacy and in turn fosters better understanding and greater political knowledge. But for Greider, the most utopian aspect of Hu's thought was his vision of the intellectual detachment of the individual who stood apart from both government and society. Such individuals required freedom to work. Such individuals had the ability to see beyond the existing reality and the duty to construct the frameworks necessary to critique it and to transcend it. Hu was skeptical of claims to absolute truth but had a deep faith in the power of rationality.[134]

If Chen Duxiu responded just to Dewey's vision of participatory democracy, Hu Shi applied Deweyan experimentalism to all of China's problems. Hu regarded social questions as amenable to experimental testing as were the physical sciences. Experimentalism represented the essence of the scientific spirit (*kexue jingshen*). Experimentalism was not random but a progressive, continuous process. As an approach to ethical questions, it provided grounds for criticizing Confucianism, but also grounds for testing what aspects of traditional culture could be usefully adapted to the modern age. Hu Shi's self-appointed task of "reordering the national heritage" (*zhengli guogu*) was essentially a heritage project that allowed him to propose a middle path between conservatism and radicalism. In a sense, Hu despised all grand theories, unless experimentalism—really, just judging policies by their results—is considered a grand theory. Like Dewey, he criticized both laissez-faire capitalism and Marxist communism. The utopian impulse in Hu took the form of believing that experimentalism guaranteed a more or less steady, ameliorative path toward just social arrangements. It was apparently a universally applicable methodology. And, though neither Hu Shi nor Dewey, so far as I know, ever quite thought of experimentalism in this way, it rested on a utopian faith in reason (which Dewey generally called "intelligence"), because without reason experimentalism was impracticable. Later generations might criticize Hu and Dewey for failing to realize that reason cannot account for the satisfactions of finding and hating the enemy, which was central to fascist and communist ideology. Dewey presented himself as neither purely a materialist nor an idealist, but insisted that theories have real effects, for good or ill. He denied he was an idealist since his theories were based on the concrete facts of individual cases. This is why he opposed both attacks against and defenses of existing institutions in toto. The obvious question for China was whether this approach, which combined radical critique with cautious policies in ways more or less suitable for a prosperous democracy like America, could work in a failed state such as China.[135]

Granted, as many scholars have commented, Hu Shi did not fully understand Dewey's ideas, or he deliberately changed them. Critics have also rubbished Hu's scholarship, though some carping may reflect the natural rivalry of men of letters, as Shen Songqiao points out.[136] Here, I simply want to emphasize that there are good reasons Hu had different things to say in some respects than did Dewey; and after all, Hu simply claimed to be an experimentalist, not Dewey's spokesman.[137] Obviously, Dewey was much more critical of American society and politics than was Hu, though I believe Hu's extraordinarily rosy remarks on America were strategically meant as a goad to his fellow citizens and he was perfectly aware that America in reality was not a utopia.[138] Hu found a sense of delight in the process of testing hypotheses, and his conviction that this led to progress followed. Perhaps Hu was prone to greater intellectualism and scientism than Dewey, and he certainly held a greater disdain for direct political involvement, at least through the 1930s.[139] Dewey more than once commented that the Chinese should build their new institutions while preserving aspects of traditional culture, at a time when Hu was advocating Westernization. And as Jerome Grieder points out, Dewey and Hu held profoundly different views of religion. Dewey was skeptical of a vision of humanity somehow apart, much less conqueror of nature, while Hu Shi continued to believe in the mastery of nature.[140] In his magisterial survey of pragmatism in China, Gu Hongliang rightly suggests that Chinese, including Hu, "misread" Dewey but did so in creative, productive ways.[141]

Without differences or even misunderstandings between them, there would have been no conversation between Dewey and Hu. Each man was learning from the other from their very different positions. And it was, after all, Hu Shi who inspired Dewey's decision to grapple with political and social philosophy more systematically than he had in the past. For Hu, Dewey provided a model for asking questions and testing answers, not any answers themselves.

Conclusion

Utopianism was a key feature of modern Chinese political thought, and a utopian impulse lay behind much Chinese work on politics that was not, at first glance, utopian. As China was drawn into a global capitalist system, it is scarcely surprising that it would participate in global cultural trends. Visions of a qualitatively better world dominated much of the early twentieth century. Egalitarian, socialist, and democratic imaginings about alternative futures were enormously influential. This study of four Chinese intellectuals in the last decade of the nineteenth century and first few decades of the twentieth century show how they developed their politics through the use, in part, of utopian ideals. It has also highlighted key dialogs between Chinese and Western thinkers. I have necessarily been selective about which dialogs to explore. Obviously, the Chinese thinkers confronted different questions and problems than their Western counterparts in the twentieth century, much less earlier centuries. And obviously, they found something useful and provocative in their Western counterparts. Whether we regard the problems today of the twenty-first century as new problems or as the heightened effects of the global capitalism of the nineteenth century, we too may find something useful and provocative in the alternative imaginings of the Chinese thinkers discussed in the pages above.

Kang Youwei, Cai Yuanpei, Chen Duxiu, Hu Shi: they were none of them purely armchair philosophers but were all politically active, though I have had little to say about their careers. In addition to the question of *how* their political views were constructed, I have said something about *why* they came to believe what they believed—the contexts in which they operated: the conditions to which they were responding. I have said nothing about whether their ideas were good or bad, right or wrong. That kind of evaluation is simply beyond the scope of this book (and my abilities). Perhaps readers can come to their own judgments. I should say (I don't know if it is obvious) that I admire these four men and their writings. I do not suffer from what David Estlund has usefully labeled utopophobia.[1]

Much of what the Chinese intellectuals I discuss were doing could fall under the rubric of what Estlund, following Rawls, calls ideal theory. However, they were not interested primarily in formulating fundamental principles of justice or democracy that reality or proposals could be measured against, as in ideal theory. Rather than starting with an ideal definition of a particular concept, they started with political programs that were partly inspired by glimpses of perfect societies that lacked the structures—boundaries—of today. In trying to get from point A to point B, they synthesized what might have been two questions into one. The two questions were: first, how to get from A to B (and no one thought it desirable or even possible to stay in point A), and second, what point B should look like. Means and goals were thus jumbled together. This jumbling together—we can think of it as a refusal to accept the artificial distinction between means and goals—was itself a way of doing realistic political theory. By this I mean political theory that was meant one way or another to inspire direct political action. The intellectuals/activists I have discussed in the pages above cannot be dismissed as "utopian dreamers" or mere fantasists. They were all, as in Wang Hui's defense of Kang Youwei, "deeply anchored in the evolving contexts and inner contradictions of modern history," facing up to "the contradictions of the modern world."[2] They responded to that world with new moral visions.

Kang Youwei began dreaming of a world of perfect equality in the 1880s. He eventually came up with the notion of "abolishing boundaries": the boundaries that arbitrarily separate nations, classes, races, and the genders, and make prisons of country and family. Few Western utopian thinkers had gone so far as to imagine racial and gender equality. Edward Bellamy, for example, assumed that Europe and America would build new societies based on the industrial army while the rest of the world remained in more backward conditions. Other utopian thinkers simply ignored one of the greatest questions of the nineteenth century. It is true that Kang's vision of racial equality was fully based on the widely shared assumption of the biological inequality of the races—he thought the inferior brown and black races would probably die out (or even should be sterilized, although Kang also implied they might be improved by migration to temperate climates). More explicitly, Kang advocated the interbreeding of the white and yellow races to produce a kind of hybrid vigor. This latter view was not uncommon at the time, though usually approached with nationalist goals based on social Darwinist assumptions.[3] Nonetheless, it is clear that for Kang, equality among nations, classes, and races meant homogenization. Kang could not dissolve gender boundaries in quite the same way, but abolition of the family—public nurseries and temporary marriage contracts—guaranteed women an equal place in the working, political, and social realms.

Both the details and the overall vision of Kang's Datong strike many readers as more dystopian than utopian. Be that as it may, Kang's work must be understood on at least three levels: the global utopian imaginary as seen in the likes of Edward Bellamy (another very proscriptive writer); the ancient notion of the Great Commonweal as it unfolded in the Confucian, Daoist, and Buddhist traditions; and the sense of crisis and anomie that Chinese intellectuals felt as the Qing empire crumbled. Like Zhang Binglin, Kang moved beyond the secular imaginary to conceive of a world without any distinctions whatsoever. Biological species, cosmic dust, buddhas: all—not exactly merge, but—shape-shift. Kang's concept of "humaneness" formed the basis of his belief in the interconnectedness of everything in the universe. Kang considered that the Chinese people were not ready to hear this religious, or metaphysical, belief. The first tasks leading toward the Great Commonweal remained secular. The advancement of technology, which would free humanity from the necessity of labor, was not the least of these tasks.

Cai Yuanpei's utopianism had much in common with Kang's and the temper of the times. His 1904 short story "New Year's Dream" had a more distinctly revolutionary cast, however. Cai imagined a world where a unified China would lead the war against imperialism, giving rise to a cosmopolitan world order that was democratic and that revolved around public institutions. At the time, Cai's story would have been read as an anti-Manchu and anti-imperialist screed. Today, its cosmopolitanism and metaphysical imaginings stand out. In describing the language of the future, Cai imagined an entirely different kind of society. There would be no terms of value (like "good" and "evil"); no terms of emotions involving social relations (like "kindness" and "resentment"). There would not even be a way to differentiate between "I" and "you." If this was not Kang Youwei's land of celestial peregrinations, it lay just across that particular border.

After Cai's studies in Germany, he developed his metaphysics of the abolition of the distinction between self and other. He did not mean this to describe an otherworldly utopia, however. He meant to describe a process through which people could learn to extinguish their egos (to translate Cai into Buddhist terms) and acquire something like absolute empathy. Working out his ideas over the 1910s and 1920s, Cai used Kant's distinction between the phenomenal and noumenal worlds and a peculiar interpretation of Kantian aesthetics in order to imagine a kind of cosmic unity. He started, at least, with Kant's and Schiller's understanding that aesthetic experience could produce a state of transcendence. This state of transcendence, Cai more or less associated with the noumenal world of ultimate reality, where the distinction between self and other had no meaning. Using traditional vocabulary, Cai called this achievement the "great self" or the human community as such. Cai's campaign to replace religion with aesthetics was the most extreme—but also the most positive—of a broad and deeply rooted effort on the part of intellectual and political elites to eradicate that they called superstition among the populace.

As a professional educator, Cai did much to encourage art education in the schools, support art and music clubs, and advocate for museums and parks to bring aesthetics into the lives of ordinary people. Cai's vision of a beautiful world filled with beautiful people was simultaneously transcendental and secular. He spoke of the need to plant street trees and, in a more clearly utopian fashion, of full employment with everyone working to the best of their abilities. He believed that schooling and life should combine physical and mental labor. He was deeply committed to the general goal of "science and democracy" even while he did not think these institutions could provide all the answers to the meaning of life.

Kang Youwei was born in 1858, Cai Yuanpei a decade later. They both passed the highest level of the traditional examination system. They were both naturally metaphysical thinkers, and both were cosmopolitan thinkers and travelers. Yet Cai lived in a mental world that is recognizably modern in a way that Kang's is not. There is no doubt of the power and originality of Kang's thought, but it is not conventionally philosophical, as Cai's is. Cai himself identified as a "philosophical anarchist" in spite of his later support for the Guomindang.[4] It may be that by the 1930s, Cai's notion of replacing religion with aesthetics had lost its original radical thrust, but an essentially emancipatory metaphysics continued to shape his liberal political views.

For Chen Duxiu, metaphysics simply did not enter into the picture. He consistently believed in the human capacity to make this world a better place—and to abolish the boundaries of class and gender and eventually of nations and races—by building better social institutions. Chen changed his mind about those institutions over the course of his life, but he never shied away from pursuing their revolutionary implications. On the one hand, Chen was a utopian thinker as defined by his unquenchable optimism in the future. This is perhaps most evident during his Leninist phase between 1920 and 1928, as he led the Communist Party and explored the laws of historical materialism. On the other hand, Chen was less precise about the glories of the future during his earlier liberal and later Trotskyist phases. Nonetheless, his democratic views rested on his utopian impulse. During his liberal phase, Chen's vision of democracy was based on a Deweyan vision of uncertainty. That is, that the only way to build a democratic order was to start with the messy decision-making processes of small-scale organizations that were voluntary and treated all members equally. There were many such grassroots associations that emerged in the 1910s, though Chen also seems to have been thinking about local self-government organs and workplace guilds. Chen's utopian assumption at this time was that egalitarian self-government would evolve naturally once China ridded itself of warlords and officials. But the fundamental point for Chen was that there should be no (or only minimal) delegation of powers. He was dubious of representation; rather, all persons should participate in the public sphere to the extent possible.

Chen's conversion to Marxism was a real break with his previous views. Chen's Marxism might be seen as new means to old ends—constructing a "new culture" to improve the lot of the Chinese people and humanity in general through "science and democracy." However, he now harshly rejected the quasi-anarchist approaches that he had previously supported, he dismissed democracy as inherently the political form of capitalism, and he looked forward to the "dictatorship of the proletariat." This amounted to an entirely new and favorable view of strong and centralized power. However, in the wake of the White Terror and the Stalinization of the Comintern, Chen turned to Trotsky to help him explain what had happened and what should be done. Chen, of course, remained committed to Marxist revolution. Tactically, he urged the party to go underground and attempt to unite with the proletariat by calling for democratic reforms through a national assembly that would fight for the eight-hour day and land reform. It would take a long time to build up a democratic movement as the bourgeoisie grew disillusioned with the Guomindang's autocratic rule, but once it was in place it would form the launching pad for the communist revolution. There would be no "bourgeois stage" to the revolution, as the Comintern proposed, but a continuous revolution leading to soviets governed by what Trotsky called the "democratic dictatorship of the proletariat and peasantry." Be that as it may, as early as 1930 Chen began rethinking the historical role of democracy. First, he postulated that proletarian democracy was the natural heir of bourgeois democracy—democracy of the true majority must result in the overthrow of capitalism and imperialism. Second (like Marx), Chen saw bourgeois democracy as progressive in its own time, overthrowing feudal power structures. And third, by the late 1930s, Chen specified that proletarian democracy must include the individual liberties that bourgeois democracy had secured, however inadequately, such as the freedoms of thought, religion, press, assembly, speech, and the like. And that the government's powers must be limited by an independent judiciary and democratic checks. The truly utopian aspect of Chen's late political thought was not his resolute confidence in the future but his belief that democracy was a kind of historical force in its own right—to be attained through class struggle but not in the end defined by class identity.

If Kang Youwei and Cai Yuanpei sought to abolish boundaries in a metaphysical sense—to create a new world without even consciousness of difference, Chen Duxiu's goal was less ambitious or, from a certain perspective, saner. He sought to build democratic institutions that would abolish the boundaries by creating inclusive, participatory communities. It is true that Chen largely neglected the problem of scaling up—how can participatory democracy work on a national basis?—but there is in fact growing work on this problem.[5] The case of Hu Shi initially looks more modest yet. But Hu believed that technological progress would enable humanity eventually to conquer Nature, or at least to lead to ever-increasing command of natural forces, which is hardly a modest goal. And even more striking is the conclusion Hu reached about the kind of society that would result. With poverty and disease no more, humanity would become a more moral and spiritual species. Hu also believed that the scientific culture on which technological development was based, was an open-ended, glorious pursuit of truth through "experimentalism." Whatever Hu did or did not learn from John Dewey, he understood the intimate links between democratic practice and education. People learn by testing hypotheses against facts. No dogma was unchallengeable. In the political sphere, no authority was beyond question. But while Hu did not believe in ultimate truths, he believed in the human capacity to build new societies through working hypotheses that, when tested, would lead to even better working hypotheses, in infinite progress.

Hu Shi's vision of "science and democracy" differed from that of Chen Duxiu (the great promoter of the slogan) insofar as Hu emphasized its unending nature. Hu's vision was, then, of a kind of processual utopia, providing joy in the pursuit of improvement. The road to moral and spiritual improvement for Hu lay in improving material life. For Hu, not class divisions, nor imperialism, nor exploitation appeared to be humanity's greatest enemies, but superstition, disease, and poverty. The boundaries Hu sought to abolish were those that prevented people from reaching their potential as individuals and as members of society. His immediate goal was not to foster empathy or, as Cai Yuanpei might say, to lessen the distinction between self and other, but to improve the material conditions of everyone. At that point, Hu had faith: empathy would follow. Similarly, Hu did not believe that the moral qualities of the people could be raised—or needed to be raised—before democratic institutions could be instituted. While the Guomindang government of the 1930s insisted that a period of "tutelage" or party-state dictatorship was necessary before the promised democratization could occur, Hu replied that only through democratic reforms would the level of the people be raised. He envisioned a process of step-by-step reforms, and he certainly opposed revolution: so in one sense Hu remained a moderate who was explicitly critical of the radicals of his day, while in another sense Hu was a radical who favored deep and fundamental reform of the political, as well as the social and cultural, institutions of his day. Democracy, for Hu, was education: the political form of rational thought. And the essence of rationality was experimentalism: formulating a clear hypothesis and carefully considering the results.

The utopian impulse found in the political theories of Kang, Cai, Chen, and Hu reflected their genuine cosmopolitanism. I mean cosmopolitanism in two senses: first, their natural tendency to think in terms of humanity and universal processes; second, their participation in global circulation of discourses they absorbed by both reading and traveling. This is not to say these four men floated above China's political and cultural wars. They lived through the crises facing China; they responded to the tumultuous global strains of Victorian optimism and the pessimism that followed the Great War. The tensions between utopianism and ideology, or the ideological uses of utopianism, are clear in hindsight.

Cosmopolitanism—taking the form of a universalistic language—could never quite mask particularistic concerns. These four men sought to improve the human condition but also, understandably, to strengthen their own country. Even so, difference had a way of slipping away in visions of humanity as one. Most obviously, in the Great Commonweal, Kang dissolved racial boundaries by creating a white-yellow hybrid directly at the expense of other races. In seeking to dissolve the boundaries between the genders, none of these four men considered the meaning of difference but simply assumed that, once freed of traditional restraints, women would emerge as full members of the public sphere. They tended to seek technological solutions to the problem of the peasants and workers. All that said, of course they could not completely transcend existing society. But their utopianism allowed all four men to do something more than merely build fantasy palaces or merely criticize their society. They built bridges to the future.

✦

Since the 1940s, China has experienced three sharply utopian experiments, none without both pleasures and pains. These were Great Leap Forward of 1958–60, the Cultural Revolution of 1966–69, and the radical capitalist reforms of the 1980s and especially the early 1990s. The utopian impulse that lay behind these particular outbursts of vast social mobilization were diverse but followed logically from one another. They were also rooted in the utopian impulses seen earlier in the century. Maoism, a complex set of political doctrines, was of course thoroughly imbricated with utopianism, much of it derived from Mao's study of Marxism and much of it derived from the ongoing tradition of Chinese utopian thinking.[6] I hope it is not necessary to say that I do not think there is any kind of straight line from the four intellectuals that the previous chapters focus on and the rise and destruction of Maoism. But there may be some crooked paths.

Ci Jiwei considers the entire Maoist period from 1949 to 1976 as utopian in ways distinct from what preceded it and what followed it, though of course the intensity and direction of utopian hopes changed over this period.[7] Unprecedented, because such devotion to the future rather than the past and present was new. The essence of the Maoist promise, in Ci's view, was not revolutionary puritanism or asceticism but a land of plenty. Chinese fervently sought a way out of poverty, which was directly promised in the GLF. Puritanism, asceticism, self-sacrificing labor—these were values, these were required, but the promise was they would lead to wealth and leisure for all. The Cultural Revolution did not directly make this promise, but it was, in Ci's reading, an "outlet for hedonistic and destructive impulses."[8] Like the GLF, the Cultural Revolution was based on an outburst of energy. Now in my view, the Great Leap Forward and the Cultural Revolution should be distinguished on several grounds. The GLF was an immense collective effort to jumpstart agricultural and industrial production through a relatively brief period of extra hard, sleepless work and sacrifice. The promise of the Cultural Revolution was not so straightforward. Its rhetoric was thoroughly ascetic and, unlike the GLF, the self-sacrifice that the Cultural Revolution ecstatically called for did not have a time limit. But the two movements shared a belief that the people can make history, that revolution was a continuous process, and that the highest good lay in devotion to the collective. In Ci's words, "If the Great Leap Forward was an openly and straightforwardly hedonistic project pursued by ascetic means, the Cultural Revolution was hedonistic only in its anarchic negation of the status quo and the psychological release such negation afforded."[9] Both movements, nonetheless, amounted to attacks on the very non-utopian status quo.

Therefore, for Ci, the initial period of Dengist reforms in the 1990s were a continuation of Maoist utopianism, though proffering more sober means. After the brutal suppression of the democracy movement in 1989—itself a utopian outburst—the economic growth that the government managed to foster in the 1990s, in Ci's reading, created a culture of "crude hedonism." Political consciousness and demands dissipated. Nonetheless, I would argue that the early 1990s saw a brief revival of a particular kind of utopian impulse in the arguments for economic liberalism, if nothing as recognizably utopian in terms of sentiments of equality and communitas. That is to say, the second phase of reforms began with the promise of a good life for all through a magical combination of management and markets: the promise was that politics was unnecessary.

Ci essentially argues that the failure of Maoism to lift the Chinese out of poverty after thirty years resulted in nihilism by the 1970s—a sense of the loss of meaning—which manifested itself in cynicism, apathy, and hedonism. But then what I am calling a third moment of utopianism arrived: the Dengist reforms of the 1980s, which along with the loosening of ideological restraints, gave rise, in Ci's account, to both liberalism and hedonism. Ci argues that these two trends were closely related, that liberalism was both the sublimation of a hedonism that had been only partly legitimated and that liberalism was the ideology of hedonism. In the wake of the government's suppression of the democracy movement of the 1980s, it "de-sublimated" liberalism by further legitimating the individual pursuit of wealth and material satisfactions.

Be that as it may, Ci seems to suggest that the move toward capitalism cannot be regarded as utopian, because it was, at least in part, a cynical ploy by the government, promised private rather than social or collective good, and had abandoned any ideals outside of material wealth. That is, if I understand Ci correctly, it still reflected the nihilism that Maoism had ultimately produced. Nonetheless, in my view, many Chinese interpreted the Dengist lunge toward privativization in the early 1990s as a promise of wealth for all. If Deng wanted to "let some people get rich first," the implication—the promise—remained that all would get rich eventually. Thus, as Maoist utopianism was rooted in hedonistic promises, the Dengist road toward capitalism (however disguised as "socialism with Chinese characteristics") was paved with a utopian impulse: the impulse of straightforward hedonism. It may be, as Ci argues, that Maoism was more idealistic just in the sense that it had no way of realizing its hedonist promises in reality as opposed to imagining a world of plenty (or at least had not done so before the collapse of the Cultural Revolution and Mao's death). It is not clear to me if Ci is assuming that hedonism cannot supply meaning and is therefore itself a form of nihilism. If this were the case, hedonism is not reflecting what is normally called a utopian vision but a dystopian nightmare of an endless but ultimately unsatisfying pursuit of pleasure.

Writing in the early 1990s, Ci observed a China that was still just beginning down the road of what would turn out to be fantastic economic growth. Yet he was struck by a certain loss of faith in the future: "By purely material standards, however, reality has improved, but not by the standards of heightened, utopianized consciousness. Thus, not only has utopian consciousness been let down by reality, but equally, reality has been betrayed and darkened by utopian consciousness."[10] Even given the wealth accumulated in China since Ci wrote these words—or perhaps because of that wealth—the existential problem of finding meaning has only grown. Of course, it is better to search for meaning on a full stomach than an empty one, and the younger generations may care little for the utopian euphoria that marked moments of the Maoist years—or, for that matter, their grandfathers' capitalism. Insofar as history moves ironically, we can note that the Maoist promise to lead the Chinese people out of poverty has been achieved (to a considerable degree, anyway). That a society of plenty would be a society of equality and freedom, however, has not been achieved.

Faith in capitalism flamed up for a very brief moment, but in the twenty-first century we can hardly conclude that faith in capitalism has replaced the earlier faith in communism.[11] If capitalism promised wealth and, through wealth, freedom, it neglected the utopian goal of equality that had so marked most of the twentieth century. Perhaps the promise of capitalism—initially labeled "socialism with Chinese characteristics" and still dominated by the state—was egalitarian up to a point: the implication of Deng Xiaoping's acceptance of "some people getting rich first" was that the rest of the population would catch up in a reasonable amount of time. But even as the rates of extreme poverty have been slashed, the gap between rich and poor has grown to be among the highest in the world. The ideological tension in official discourse was between the promise to maintain a degree of socialism and the admission, in Marxist terms, that China had to undergo the capitalist "stage" before it could embark on truly socialist policies. This resulted in the de facto creation of a semi-kleptocracy.

If China's commitment to capitalism looks like a hesitant, two-steps-forward-one-step-back process that took a full generation and even now is obviously distinct from the Anglo-American model, nonetheless we can read the trial of the "Gang of Four" in 1980 as a turning point away from Maoism to a theoretically depoliticized, rational state.[12] The Anglo-American model relies on the state to guarantee the rights of ownership, and enforce certain limits on those rights, but above all to clarify the rules of the flow of profits. Ownership (or "property rights") in China has remained less clarified than in the Anglo-American model, while marketization and liberal-capitalist ideology had intensified by the twenty-first century. Whether this marks a distinct "China model" is open to question. It has led to a second ideological tension. In addition to the tension between socialism-with-Chinese-characteristics and capitalism, there is a tension between the kind of Hayekian view of markets taught in economics departments and think tanks on the one hand, and the actual economic powers given to state actors on the other. Yet regardless of these tensions, by the 1990s China had become a fully paid up member of the global economy, and the essential structure of the Chinese economy was reshaped to fit into the neoliberal order.[13] However, whether

China has fully accepted neoliberal theory and practice is open to some debate, as it has become debated in other parts of the world as well.

Still, now that China has "joined tracks with the world," utopianism is in no better shape there than elsewhere. The current phase of reform might be called, "Forget the class struggle, dream of consumption." The violent misuse of the concept of class struggle in the Cultural Revolution has made it impossible to utter at this moment of heightened class exploitation. If the mobilization of the Chinese people—in some ways going back to the end of the nineteenth century—was increasingly based on the desire, "We don't want to be poor anymore," then the continuity of this basic movement is evident across the political chaos of the entire twentieth century and is flourishing today. At the same time, however, the shift away from conceptions of public good to private interest is at least as clear. It is perhaps capitalism's legitimation of private interest that disqualifies it as a utopian ideology, regardless of the hopes placed in it. Yet there is another aspect of Chinese capitalism that speaks to a deep historical continuity and is inhospitable to utopianism. That is the importance of state-building and economic development. It is not that political leaders and intellectual elites necessarily thought that capitalism was the only basis of state-building—on the contrary—but that capitalism, when it developed, has done so in tandem with corporatist policies and the encouragement of nationalist sentiment. If not logically impossible, it has proved difficult to integrate nationalist sentiment with cosmopolitan concern for humanity as a whole.

Today's Chinese state stands ready to check the undesirable activities of companies and is very quick to suppress independent unions (and officials profit enormously from their government positions). Liberal economists sometimes doubt whether China deserves to be called "capitalist" at all, but of course China has simply become one type of capitalist state, part of a global capitalist (or neoliberal) order.[14] In any case, the point here is that Chinese economic development in the twenty-first century has resulted in two trends inimical to utopianism. First, facing the inability of materialism to satisfy their spiritual needs, many people are turning to religion.[15] If religion has some ability to inspire utopian longings, they are eschatological and not of this world. And second, capitalist competition, whether leading to triumph or, more often, to a kind of nervousness over what might constitute success, fails to invoke any kind of higher ideal. Increasingly, official and public discourse alike has evolved (or devolved) away from "socialism with

Chinese characteristics" and "market socialism" to "harmonious society" and "prosperous (*xiaokang*) society." Coincidentally or not, *xiaokang* was what Kang Youwei called the general stage of social progress *before* it entered into the Datong.

ॐ

As I noted at the beginning of this study, scholars of China inside and outside of the country have often detected utopianism here, there, and everywhere. Yet there have been few systematic studies. In the modern period, from Liang Qichao and Yan Fu to Chiang Kai-shek and Mao Zedong, many persons displayed utopian impulses at one time or another, even while few figures identified themselves as utopian thinkers.[16] I hope my study has highlighted cases where a strain of utopianism wove its way in and out of modern political thought. At the same time, it is clear that for all its importance, utopianism was *not* the *basis* of Chinese political thinking.[17]

The most thorough claim to the ubiquity of utopianism in Chinese thinking is Thomas Metzger's exploration of "epistemological optimism." By this term, Metzger essentially refers to the belief that knowledge—moral as well as technical—is available to a number of persons especially equipped to discover it, and as a corollary that those persons can rectify the state and should lead society.[18] Creating the perfect state is thus a practical goal, and here, for Metzger, lies the essence of Chinese utopianism. Metzger contrasts this fundamental cultural disposition to "epistemological pessimism," which he associates with the modern West and which entails thoroughgoing skepticism about truth claims, a tragic view of history and human potential, and a turn to the negative freedoms of markets rather than reliance on leaders (who are always fallible). In essence, then, Metzger believes that all modern Chinese ideologies are founded on epistemological optimism and are therefore utopian. Even Chinese liberals believe that liberalism "is a basically definitive theory," rather than an acknowledgment of limits, and "that its implementation in the West has greatly reduced the impact of selfishness and irrationality on public life." If liberal utopianism in China seems relatively moderate, it still derives socio-moral standards from supposedly objective, rational truths—the mark of epistemological optimism and hence irredeemably utopian.[19] According to Metzger, *all* leading modern Chinese ideologies shared a fundamental optimism.

> Convinced that the corrigible state could be a vehicle of progress free of selfish interests and tyrannical tendencies, they saw no need to accept any risk of moral-intellectual dissonance. Thus they all insisted on a utopian, Rousseauistic ideal of a government fusing together knowledge, morality, political power and an effective concern with the freedom of the individual. . . . [T]hey all looked to an intellectually guided transformation of "Chinese culture" and the resulting use of the educational system to produce morally and intellectually reformed citizens. These citizens would realize what Isaiah Berlin had called "positive freedom."[20]

Powerful as it is, there are several problems with Metzger's analysis, however. The all-encompassing ideal of selflessness that, in different ways, arguably does describe Maoists and the New Confucians, is certainly a key to Chinese utopianism. But it was not important for all thinkers in China, or was only a secondary concern. Distrust of government was deeper than Metzger acknowledges, seen not only in the anarchist movement but in the late Qing proposals for local self-government and the creation of numerous independent civic associations. Metzger barely acknowledges the calls both strident and sober for individualism and liberation. Nor, as Ci Jiwei has pointed out, does Metzger analyze the actual functions of freedom in Western societies, where, for example, it is capable of producing conformity as well as license.[21] Whether in China or a Western nation, freedom functions in different ways to simultaneously achieve two objectives: individual agency and social order. An even more pressing issue, for my purposes, is Ci's refutation of Metzger's linkage of epistemological optimism to utopianism.[22] For regardless of their putative epistemologies, generations of Chinese thinkers and political actors looked back to centuries of highly nonutopian reality, and had come to the understanding that utopian hopes were not in fact realistic or practicable. Therefore, in Ci's terminology, what Metzger took to be an enduring utopianism in Chinese discourse was in fact an ideological discourse. That is, a discourse affirming the status quo; as for example, optimism about elites legitimates their claims to authority. We may question whether epistemology is simply all that important.[23]

Still, we are left with a major question. Metzger believed that through the 1990s "modern Chinese dynamism . . . entailed a kind of utopianism at odds with the functional requirements of modernization."[24]

Although I am not quite sure whether Metzger would put it precisely in these terms today, in essence this view remains a widely shared, commonsensical judgment of utopianism.[25] The fundamental problem with utopianism in this view is that, even if it acknowledges the legitimacy of fallible institutions, it cannot admit that private interests can ever be fully legitimate. Therefore, utopianism is incompatible with modernity; of course, this is to define modernity in terms of the capitalist world order. Yet China *has* modernized; has it suddenly abandoned epistemological optimism? Whether Chinese thought has bent toward epistemological optimism, whether China is truly capitalist or truly modern, whether Maoism was a utopian dead end: these issues beg the question: Is there an alternative to capitalist modernity? Given the dangers of complacency as twenty-first century unfolds, we are entitled to reverse the question: Is there a decent alternative to the utopian imagination? Kang Youwei, Cai Yuanpei, Chen Duxiu, and Hu Shi might show us how it's done.

Glossary

ai 愛
benti 本體
buduan de geming 不斷的革命
Buren 不忍
buren 不仁
Cai Yuanpei 蔡元培
chaotuo 超脫
Chen Duxiu 陳獨秀
Dao 道
Datong 大同
datong zhuyi 大同主義
dawo 大我
difang zizhi 地方自治
dongfanghua 東方化
gangda zhi mei 剛大之美
ganqing 感情
gao 高
gongli 公理
gongtong shenghuo 共同生活
gonggong yizhi 公共意志
guanzhi 官治
guomin huiyi 國民會議
guomin jiaoyu 國民教育
Guomindang 國民黨
Hu Shi 胡適
Huaxu 華胥
Inoue Enryō 井上圓了
jianrong bingbao 兼容並包

jiben de yuwang 基本的慾望
jinhua 進化
jixie nuli 機械奴隸
jun wupin 均無貧
Kang Youwei 康有為
kexue jingshen 科學精神
kongxiang 空想
Laozi 老子
Li Shizeng 李石曾
Liang Qichao 梁啟超
Liezi 列子
Liji 禮記
Liu Shipei 劉師培
"Liyun" 禮運
lixian huiyi 立憲會議
lizhihua 理智化
meigan 美感
meigan zhi jiaoyu 美感之教育
meishu 美術
meishu de jiaoyu 美術的教育
meixue 美學
minquan 民權
minzhi 民治
minzhu zhuyi 民主主義
pingmin zhengzhi 平民政治
pingmin zhuyi 平民主義
pupian 普遍
qin'ai 親愛
quan minyi 全民意
ren 仁
rendao zhuyi 人道主義
renge 人格
renmin zhijie de shiji de zizhi yu lianhe 人民直接的實際的自治與聯合
renquan 人權
qi 氣
qiangquan 強權
sandai 三代
sanshi 三世
santong 三統
shehuihua 社會化

shen 神
shenming 神明
shi 勢
shijie zhuyi 世界主義
shijieguan jiaoyu 世界觀教育
Shinshū 真宗
shiti 實體
shiyan 試驗
shu 恕
Suehiro Tetchō 末広鐵腸
taiji 太極
Tan Sitong 譚嗣同
tianxia wei gong 天下為公
tong (undifferentiatedness) 同
tong (interconnectedness) 通
tongye lianhe 同業聯合
wangguo 亡國
woxiang 我相
wuduan zhuyi 武斷主義
wutuobang 烏托邦
wuyu 無欲
xianshi 現世
xiaokang 小康
xiaowo 小我
xin 心
xin shijie 新世界
Xin shitou ji 新石頭記
Xin Zhongguo weilai ji 新中國未來記
"Xinnian meng" 新年夢
Xiong Shili 熊十力
Xixue Zhongyuan 西學中源
Xu Xing 許行
Xu Zhimo 徐志摩
xunzheng 訓政
Yan Fu 嚴復
yi 義
yijuequan 議決權
yishi 意識
yizhi 意志
you yishi de lifa 有意識的立法

Zhang Binglin 章炳麟
zhengjiao 政教
zhengli guogu 整理國故
zhenmei 真美
zhi 智
zhishi 知識
Zhongguo yi min 中國一民
zhuanjixing 專己性
ziyouquan 自由權
zizhi 自治
zizhu zhi quan 自主之權
zunyan 尊嚴

Notes

Chapter 1

1. Krishan Kumar, "The Ends of Utopia," *New Literary History* 41, no. 3 (Summer 2010): 549–69; Gregory Claeys, "The Origins of Dystopia: Wells, Huxley and Orwell," in *The Cambridge Companion to Utopian Literature*, ed. Gregory Claeys (Cambridge: Cambridge University Press, 2010), 107–32; Leonidas Donskis, "The End of Utopia?" *Soundings: An Interdisciplinary Journal* 79, no. 1/2 (Spring/Summer 1996): 197–219.

2. Cornelius Castoriadis, *The Imaginary Institution of Society* (Cambridge: MIT Press, 1998), 156.

3. For a critical but balanced view, see Ya-pei Kuo, "The Making of The New Culture Movement: A Discursive History," *Twentieth-Century China* vol. 42, no. 1 (2017), pp. 52–71.

4. The rise of the modern humanist movement is beyond the scope of this book. It is worth noting that John Dewey, discussed in the following chapters, was a signatory of the "Humanist Manifesto" of 1933, essentially an effort to reconstitute traditional religion in a nontheistic direction and to foster the "complete realization of human personality." *New Humanist*, May–June 1934.

5. Joachim Kurtz, "Cosmopolitanism, in Late Qing China: Local Refractions of a Global Concept," in *Reading the Signs: Philology, History, Prognostication: Festschrift for Michael Lackner*, ed. Iwo Amelung and Joachim Kurtz (München: Iudicium, 2018), 379.

6. I exclude what might count as utopian visions but that are not based on egalitarianism or some sense of universal *communitas* (fascism, Nazism, capitalism, and certain religious utopias that are hierarchical). See Russell Jacoby, *Picture Imperfect: Utopian Thought for an Anti-Utopian Age* (New York: Columbia University Press, 2005) for a view of utopianism as a a general commitment to universal brotherhood and communal work, excluding doctrines that celebrate violence or terrorism, or promote racial or religious exclusionism, even if they make some gesture to utopian ideas (ix–xiii). The definition of utopianism can

easily—and perhaps with greater internal coherence—be broadened to include ancient visions of the perfect society going back at least to Plato and to include religious visions of various heavens and their associated millenarian movements. However, utopianism in its modern sense is derived from Thomas More's 1516 *Utopia* with its distinctively egalitarian focus. See Krishan Kumar, *Utopianism* (Minneapolis: University of Minnesota Press, 1991), 20–41.

7. See Martin Buber, *Paths in Utopia*, trans. R. F. C. Hull (London: Routledge and Kegan Paul, 1949), especially Buber's discussions of Proudhon and Kropotkin.

8. Frank E. Manuel and Fritzie P. Manuel, *Utopian Thought in the Western World* (Cambridge: Belknap Press, Harvard University Press, 1979), 1–29. The question of whether premodern societies outside of the West developed utopianism need not detain us here (I will mention relevant instances in the following pages, but by and large this is a story of the twentieth century). As I noted above, for my purposes, utopianism is a modern phenomenon and global in its extent. For the general question, see Kumar, *Utopianism*, 32–37; and Jacquelin Dutton, " 'Non-Western' Utopian Traditions," in *The Cambridge Companion to Utopian Literature*, ed. Gregory Claeys (Cambridge: Cambridge University Press, 2010), 223–58. For China, see Wolfgang Bauer, *China and the Search for Happiness: Recurring Themes in Four Thousand Years of Cultural History*, trans. Michael Shaw (New York: Seabury Press, 1976); Douwe Fokkema, *Perfect Worlds: Utopian Fiction in the China and the West* (Amsterdam: Amsterdam University Press, 2011); and Zhongguo kexueyuan zhexue yanjiusuo Zhongguo zhexueshizu 中國科學院哲學研究所中國哲學史組, ed., *Zhongguo datong sixiang ziliao* 中國大同思想資料 (Beijing: Zhonghua shuju, 1959).

9. See Kumar, *Utopianism*, 23–32, 41–42; Kumar also emphasizes the importance of secularity to his definition of utopianism as a modern phenomenon.

10. Krishan Kumar, *Utopia and Anti-Utopia in Modern Times* (Oxford: Basil Blackwell, 1987).

11. Krishan Kumar, "The Ends of Utopia," *New Literary History* 41, no. 3 (Summer 2010), 555–56; Frank and Fritzie Manuel, *Utopian Thought in the Western World*, 2.

12. Catherine Vance Yeh, *The Chinese Political Novel: Migration of a World Genre* (Cambridge: HUAC, Harvard University Press, 2015); Lorenzo Andolfatto, *Hundred Days' Literature: Chinese Utopian Fiction at the End of Empire, 1902–1910* (Leiden: Brill, 2019).

13. The Filipino José Rizal's *Noli Me Tangere* (1886) was an early example. The Italian case, marked by the emancipatory drive for national unity, is perhaps more comparable to the Philippines than the "West," but the general point holds. Yeh shows that in the case of Japan, political novels of the day spoke to themes of liberty, including women's equality, and of democracy. Yeh, *The Chinese Political Novel*, 53–72.

14. Yeh, *The Chinese Political Novel*, 127–35; Lorenzo Andolfatto, *Hundred Days' Literature*; and David Der-wei Wang, *Fin-de-siècle Splendor: Repressed Modernities of Late Qing Fiction, 1849–1911* (Stanford: Stanford University Press, 1977); "Utopian Dream and Dark Consciousness: Chinese Literature at the Millennial Turn," *Prism* 16, no. 1 (2019): 136–56; and "Panglossian Dream and Dark Consciousness: Modern Chinese Literature and Utopia," in *Utopia and Utopianism in the Contemporary Chinese Context* (Hong Kong: Hong Kong University Press, forthcoming). See also Xiaobing Tang, *Chinese Modern: The Heroic and the Quotidian* (Durham: Duke University Press, 2000); Mingwei Song, *Young China: National Rejuvenation and the Bildungsroman, 1900–1959* (Cambridge: HUAC, Harvard University Press, 2015); Yan Jianfu 顏健富, *Cong "shenti" dao "shijie": wan-Qing xiaoshuo xingainian ditu* 從「身體」到「世界」：晚清小說新概念地圖 (Taibei: Taiwan daxue chuban zhongxin, 2014), 137–207; and Guangyi Li, "'New Year's Dream': A Chinese Anarcho-cosmopolitan Utopia," *Utopian Studies* 24, no. 1 (2013): 89–104.

15. Vance Yeh, *The Chinese Political Novel*, 115.

16. C. S. Goto-Jones, "Transcending Boundaries: Nishida Kitarō and K'ang Yu-Wei, and the Politics of Unity," *Modern Asian Studies* 39, no. 4 (2005): 793–816.

17. Karl Mannheim, *Ideology and Utopia*, trans. Louis Wirth and Edward Shils (New York: Harcourt, Brace and World, 1936), 192.

18. Ibid., 193.

19. See Reinhart Koselleck, "The Temporalization of Utopia," in *The Practice of Conceptual History: Timing History, Spacing Concepts*, trans. Todd Presener et al. (Stanford: Stanford University Press 2002), 84–100.

20. See also Paul Ricoeur, *Lectures on Ideology and Utopia* (New York: Columbia University Press, 1986), 274–75.

21. Anna Gustafsson Chen, "Dreams of the Future: Communal Experiments in May Fourth China," PhD dissertation, Lund University, 1998; Shakhar Rahav, *The Rise of Political Intellectuals in Modern China: May Fourth Societies and the Roots of Mass Politics* (Oxford, Oxford University Press, 2015). For general remarks on the ubiquity of utopia, see Ernst Bloch, *The Principle of Hope*, trans. Neville Plaice, Stephen Plaice, and Paul Knight (Cambridge: MIT Press, 1986); Ruth Levitas, *The Concept of Utopia* (Oxford: Peter Lang, 2010); and Davina Cooper, *Everyday Utopias: The Conceptual Life of Promising Spaces* (Durham: Duke University Press, 2014).

22. Shakhar Rahav, "Scale of Change: The Small Group in Chinese Politics, 1919–1921," *Asian Studies Review* 43, no. 4 (2019): 674–90; Margherita Zanasi, "Western Utopias, Missionary Economics, and the Chinese Village," *Journal of World History* 24, no. 2 (June 2013): 359–87.

23. Related to the utopian impulse, in my view, is what Jay Winter calls "minor utopias" or "imaginings of liberation usually on a smaller scale." Jay Winter, *Dreams of Peace and Freedom: Utopian Moments in the Twentieth Century* (New

Haven: Yale University Press, 2006), 4–6. Minor utopias do not aim to remake everything but are relatively focused on a particular problem: national unity, peace, human rights, and the like. In Winter's analysis, major utopias—what I call totalistic visions—are in contrast marked by great detail, by massive scale, and often by their distance in future. Major utopias always, and minor utopias to a considerable extent, are based on a particular historical view that gives confidence in the future. In comparision to minor utopias, the utopian impulse is both broader and narrower. Broader, because not limited to a specific political aim but rather intrinsic to a whole ideological position. But narrower, because only one part of the edifice on which an ideology is based.

24. Frederic Jameson, *Archaeologies of the Future: The Desire Called Utopia and Other Science Fictions* (London: Verso, 2005), 1; my emphasis.

25. Ibid., 11.

26. Luo Zhitian 羅志田, "Lixiang yu xianshi: Qingji minchu shijie zhuyi yu minzu zhuyi de guanlian hudong" 理想與現世——清季民初世界主義與民族主義的關聯互動, in Wang Fansen et al. 王汎森 等, *Zhongguo jindai sixiang de zhuanxing shidai: Zhang Hao yuanshi qizhi zhushou lunwenji* 中國近代思想史的轉型時代: 張灝院士七秩祝壽論文集 (Taipei: Lianjing Press, 2007), 271–314.

27. I return to the issue of "epistemological optimism," most closely associated with the work of Thomas Metzger, in the conclusion of this book.

28. For Chinese fascism, see Maggie Clinton, *Revolutionary Nativism: Fascism and Culture in China, 1925–1937* (Durham: Duke University Press, 2017); Brian Tsui, *China's Conservative Revolution: The Quest for a New Order, 1927–1949* (Cambridge: Cambridge University Press, 2018).

29. Aside from the literary studies cited above, see Longxi Zhang, "The Utopian Vision, East and West," *Utopian Studies* 13, no. 1 (Winter 2002): 1–21; Maurice J. Meisner, *Marxism, Maoism, and Utopianism: Eight Essays* (Madison: University of Wisconsin Press, 1982); Shiping Hua, *Chinese Utopianism: A Comparative Study of Reformist Thought with Japan and Russia, 1898–1997* (Washington, DC: Woodrow Wilson Center Press, 2009); Dorothy Ko, "Bodies in Utopia and Utopian Bodies in Imperial China," in *Thinking Utopia: Steps into Other Worlds*, ed. Jörn Rüsen, Michael Fehr, and Thomas W. Rieger (New York: Berghahn Books, 2005), 89–103. An eloquent study of utopian movements that centered on the city of Nanjing and sometimes radiated out from it in the nineteenth century and the late Qing is Chuck Wooldbridge, *City of Virtues: Nanjing in an Age of Utopian Visions* (Seattle: University of Washington Press, 2015).

A good deal of scholarship in Chinese touches on utopianism, though it seldom analyzes what I am calling the utopian impulse. Broadly conceived studies include Zhou Ning 周宁, *Xiangxiang Zhongguo: cong "kongjiao wutuobang" dao "hongse shengdi"* 想像中国: 从"孔教乌托邦"到"红色圣地" (Beijing: Zhonghua shuju, 2004); Li Shuqiao 李書巧, *Lixiang zhixu de tanqiu: jindai Zhongguo wutuobang sixiang yanjiu* 理想秩序的探求: 近代中國烏托邦思想研究 (Xinbeishi, Taiwan:

Hua Mulan wenhua chubanshe, 2013); and Lin Yüsheng 林毓生, "Ershi shiji Zhongguo de fanchuantong sichao yu Zhongshi malie zhuyi yu Mao Zedong de wutuobang zhuyi" 二十世紀中國的反傳統思潮與中式馬列主義及毛澤東的烏托邦主義, *Xin shixue* 6, no. 3 (Sept. 1995): 95–154.

30. Zhang Hao 張灝, "Zhuanxing shidai Zhongguo wutuobang zhuyi de xingqi" 轉型時代中國烏托邦主義的興起, *Xinshixue* 新史學 46, no. 2 (June 2003): 1–42 is the most acute and complete analysis of Chinese utopianism in what Chang calls the transitional period (c. 1895–1925).

31. For Zhang's methodolical approach to fundamental political change, see Leigh Jenco, *Making the Political: Founding and Action in the Political Theory of Zhang Shizhao* (Cambridge: Cambridge University Press, 2010).

32. See Axel Schneider, "Nation, History, and Ethics: The Choices of Post-Imperial Chinese Historiography," in *Transforming History: The Making of a Modern Academic Discipline in Twentieth-Century China*, ed. Brian Moloughney and Peter Zarrow (Hong Kong: Chinese University Press, 2012), 271–302.

33. For the intellectual milieu that most fundamentally shaped Kang, see Benjamin A. Elman, *Classicism, Politics, and Kingship: The Chang-chou School of New Text Confucianism in Late Imperial China* (Berkeley: University of California Press, 1990).

34. See Rudolf G. Wagner, "The Free Flow of Communication between High and Low: The *Shenbao* as Platform for Yangwu Discussions on Political Reform 1872–1895," *T'oung Pao* 104, no. 1–3 (2018): 116–88; "The *Zhouli* as the Late Qing Path to the Future," in *Statecraft and Classical Learning: The* Rituals of Zhou *in East Asian History*, ed. Benjamin A. Elman Martin Kern (Leiden: Brill, 2010), 359–87; and Wagner, "A Classic Paving the Way to Modernity: The *Ritual of Zhou* in the Chinese Reform Debate Since the Taiping Civil War," in *Modernity's Classics*, ed. Sarah C. Humphreys and Rudolf G. Wagner (Berlin: Springer-Verlag, 2013), 77–99.

35. Tan Sitong, ed. and trans. Sin-wai Chan, *An Exposition of Benevolence: The* Jen-hsüeh *of T'an Ssu-t'ung* (Hong Kong: The Chinese University Press, 1984). See also Hao Chang, *Chinese Intellectuals in Crisis: Search for Order and Meaning, 1890–1911* (Berkeley: University of California Press, 1987), ch. 3. "Humaneness" is further discussed in chapter 2 below.

36. Liu Shipei 劉師培, "Renlei junli shuo" 人類均力說, *Tianyi bao* 天義報 no. 3 (July 1907), 24–36.

37. A profound recent study that brings out Chinese intellectuals' anxious exploration in a suddenly enlarged and dangerous world, though from a different perspective, is Theodore Huters, *Bringing the World Home: Appropriating the West in Late Qing and Early Republican China* (Honolulu: University of Hawai'i Press, 2005).

A metho-historiographical note: This study attempts to study particular ideas in particular contexts. I believe that the "impact-response" models associated with the so-called Fairbank school of the 1950s-'60s remain valuable up to a point. As Jiwei Ci put it, not "everything of moment that has happened in Chian since 1840 has been the result of the 'Western impact,'" but "impact" in effect remains a useful metaphor, especially when viewed "as an ongoing causal chain." Jiwei Ci, *Dialectic of the Chinese Revolution: From Utopianism to Hedonism* (Stanford: Stanford University Press, 1994), 248–49. In the intellectual sphere, this model highlights "influences" from the putative West to China. Its deficiencies have been perceptively critiqued for decades and do not need to be reviewed here. Surely, the alternative model that emphasizes the relevance of ongoing intellectual movements with centuries-old roots has rightly corrected the "impact-response" model—but not, I think, entirely replaced it. Outstanding research on these lines ranges from Hao Chang's work starting in the 1970s (*Liang Ch'i-ch'ao and Intellectual Transition in China, 1890–1907* [Cambridge: Harvard University Press, 1971]) to Wang Hui's 汪晖 *Xiandai Zhongguo sixiang de xingqi* 现代中国思想的兴起 (Beijing: Sanlian, 2004). Both models—impact-response and "evolving tradition," if I may so term it—are essential frameworks. But here I want to add a third framework, the "global circulation of ideas"—which I mean in a literal or "material" sense (the movements of texts, teachers, translations, and so forth) and in a kind of "idealist" sense: it is sometimes worthwhile to look at the same (?) idea in entirely different contexts that have no direct relation to one another. (This is another historiographical metaphor: ideas do not literally circulate: texts and people do, which is how ideas constantly evolve.)

38. The possibilities of cross-cultural dialog and political thought have inspired a generation of theorists too numerous to list here; an example directly relevant to this book is Joseph Grange, *John Dewey, Confucius, and Global Philosophy* (Albany: State University of New York Press, 2004).

39. See chapter 2 below.

40. *Tianyanlun* "天演論" in Wang Qingcheng 王慶成 et al., eds., *Yan Fu heji* 嚴復合集 (Taibei: Gu Gongliang wenjiao jijinhui, 1998), vol. 7, 13–14. It seems a strange translation decision, because Yan could simply have used a standard translation for the "garden of Eden," which would have made more sense in conveying Huxley's point about the differences between Nature and human civilizations (for which agriculture/gardening served as an example and metaphor), though Yan may have wished to avoid Christian references. As well, Yan's translation was very free; in addition to inserting commentaries to supplement his translation, he did not shrink from adding his own statements to the translation itself. For greater detail on translation issues, see Peter Zarrow, "Adventures of 'Utopia' (烏托邦) in Republican China: Setting the Stage for May Fourth Idealism," *Sixiangshi* 思想史 (Taipei) no. 9 (Dec. 2019): 265–312.

Huaxu referred to a dream-land first recorded in the *Liezi*. According to legend, the Yellow Emperor dreamed of a country where the people were simple farmers whose needs were met and who felt no greedy desires for more. They had no conflicts and no need for rulers. This description of Huaxu reflected some of the ideas of the "Liyun" that inspired Kang Youwei and of the *Laozi*.

41. Yan Fu, "Yuanfu (xia)" 原富 (下), in *Yan Fu heji* vol. 9, 472.

42. In other words, the phenomenon can exist without the term. Reinhart Koselleck notes: "[E]very semantics posits beyond itself, even if no subject area can be apprehended and experienced without the semantic performances of language . . . the meaning and usage of a word never have a one-to-one relationship with so-called reality. . . . [C]oncepts and reality change at variable speeds, so that on occasion it is the conceptuality that outpaces the reality, and sometimes the other way around." "On the History of Concepts and the Concept of History," in *Disseminating German Tradition: The Thyssen Lectures*, ed. Dan Diner and Moshe Zimmermann (Leipzig: Lepziger Universität, 2009), 40. Relevant here is Koselleck's further observation: "Furthermore, there are concepts in modernity that are essentially utopian—that is to say, not based in any existing 'reality' at all—and thus purely about creating expectations (*Erwartungsbegriffe*)." Koselleck was referring to modern basic concepts—the "isms" central to political thought since the eighteenth century—that inspire action: "new concepts that help transform the old ones into a new reality." Thus, "temporally speaking, they no longer rest solely on experiences that they are reflecting. What they seem to be aiming at instead, is a constitutional change in social, political, as well as in religious terms" (40–43).

43. Karl Mannheim, *Ideology and Utopia*, 209.

44. Lorenzo Andolfatto, *Hundred Days' Literature*, 7.

Chapter 2

1. Kwame Anthony Appiah, "Cosmopolitan Patriots," *Critical Inquiry* 23, no. 3 (April 1997): 617–39.

2. This is not to say that the historical Confucius ever said any such thing, but the text periodically emerged as central to Confucian idealism. For general discussions, see Benjamin A. Elman and Martin Kern, eds., *Statecraft and Classical Learning: The Rituals of Zhou in East Asian History* (Leiden: Brill, 2009), and Michael Nylan, *The Five "Confucian" Classics* (New Haven: Yale University Press, 2014).

3. Laurence G. Thompson, trans. and ed., *Ta T'ung Shu: The One-World Philosophy of K'ang Yu-Wei* (London: George Allen and Unwin, 1958). The translation is somewhat abridged by paraphrasing or omitting some of Kang's repetitive passages.

4. There may have been many utopian visions (and longings) in the traditional literature, but these were not worked out in any particular detail or made part of a secular reform program. Wolfgang Bauer, *China and the Search*

for Happiness. See also the Introduction above. The speaking picture utopia, with its sometimes arbitrary details of daily life, is distinguished not merely from the utopian sketch but also from utopian political theory; it has thus largely taken novelistic form from Thomas More's *Utopia* (1516) onward. See Krishan Kumar, *Utopianism*; "speaking picture" utopia is from Frank and Fritzie Manuel, *Utopian Thought in the Western World*, 2. Although *The Great Commonweal* is not a novel, it shares more in common with utopian novels, particularly those of Euro-America's late nineteenth century, than with political theory. (Conversely, utopian novels have little by the way of character development and plot but much political sermonizing and ethnographic description of vastly preferable alien societies.)

5. Dating *Datongshu* is tricky, not least because Kang's remarks on when he wrote it are unreliable, and he continued tinkering with it for many years. It was not published in its entirety until 1935, after his death; the first part of the book (its less radical portions) was published in Kang's journal *Buren* in 1913. Tang Zhijun 汤志钧, *Kang Youwei yu wuxu bianfa* 康有为与戊戌变法 (Beijing: Zhonghua shuju, 1984), 108–33; Richard C. Howard, "K'ang Yu-wei (1858–1927): His Intellectual Background and Early Thought," 294–316 in *Confucian Personalities*, ed. Arthur F. Wright and Denis Twitchett (Stanford: Stanford University Press, 1962), 306–14; and Kung-chuan Hsiao, *A Modern China and a New World: K'ang Yu-wei, Reformer and Utopian, 1858–1927* (Seattle: University of Washington Press, 1975), 408–13.

6. While Kang's major trips to Europe remained in the future, we can find many traces of foreign models in *The Great Commonweal*. While the main scholarly debate over Kang's sources has taken the arid form of "Buddhism versus Confucianism," his inclusive intellectual curiosity has received less attention.

7. Wang Fansen 王汎森, *Gushibian yundong de xingqi* 古史辨運動的興起 (Taibei: Yunchen wenhua gongsi, 1987).

8. Anne Cheng, "Nationalism, Citizenship, and the Old Text/New Text Controversy in Late Nineteenth Century China," in *Imagining the People: Chinese Intellectuals and the Concept of Citizenship, 1890–1920*, ed. Joshua A. Fogel and Peter G. Zarrow (Armonk, NY: M. E. Sharpe, 1997), 61–81; Benjamin A. Elman, *Classicism, Politics, and Kingship: The Chang-chou School of New Text Confucianism in Late Imperial China* (Berkeley: University of California Press, 1990); and see also Kung-chuan Hsiao, *A Modern China*, 41–136 passim.

9. Kang Youwei, *Datongshu* (Taibei: Longtian, 1979), 11; cf. Laurence G. Thompson, *Ta T'ung Shu*, 72.

10. Herbert Spencer, *Essays: Scientific, Political, and Speculative*, vol. 1 (New York: D. Appleton, 1916), 9. The quotation is from an early expression of Spencer's progressivism first published as "Progress: Its Law and Cause" in 1857.

11. This description of Spencer's thought is of course highly simplified. Nonetheless, it remains somewhat ironic that Chinese reformers used Spencer to

justify state-building projects. The classical work on the subject is Benjamin I. Schwartz, *In Search of Wealth and Power: Yen Fu and the West* (Cambridge: Belknap Press, Harvard University Press, 1964); see also Jilin Xu, "Social Darwinism in Modern China," *Journal of Modern Chinese History* 6, no. 2 (2012): 182–97.

12. Han Chenghua 韓承樺, "Sibinsai dao Zhongguo—yige fanyishi de taolun" 斯賓塞到中國——一個翻譯史的討論, *Bianyi luncong* 編譯論叢 3, no. 2 (Sept. 2010): 33–60. Yan Fu began publishing reformist essays in 1895, and translations on social Darwinism starting in 1896; his translation of Spencer's *The Study of Sociology* came out in 1903, though he had been studying Spencer since the early 1880s.

13. Don C. Price, *Russia and the Roots of the Chinese Revolution, 1896–1911* (Cambridge: Harvard University Press, 1974).

14. Peter Zarrow, "The Reform Movement, the Monarchy, and Political Modernity," in *Rethinking the 1898 Reform Period: Political and Cultural Change in Late Qing China*, ed. Rebecca E. Karl and Peter Zarrow (Cambridge: HUAC, Harvard University Press, 2002), 24–33.

15. Kang Youwei, *Kangzi neiwaipien* 康子內外篇, *Kang Youwei quanji* 康有為全集 (Shanghai: Shanghai guji chubanshe, 1987), 1: 165–200.

16. Wen Yu, "The Search for a Chinese Way in the Modern World: From the Rise of Evidential Learning to the Birth of Chinese Cultural Identity," PhD dissertation, Harvard University, 2018, ch. 4.

17. For those who have found it difficult to reconcile Kang's conservatism with his radical ideas, it seems one or the other must be marginal. See Qian Mu 錢穆, *Zhongguo jinsanbainian xueshushi* 中國近三百年學術史 (Shanghai: Shangwu, 1937), vol. 1, 664.

18. See Li Zehou 李泽厚, *Zhongguo jindai sixiang shilun* 中国近代思想史论 (Beijing: Renmin, 1986), 127–60; Tang Zhijun, *Kang Youwei yu wuxu bianfa*, 96–107, 134–71. Tang thinks Kang's utopia marks an important moment in Chinese intellectual history and seems to acknowledge the work's power, but he concludes that it was a reactionary text, hindering revolutionary efforts, and with no positive impact. Li, on the contrary, judges the historical function of *The Great Commonweal* in particular and Kang's utopian thought in general as highly progressive, both as a critique—unmasking—of feudalism and as a reflection of the bourgeois faith in material progress.

19. See Kung-chuan Hsiao, *A Modern China and a New World: K'ang Yu-wei, Reformer and Utopian, 1858–1927* (Seattle: University of Washington Press, 1975), 409–12; and Wang Hui, *Xiandai Zhongguo sixiang de xingqi*, vol. 1B, 745–47. As Wang suggests, both Chinese nationalism (or reformism) and utopian universalism (or "cosmopolitanism") were forms of resistance against Western imperialism, and utopianism in particular a form of resistance against the Eurocentric universalism of global capitalism. However, this fails to resolve the tensions in Kang's thought, if that is what they were.

20. Jianhua Chen, "World Revolution Knocking at the Heavenly Gate: Kang Youwei and His Use of *Geming* in 1898," *Journal of Modern Chinese History* 5, no. 1 (2011): 89–108.

21. Kang Youwei, *Shili gongfa quanshu* 實理公法全書, *Kang Youwei quanji*, 1: 245–306; cf. San-pao Li, "K'ang Yu-wei's Shih-li kung-fa ch'üan-shu, *Zhongyang yanjiuyuan jindaishi yanjiusuo jikan* no. 7 (June 1978): 683–725.

22. Hao Chang, *Chinese Intellectuals in Crisis: Search for Order and Meaning, 1890–1911* (Berkeley: University of California Press, 1987), 35–37. See also Federico Brusadelli, "Transforming Benevolence: Classicism, Buddhism, and Politics in Kang Youwei's Lecture on 'Ren' 講仁字 (1897)," *Archiv Orientalni* 85, no. 1 (2017): 99–117; and Song Rongpei 松榮培, "Kang Youwei 'ren' de zhexue yu datong wutuobang" 康有為「仁」的哲學與大同烏托邦, *Ehu yuekan* 鵝湖月刊 38, no. 1 (July 2012): 13–21.

23. Wen Yu, "The Search for a Chinese Way," citing "Lixue pian" (理學篇), *Kangzi neiwai pian*, 100.

24. Kang Youwei, *Datongshu*, 104; Laurence Thompson, *Ta T'ung Shu*, 84.

25. Liu Shipei, "Renlei junli shuo." See Peter Zarrow, *Anarchism and Chinese Political Culture* (New York: Columbia University Press, 1990), 83–88.

26. Kang Youwei, *Datongshu*, 431; Laurence Thompson, *Ta T'ung Shu*, 264.

27. Kang Youwei, *Datongshu*, 452–53; Laurence Thompson, *Ta T'ung Shu*, 275–76.

28. Kang spoke of the Three Ages here in terms of the extension of "humaneness" from kin (age of Chaos) to all of humanity (age of Lesser Peace), but did not use the term *humaneness* to describe the "love" (*ai*) of all creatures that would mark the Great Commonweal. Kang Youwei, *Datongshu*, 435; Laurence Thompson, *Ta T'ung Shu*, 266.

29. Kang Youwei, *Datongshu*, 441–53; Laurence Thompson, *Ta T'ung Shu*, 271–80.

30. Kang Youwei, *Datongshu*, 452–53; Laurence Thompson, *Ta T'ung Shu*, 275–76.

31. Taiyan 太炎, "Wuwulun" 五無論, *Minbao* no. 16 (25 September 1907), 1–22.

32. Kung-chuan Hsiao, *A Modern China*, 168–79.

33. Kang Youwei, *Ziding nianpu*, 11; cf. Jung-pang Lo, ed., *K'ang Yu-wei: A Biography and a Symposium* (Tucson: University of Arizona Press, 1967), 36.

34. Kang Youwei, *Ziding nianpu*, 11–12; Jung-pang Lo, *K'ang Yu-wei*, 38.

35. Young-tsu Wong, "The Search for Material Civilization: Kang Youwei's Journey to the West," *Taiwan Journal of East Asian Studies* 5, no. 1 (June 2008): 39–59 (quote from 36).

36. In Young-tsu Wong's formulation, "Unquestionably, this world tour reinforced Kang's commitment to promoting constitutional monarchy, thus giving it higher priority than his utopian vision of a 'Great Community' in the distant future"—ibid., 39. However, this is to set up a false dichotomy.

37. Kang Youwei, "Wuzhi jiuguo lun" 物質救國論, *Kang Youwei quanji*, 8: 61–101.

38. Ibid., 59.

39. John Fitzgerald, *Awakening China: Politics, Culture, and Class in the Nationalist Revolution* (Stanford: Stanford University Press, 1996), 67–76.

40. Hao Chang, *Chinese Intellectuals in Crisis*, 50–54. "Seen in this light, Kang's evolutionary view of history is obviously not just an ideological instrument to justify his political reformism. . . . Rather, it is a conceptual framework that he finally discovered after years of intellectual search, enabling him to weave together and integrate into an overall synthesis all the major elements of his thinking." See also Zhang Hao 張灝 (Hao Chang), "Zhuanxing shidai Zhongguo wutuobang zhuyi de xingqi" 轉型時代中國烏托邦主義的興起, *Xinshixue* 新史學 46, no. 2 (June 2003): 8–16.

41. Kang Youwei, *Datongshu*, 1–3; Laurence Thompson, *Da T'ung Shu*, 62–63.

42. Background on Kang's chronological autobiography is given in Jung-pang Lo, ed., *K'ang Yu-wei*, 17–20.

43. Kang Youwei, *Ziding nianpu*, 1; Jung-pang Lo, *K'ang Yu-wei*, 21.

44. Kang Youwei, *Ziding nianpu*, 2, 4; Jung-pang Lo, *K'ang Yu-wei*, 23, 26. Ages are given in Chinese *sui*.

45. Kang Youwei, *Ziding nianpu*, 9; Jung-pang Lo, *K'ang Yu-wei*, 32 mod.

46. Kang Youwei, *Ziding nianpu*, 14–15; Jung-pang Lo, *K'ang Yu-wei*, 39–42.

47. Kang Youwei, *Ziding nianpu*, 18; Jung-pang Lo, *K'ang Yu-wei*, 45.

48. Kang Youwei, *Ziding nianpu*, 18; Jung-pang Lo, *K'ang Yu-wei*, 47.

49. Kang Youwei, *Ziding nianpu*, 27–28; Jung-pang Lo, *K'ang Yu-wei*, 60–61.

50. Kang Youwei, *Ziding nianpu*, 74, 72–73; Jung-pang Lo, *K'ang Yu-wei*, 138, 135–36.

51. See John Fitzgerald, *Awakening China*, 58–61.

52. Douwe Fokkema, *Perfect Worlds*, 278.

53. (Timothy Richard), *Huitoukan jilue* 回頭看紀略, *Wanguo gongbao* 萬國公報 (1891–92). See Kenny K. K. Ng, "Ending as Beginning: Chinese Translations of Edward Bellamy's Utopian Novel *Looking Backward*," *Frontiers of Literary Studies in China* 10, no. 1: 9–35; Catherine Vance Yeh, *The Chinese Political Novel*, 38–41.

54. Krishan Kumar, *Utopia and Anti-Utopia in Modern Times* (Oxford: Basil Blackwell, 1987), 133–36. Nationalist clubs inspired by *Looking Backward* were formed abroad as well as in the United States—Sylvia E. Bowman et al., *Edward Bellamy Abroad: An American Prophet's Influence* (New York: Twayne, 1962).

55. Kumar, *Utopianism*.

56. The plot, in summary: One night in Boston in the 1880s Julian West, a well-to-do man of thirty engaged to a woman named Edith, goes to sleep. He wakes up in the year 2000 having aged not at all. The family of the retired Dr. Leete takes him in and shows and explains the new Boston to him. West falls

in love with Leete's daughter Edith, who he learns at the end of the novel is the great-granddaughter of his original fiancée. The only tension in the plot is provided when West thinks he is back in the Boston of the 1880s having only dreamed of the Leetes and the perfect society of the twenty-first century; however, this is but a dream from which he wakes in the twentieth century after all.

57. For a single example, see the description of the fates of soldiers in war: "They may meet with arrows, stones, lances, cannon, poison gas. And then again, they may be disemboweled or decapitated, their blood splashed on the field, their limbs hung in the trees. Sometimes they are thrown into a river, dragging each other under" (Kang Youwei, *Datongshu*, 83; Laurence Thompson, *Da T'ung Shu*, 81 mod.). *The Great Commonweal* is full of such evocative passages.

58. Edward Bellamy, *Looking Backward*, 167. The sermon even ends on a mystical-evolutionary note: "Do you ask what we look for when unnumbered generations shall have passed away? I answer, the way stretches far before us, but the end is lost in light. For twofold is the return of man to God 'who is our home,' the return of the individual by the way of death, and the return of the race by the fulfillment of the evolution, when the divine secret hidden in the germ shall be perfectly unfolded" (173). Yet Bellamy displayed no sense that social institutions such as the family would change in any fundamental way.

59. Ibid., 56–57.

60. Ibid., 98.

61. Ibid., 161.

62. Kumar, *Utopia and Anti-Utopia*, 132–67.

63. Edgar Snow, *Red Star over China* (New York: Grove Press, 1961), 133, 135.

64. It is understandable that readers are impressed by Kang's political cosmopolitanism—his vision of a democratic, apparently federalist world government. And in a recent appreciation of Kang, Ban Wang notes a parallel between the moral cosmopolitanism of Immanuel Kant (which I discuss in the next chapter) and Kang: "Like Kant, Kang Youwei thought of the world in terms of morality and the aesthetic. To him the aesthetic consists in learning from immersing oneself in diverse culture in a way that involves all senses and the soul." Ban Wang, "The Moral Vision in Kang Youwei's *Book of the Great Community*, in *Chinese Visions of World Order: Tianxia, Culture, and World Politics*, ed. Ban Wang (Durham: Duke University Press, 2017), 94. But this is to confuse sensual pleasures, which Kang certainly advocated, with aesthetics, and to posit a link between aesthetics and morality that misreads the structure of Kang's thinking.

65. Evans Chan 陳耀成: "Datong: Kang Youwei zai Ruidian" 大同: 康有為在瑞典 (2011); *Datong: The Chinese Utopia* (Hong Kong: Hong Kong Arts Festival Society, 2016).

66. This is not to say treatments of Kang are entirely uncritical, but he is being firmly put back into the genealogy of New Confucianism. See, e.g.,

works by the Beijing Philosophy Department professor Gan Chunsong 干春松: *Baojiao liguo: Kang Youwei de xiandai fanglue* 保教立国: 康有为的现代方略 (Beijing: Sanlian, 2015); *Kang Youwei yu Ruxue de "xinshi": cong Ruxue fenqi kan Ruxue de weilai fazhan lujing* 康有为与儒学的"新世": 从儒学分期看儒学的未来发展路径 (Shanghai: Huadong daxue chubanshe, 2015). Translated economiums to Kang and Kang-style Confucianism are available at the "Reading the China Dream" project run out of the Université de Montréal by Professor David Ownby and colleagues (https://www.readingthechinadream.com/about.html).

Chapter 3

1. There is no full-length biography of Cai in English. See William J. Duiker, *Ts'ai Yuan-p'ei: Educator of Modern China* (University Park: Pennsylvania State University Press, 1977), and Chaohua Wang, "Cai Yuanpei and the Origins of the May Fourth Movement: Modern Chinese Intellectual Transformations, 1890–1920," PhD dissertation, University of California-Los Angeles, 2008. In Chinese, useful studies include Cai Jianguo 蔡建国, *Cai Yuanpei yu jindai Zhongguo* 蔡元培与近代中国 (Shanghai: Shanghai shehui kexue chubanshe, 1997); Zhang Xiaowei 张晓唯, *Cai Yuanpei pingzhuan* 蔡元培评传 (Nanchang: Baihuazhou wenyi chubanshe, 1993).

2. Cai Yuanpei, "Zixie nianpu" 自寫年譜, *Cai Yuanpei wenji* 蔡元培文集 (Taibei: Jinxiu chuban, 1995), *zizhuan* 自傳, 47–50, 101–106 n. 167; "Zhuanlue" 傳略, in *Cai Yuanpei wenji, zizhuan*, 126–27.

3. Pingyuan Chen, *Touches of History: An Enquiry into 'May Fourth' China*, trans. Michel Hockx et al. (Leiden: Brill, 2011), 162.

4. Cai Yuanpei, "Xinnian meng" 新年夢, in *Cai Yuanpei wenji, zhengzhi-jingji* 蔡元培文集-政治經濟, 85–98; translated in Lorenzo Andolfatto, *Hundred Days' Literature: Chinese Utopian Fiction at the End of Empire, 1902–1910* (Leiden: Brill, 2019), 199–212. For more detailed analyses, see Lorenzo Andolfatto, *Hundred Days' Literature*, 9–23; and Guangyi Li, " 'New Year's Dream,' " 89–104.

5. Arguably, this name is ambiguous if not subtle, but I follow Andolfatto in understanding Cai to mean something like "citizen" here.

6. This was a common trope among progressives at the time.

7. The reference was to the Russo-Japanese War for dominance in Manchuria that ended in 1905.

8. Cai Yuanpei, "Xinnian meng," 87; Lorenzo Andolfatto, *Hundred Days' Literature*, 15.

9. Cai Yuanpei, "Xinnian meng," 88; Lorenzo Andolfatto, *Hundred Days' Literature*, 15–16.

10. Cai Yuanpei, "Xinnian meng," 96; Lorenzo Andolfatto, *Hundred Days' Literature*, 28–29.

11. Cai Yuanpei, "Fojiao huguolun" 佛教護國論, in *Cai Yuanpei wenji, zheng-zhi-jingji*, 58–62. See Douglas M. Gildow, "Cai Yuanpei (1868–1940), Religion, and His Plan to Save China through Buddhism," *Asia Major* 31, no. 2 (2018): 107–48; and Wang Chaohua, "Cai Yuanpei and the Origins of the May Fourth Movement," 232–36. Cai's essay is excellently translated by Gildow, 139–49.

12. Tan's posthumously published *Renxue* 仁學 electrified China's radical reformers. Chan Sin-wai, trans. and ed., *An Exposition of Benevolence: The Jen-hsueh of T'an Ssu-t'ung* (Hong Kong: Chinese University Press, 1984).

13. Cai Yuanpei, "Fojiao huguolun," 61; cf. Chaohua Wang, "Cai Yuan-pei," 235–36.

14. Cai Yuanpei, "Laogong shensheng" 勞工神聖, Cai Yuanpei, *Cai Yuanpei xiansheng yiwen leichao* 蔡元培先生遺文類鈔, ed. Sun Dezhong 孫德中 (Taibei: Fuxing shuju, 1966), 469.

15. Cai Yuanpei, "Huagong xuexiao jiangyi" 華工學校講義, in ibid., 351.

16. Cai Yuanpei, "Ziyou yu fangzong" 自由與放縱, in ibid., 421–22.

17. Cai Yuanpei, "Qingong jianxue xu" 勤工儉學序 [Oct. 1915], in ibid., 288–90. Cai began with a hoary quote from Mencius, deliberately decontextualized: "Further, to make for yourself, in a single lifetime, all the things that the myriad craftsmen make (if you insist that all you use should be made by yourself) would have everyone completely worn out." W. A. C. H. Dobson, trans., *Mencius* (Toronto: University of Toronto Press, 1969), 117. Pointedly, Cai neglected Mencius's previous point that "[t]here are pursuits proper to great men, and pursuits proper to lesser men," and his followup: "Therefore it is said, 'Some labor with the hands, and some labor with the minds. Those who labor with the minds govern others. Those who labor with the hands are governed by others.'" Cai's use of classical references is discussed below. Li Shizeng (1881–1973) had been a revolutionary anarchist in the years leading up to the 1911 Revolution and later worked in educational circles.

18. Cai Yuanpei, "Qingong jianxue xu," in *Cai Yuanpei xiansheng yiwen leichao* 289.

19. Cai Yuanpei, "Heian yu guangming de xiaozhang" 黑暗與光明的消長, in ibid., 22.

20. Ibid., 21–24.

21. In using the term *pingmin zhuyi*, Cai was signaling his rejection of liberal representative democracy (*minzhu zhuyi*).

22. Cai Yuanpei, "Heian yu guangming de xiaozhang," 23–24.

23. Ibid., 24.

24. On 4 May 1919, some three thousand Beijing students demonstrated against the Versailles Treaty. That day resulted in the arrests of students, the return of more protestors to the Beijing streets, the spread of demonstrations to other cities, and strikes and boycotts lasting several weeks. As Timothy Weston shows, already angry over agreements between the Chinese and Japanese governments,

student demonstrators had provoked Cai's first brief resignation as chancellor of Peking University in 1918 (possibly to forestall being fired and possibly as a subtle, Confucian form of protest). Cai tended to urge students to make study their first priority, but also supported political activism if it was motivated by pure, patriotic motives. Returning as chancellor in 1919, Cai worked for the arrested students' release before resigning one more time (at least partly in fear of his life), but, returning for the fall semester, he also remained anxious for students to return to the classroom. See Timothy Weston, *The Power of Position: Beijing University, Intellectuals, and Chinese Political Culture, 1898–1929* (Berkeley: University of California Press, 2004), 155–63, 175–81.

25. Cai Yuanpei, "Kexue zhi xiuyang" 科學之修養, in *Cai Yuanpei xiansheng yiwen leichao*, 474–77.

26. Cai Yuanpei, "Jiaoyu zhi duidai de fazhan" 教育之對待的發展 [1920], in ibid., 98–99.

27. For discussions of Cai's views on aesthetics, see William J. Duiker, "The Aesthetics Philosophy of Ts'ai Yuan-p'ei," *Philosophy East and West* 22, no. 4 (Oct. 1972): 385–401; Lu Shanqing 卢善庆, *Zhongguo jindai meixue sixiangshi* 中国近代美学思想史 (Shanghai: Huadong shifan daxue chubanshe, 1991), 504–49.

28. Cai Yuanpei, "Duiyu jiaoyu fangzhen zhi yijian" 對於教育方針之意見, in *Cai Yuanpei xiansheng yiwen leichao*, 77–84. For the influence of Kant and other German philosophers on Cai, discussed further below, see Li Zongze 李宗澤, "Cai Yuanpei sixiang zhong de Deguo ziyuan" 蔡元培思想中的德國資源, in *Jindai dong-xi sixiang jiaoliu zhong de chuanbozhe* 近代東西思想交流中的傳播者, ed. Yang Zhende 楊貞德 (Taibei: Zhongyang yanjiuyuan, Zhongguo wenzhe yanjiusuo, 2017), 199–229.

29. As a republican revolutionary, Chen dismissed even constitutional monarchies as essentially autocratic.

30. *Analects* 9:25; cf. James Legge, trans., *The Four Books* (Taipei: Culture Book Co., 1981), 241; Arthur Waley, *The Analects of Confucius* (New York: Vintage Books, 1938), 144.

31. *Mencius* 3B2; cf. W.A.C.H. Dobson, *Mencius* (Toronto: University of Toronto Press, 1969), 124–25.

32. *Analects* 12: 2 (James Legge, *Four Books*, 279–80).

33. To which Confucius replied that Zigong was not able to do that yet. *Analects* 5:11.

34. James Legge, *Four Books*, 29.

35. *Mencius* 1B5 (Dobson, *Mencius*, p. 19, mod.).

36. Zhang Zai 張載, "Ximing" 西銘, trans. B. W. Van Norden, https://www.google.com/search?q=zhang+zai+western+inscription&ie=utf-8&oe=utf-8; accessed April 20, 2017.

37. *Analects* 6: 28 (Legge, *Four Books*, 199; Waley, *Analects*, 122).

38. *Mencius* 4B.29 (Dobson, *Mencius*, 183–84); *Mencius* 5A.7 (Dobson, *Mencius*, 61).

39. I explore this issue in greater detail in Peter Zarrow, "Cai Yuanpei's Politico-Philosophical Languages," in *Time, Language, and Power in Late Imperial and Republican China*, ed. Ori Sela, Zvi Ben-Dor Benite, and Joshua Fogel (forthcoming).

40. There is an extensive scholarly literature that touches on this seemingly weird view. For a convincing and bracing appraisal, see Leigh Jenco, "Histories of Thought and Comparative Political Theory: The Curious Thesis of 'Chinese Origins for Western Knowledge,' 1860–1895," *Political Theory* 42, no. 6 (Dec. 2014): 658–81.

41. Isaiah Berlin, *Four Essays on Liberty* (Oxford: Oxford University Press, 1969).

42. Cai Yuanpei, "Duiyu jiaoyu fangzhen zhi yijian," 84.

43. Ibid., 78–79. The "Liyun" chapter, which described *datong*, of the classic *Liji* had become shorthand for "utopia"—see chapter 2 above.

44. Ibid., 80–81.

45. Cai concluded his essay with reflections on how the five spheres of education mutually supported one another and how the various school subjects reflected various modes. For example, mathematics was first a vocational or practical branch of learning, but if we followed Pythagoras in thinking of numbers as the source of all things, math was also an aspect of worldview, while geometry also concerned aesthetics. History and geography were primarily utilitarian, but heroic figures of the past could represent the ideal of the militant citizenry, stories of artists spoke to aesthetics, and of course these subjects touched on morality and worldview as well. This final section of the essay may have helped Cai's audience of educators to understand how to apply his theory but need not detain us here.

46. Cai Yuanpei, "Shijieguan yu renshengguan" 世界觀與人生觀 [1913], in *Cai Yuanpei xiansheng yiwen leichao*, 16–20.

47. Ibid., 17.

48. A slightly weird comparison might be made with the Christian "omega point" notion of Pierre Teilhard de Chardin—see *The Phenomenon of Man* (New York: Harper Perennial, 2008) and *The Divine Milieu* (New York: Harper and Row, 1960).

49. Cai Yuanpei, "Shijieguan yu renshengguan," 17.

50. Ibid., 18.

51. Cai Yuanpei, "Wenhua yundong buyao wangle meiyu" 文化運動不要忘了美育 (1919), in *Cai Yuanpei wenji, meiyu*, 91–92.

52. Cai used the terms *art* (*meishu*) or *art education* (*meishu de jiaoyu*) here, but he meant what is generally termed aesthetics, that is, the study and appreciation of art.

53. "Meiyu yu rensheng" 美育與人生, in *Cai Yuanpei wenji, meiyu*, 373–75.

Indeed, Cai developed a view of human psychology and social utility that led him to propose replacing religion with aesthetics, discussed below. Cai's notion of "living amid beauty" is also further discussed below.

54. Friedrich Paulsen (1846–1908) was of interest to Cai both as a philosopher and an educator. Cai translated Paulsen's *System of Ethics* in 1909 from the Japanese (discussed below), while his first direct translation from a German text was of Paulsen's introduction to his *The German University and University Study*, in 1910. Chaohua Wang, *Cai Yuanpei*, 266.

55. Joachim Kurtz, "Domesticating a Philosophical Fiction: Chinese Translations of Immanuel Kant's 'Things in Themselves,'" *Concept and Communication* 7 (2011): 165–200; quotation 166. Kurtz emphasizes the transition from a tendency to read—and domesticate—Kant in Buddhist terms to a more professional understanding of Kant in his own terms (or the terms of Western philosophical traditions), even while there were no standard translations of key Kantian concepts well into the 1920s.

56. Cai Yuanpei, "Zixie nianpu," in *Cai Yuanpei wenji, zizhuan*, 51.

57. For a review of the literature on this topic, see Cheng Tingting 程婷婷 and Gao Wenqiang 高文强, "'Yi meiyu dai zhongjiao shuo' yanjiu shuping" "以美育代宗教说"研究述评, *Zhongguo meixue yanjiu* no. 6 (Feb. 2015): 182–93. Li Zongze ("Cai Yuanpei sixiang zhong de Deguo ziyuan," 199–229) emphasizes Cai's fealty to Kant.

58. Edward Franklin Buchner, trans. and ed., *The Educational Theory of Immanual Kant* (Philadelphia: J. B. Lippincott, 1904), 90–91.

59. Paul Guyer, *Kant and the Claims of Taste* (Cambridge: Harvard University Press, 1979); Eva Schaper, "Taste, Sublimity, and Genius: The Aesthetics of Nature and Art," in *The Cambridge Companion to Kant*, ed. Paul Guyer (Cambridge: Cambridge University Press, 1992), 367–93; Paul Guyer, "Kant's Ambitions in the Third *Critique*," in *The Cambridge Companion to Kant and Modern Philosophy*, 538–87; Paul Crowther, *The Kantian Sublime: From Morality to Art* (Oxford: Oxford University Press, 1989); Hannah Ginsborg, "Kant's Aesthetics and Teleology," *The Stanford Encyclopedia of Philosophy* (Fall 2014); and Edward N. Zalta, ed., http://plato.stanford.edu/archives/fall2014/entries/kant-aesthetics/. For general context, see Douglas Moggach, "Aesthetics and Politics," in *The Cambridge History of Nineteenth-Century Political Thought*, ed. Gareth Stedman Jones and Gregory Claeys (Cambridge: Cambridge University Press, 2011), 479–520. If the writings of John Dewey, discussed in later chapters, are, to the outsider, a dense thicket lit faintly with flickering light, Kant's are a dark, impenetrable forest. However shallow the following discussion, my notes will make obvious my intellectual debts to those who have opened trails that a novice can follow. I reference J. H. Bernard, trans., *Kant's Critique of Judgement* (London: Macmillan, 1931).

60. Eva Schaper, "Taste, Sublimity, and Genius," 373.

61. *Kant's Critique of Judgement*, 56 (§6).

62. Paul Guyer, "Kant's Ambitions in the Third *Critique*," 559.

63. Paul Guyer, *Kant and the Claims of Taste*, 8–9.

64. *Kant's Critique of Judgement*, 34–35 (Introduction).

65. *Kant's Critique of Judgement*, 102 (§23).

66. Eva Schaper, "Taste, Sublimity, and Genius," 384.

67. Cited in Paul Guyer, *Kant and the Claims of Taste*, 265.

68. *Kant's Critique of Judgement*, 108–109 (§25).

69. Ibid., 116–17 (§26).

70. Ibid., 119–20 (§27).

71. Ibid., 130–31 (§29).

72. Ibid., 125 (§28).

73. Ibid., 136 (§29).

74. Ibid., 248–52 (§59).

75. Paul Guyer, "Kant's Ambitions in the Third *Critique*," 563. The issue is complex; see the discussions in Paul Guyer, *Kant and the Claims of Taste*, 351–94; and Ted Cohen, "Why Beauty Is a Symbol of Morality," in *Essays in Kant's Aesthetics*, ed. Ted Cohen and Paul Guyer (Chicago: University of Chicago Press, 1982), 221–36. According to Guyer, insofar as Kant did connect aesthetic judgment and morality, his arguments were relatively weak.

76. *Kant's Critique of Judgement*, 77 (§15).

77. Paul Crowther, *The Kantian Sublime*, esp. ch. 2; see also Hannah Ginsborg, "Kant's Aesthetics and Teleology."

78. *Kant's Critique of Judgement*, 135 (§29).

79. In Kant's words, "How is a judgment possible which, merely from one's *own* feeling of pleasure in an object, independent of its concept, estimate *a priori*, that is, without having to wait upon the agreement of others, that this pleasure is connected with the representation of the object *in every other subject?*" Cited in Paul Guyer, *Kant and the Claims of Taste* (Cambridge: Harvard University Press, 1979), 1.

80. Cai Yuanpei, "Meixue guannian," in *Cai Yuanpei wenji, meiyu*, 22–24.

81. Linda M. Brooks, *The Menace of the Sublime to the Individual Self: Kant, Schiller, Coleridge, and the Disintegration of Romantic Identity* (Lewiston, NY: Edwin Mellen Press, 1995). Conversely, it is possible that Cai was wrenching "*woxiang*" out of its Buddhist context to refer to what the neo-Kantians he read sometimes called the noumenal self, though this does not seem the best explanation to me.

82. See Hsuan Hua, *The Vajra Prajna Paramita Sutra* (Burlingame, CA: Dharma Realm Buddhist University, 2002), 45 (mod.), 63, 115–16, 146. "The Buddha told Subhuti, 'All Bodhisattvas, Mahasattvas, should thus subdue their hearts with the vow, "I must cause all living beings—those born from eggs, born from wombs, born from moisture, born by transformation; those with form, those without form, those with thought, those without thought, those not totally

with thought, and those not totally without thought—to enter nirvana without residue and be taken across to extinction." Yet of the immeasurable, boundless numbers of living beings thus taken across to extinction, there is actually no living being taken across to extinction. And why? Subhuti, if a Bodhisattva has a mark of self, a mark of others, a mark of living beings, or a mark of a life, he is not a Bodhisattva.'"

83. A. Charles Muller, comp. and trans., *The Sutra of Perfect Enlightenment: Korean Buddhism's Guide to Meditation* (Albany: State University of New York Press, 1999), 202–205. "Good sons, what is the 'trace of self' (*woxiang*)? It is that which is witnessed by the mind of sentient beings. Good sons, when you are in good health you naturally forget about your body. But when the body becomes sick, and you make an effort correct the infirmity, with the slightest application of moxibustion and acupuncture you are immediately aware of your existence as a self. Thus, it is only in reference to this 'witnessing' that you perceive and grasp to an apparent self-essence. Good sons, every kind of witnessing from this level up to the Tathāgata's perfect perception of pure nirvana, is all the 'trace of self.'"

84. Cai Yuanpei, "Meixue guannian," in *Cai Yuanpei wenji, meiyu*, 22.

85. I am indebted to Joachim Kurtz for this suggestion. See Dieter Henrich, "Beauty and Freedom: Schiller's Struggle with Kant's Aesthetics," in *Essays in Kant's Aesthetics*, ed. Ted Cohen and Paul Guyer (Chicago: University of Chicago Press, 1982), 237–57; Stephen Boos, "Rethinking the Aesthetic: Kant, Schiller, and Hegel," in *Between Ethics and Aesthetics: Crossing the Boundaries*, ed. Dorota Glowacka and Stephen Boos (Albany: State University of New York Press, 2002), 15–27; Michael John Kooy, *Coleridge, Schiller, and Aesthetic Education* (Houndmills: Palgrave, 2002).

86. Friedrich Schiller, "Letters on the Aesthetical Education of Mankind," *The Aesthetical Essays*, Project Gutenberg EBook (George Bell and Sons, 1879; web: Dec. 19, 2015).

87. W. Windelband, *A History of Philosophy: With Special Reference to the Formation and Development of its Problems and Conceptions*, trans. James H. Tufts (Taibei: Zhuangyuan chubanshe, 1969), 600–601. Windelband was a leading neo-Kantian of the late nineteenth century; the first edition of his *Geschichte der Philosophie* was published in 1892 and the English translation in 1893; the second edition in 1900 followed by the English translation in 1914. For Cai's possible acquaintance with the text, see Li Zongze, "Cai Yuanpei sixiang Zhong de Deguo ziyuan," 205.

88. W. Windelband, *A History of Philosophy*, 601.

89. Cai Yuanpei, "Meishu zhi zuoyong" 美術之作用 [1916], in *Cai Yuanpei wenji, meiyu*, 57–59. Rather bizarrely, Cai attempted to link nations to his distinction between beauty and sublime—the ancient Greeks and now the French believed in beauty, while the Germanic race and today's Germans believed in

the sublime. Writing in 1916, Cai suggested that aesthetics could explain how the easygoing French and the determined-to-the-end Germans could fight for so long. He returned to this observation in a talk to students delivered on New Year's Day in 1917. Cai did not speak of the political or economic causes of the war but rather contrasted the aesthetic-racial characters of the French and the Germans. The French, Latins, believed in loveliness and elegance while the Germans, Teutons, were tough and heroic. The French valued dignity and honor while the Germans believed in will power and determination. "Wo zhi Ouzhan guan" 我之歐戰觀, in *Cai Yuanpei wenji, zhengzhi-jingji*, 210–14, first published in *Xin qingnian* 2, no. 5 (Jan. 1917).

90. Cai Yuanpei, "Yi meiyu dai zongjiao shuo" 以美育代宗教說 in *Cai Yuanpei xiansheng yiwen leichao*, 229–32. This essay, Cai's first on the subject, was originally given as a lecture and has been translated into English by Julia F. Andrews: "Replacing Religion with Aesthetic Education," in *Modern Chinese Literary Thought: Writings on Literature, 1893–1945*, ed. Kirk A. Denton (Stanford: Stanford University Press, 1996), 182–89.

91. Cai Yuanpei, "Yi meiyu dai zongjiao shuo," 232.

92. Cai Yuanpei, "Yi meiyu dai zhongjiao" 以美育代宗教, in *Cai Yuanpei wenji, meiyu*, 277–79.

93. Cai Yuanpei, "Meiyu dai zongjiao," in *Cai Yuanpei wenji, meiyu*, 385–91.

94. Ibid., 389.

95. Cai Yuanpei, "Meixue guannian," in *Cai Yuanpei wenji, meiyu*, 22–24.

96. Cai Yuanpei, "Meishu yu kexue de guanxi" 美術與科學的關係 [1920], in *Cai Yuanpei wenji, meiyu*, 157–60.

97. Cai Yuanpei, "Zhen shan mei" 真善美 (1927), in *Cai Yuanpei wenji, zhexue*, 518–23.

98. Ibid., 518.

99. Ibid., 520.

100. Cai Yuanpei, "Meiyu" 美育 [1930], in *Cai Yuanpei wenji, meiyu*, 283–88.

101. Ibid., 285–87. As noted above, Cai had begun speaking along these lines as early as 1919 (Cai Yuanpei, "Wenhua yundong buyao wangle meiyu," in *Cai Yuanpei wenji, meiyu*, 91–92), but without the details offered here.

102. Cai Yuanpei, "Meiyu yu rensheng" 美育與人生, in *Cai Yuanpei wenji, meiyu*, 373–75.

103. *Aufklärung—Kulture—Bildung*. See Ruth-Ellen Boetcher Joeres, "The German Enlightenment (1720–1790)," in *The Cambridge History of German Literature*, ed. Helen Watanabe–O'Kelly (Cambridge: Cambridge University Press, 1997), 147–201.

104. Barry A. Jackisch, "The Nature of Berlin: Green Space and Visions of a New German Capital, 1900–45," *Central European History* 47 (2014): 307–33.

105. Claude James Rubinson, "The Production of Style: Aesthetic and Ideological Diversity in the Arts and Crafts Movement, 1875–1914," PhD dissertation, University of Arizona, 2010.

106. Sara Lyons, "The Disenchantment/Re-Enchantment of the World: Aesthetics, Secularization, and the Gods of Greece from Friedrich Schiller to Water Pater," *The Modern Language Review* 109, no. 4 (2014): 873–95.

107. Cai Yuanpei, "Zhuanlue (shang)," in *Cai Yuanpei wenji, zizhuan*, 124. Cai's "Outline of Philosophy" (*Zhexue yaolin* 哲學要領) was possibly the first translation of an introduction to Western philosophy into Chinese. See Ouyang Zhesheng 歐陽哲生, *Tanxun Hu Shi de jingshen shijie* 探尋胡適的精神世界 (Taibei: Xiuwei zixun keji gongsi, 2011), 114–15. Cai later found many mistakes in his translation, but that is not the point here.

108. Oswald Külpe, *Introduction to Philosophy* [*Einleitung in die Philosophie*, 1895], trans. W. B. Pillsbury and E. B. Titchener (London: Swan Sonnenschein, 1897), 22–23.

109. Ibid., 67–68; however, Külpe did note that although ethics evolved independently (i.e., not as, say, not merely religious sanctions), it rested on psychology, political economy, biology, etc. (ibid., 72).

110. Ibid., 81–82.

111. Ibid., 83–84.

112. Ibid., 86–90.

113. Ibid., 223–26.

114. Cai Yuanpei, "Zhuanlue (shang), in *Cai Yuanpei wenji, zizhuan*, 126–27, 143 n. 39. Cai's translation was titled *The Principles of Ethics* (*Lunlixue de yuanli* 倫理學的原理). During his years at Leipzig, Cai also wrote a major middle school textbook on ethics, *Zhongxue xiushen jiaokeshu* (中學修身教科書), and the first history of Chinese ethics, *Zhongguo lunlixue shi* (中國倫理學史).

115. Friedrich Paulsen, *A System of Ethics* [*System der Ethik*, 1889, 1899], ed. and trans. Frank Thilly (New York: Charles Scribner's Sons, 1899), 556–68.

116. Ibid., 557.

117. Ibid., 558.

118. Ibid., 558–59.

119. For background, see Thomas E. Willey, *Back to Kant: The Revival of Kantianism in German Social and Historical Thought, 1860–1914* (Detroit: Wayne State University Press, 1978); Klaus Christian Köhnke, trans. R. J. Hollingdale, *The Rise of Neo-Kantianism: German Academic Philosophy between Idealism and Positivism* (Cambridge: Cambridge University Press, 1991). "Three philosophical elements above all had to come together for neo-Kantianism to become the dominant movement in German academic philosophy at the end of the nineteenth century: theory of knowledge as the systematic concern, a new idealism as the *weltanschaulich* concern, and thirdly a new relationship with tradition." Köhnke, *The Rise of Neo-Kantianism*, 136.

120. Wilhelm Wundt, *Elements of Folk Psychology: Outlines of a Psychological History of the Development of Mankind* (London: George Allen and Unwin, 1928 [1916]). Whether or not the two men discussed its ideas in any depth, this work contributed to the proto-anthropological discussions of the origins

and development of religion that were prominent at the time, an approach reflected in Cai's writings.

121. Ibid., 10.

122. Ibid., 470–523; quotes from 470, 472; italics in original.

123. Three world religions, or just two, Christianity and Buddhism—ibid., 478.

124. Ibid., 514–15.

125. Zehou Li, *The Chinese Aesthetic Tradition*, trans. Maija Bell Samei (Honolulu: University of Hawaii Press, 2009).

126. Aleš Erjavec, ed., *Aesthetic Revolutions and Twentieth-Century Avant-Garde Movements* (Durham: Duke University Press, 2015).

127. Terry Eagleton, *The Ideology of the Aesthetic* (Oxford: Basil Blackwell, 1990). Eagleton's fundamental argument, if I understand it, is that modern thought and even social life are both thoroughly aestheticized—the eighteenth-century field of aesthetics became foundational for the understanding of society, capitalist relations, the state, and so forth. Aesthetic standards thus largely came to legitimate existing power relations, but might under certain conditions also serve to criticize them, even providing glimpses of a utopian future.

128. Ibid., 112–14.

129. I am indebted to Sarah Schneewind for suggesting this possibility to me. There is no doubt of German interest in Chinese philosophy, at least from Leibniz on. See David E. Mungello, *Leibniz and Confucianism: The Search for Accord* (Honolulu: University of Hawaii Press, 1977); Julia Ching and Willard G. Oxtoby, eds., *Discovering China: European Interpretations in the Enlightenment* (Rochester: University of Rochester Press, 1992). In a sense, Cai, of course, read Kant through Confucian eyes, but whether he responded to Chinese strains in Kantianism is beyond the scope of this chapter.

130. Joey Bonner, *Wang Kuo-wei: An Intellectual Biography* (Cambridge: Harvard University Press, 1986), 31–44.

131. Cited in Zehou Li, *The Chinese Aesthetic Tradition*, 213–14.

132. As was his commitment to the transformation of Chinese artistic practice. Cai's aesthetics were more theoretical than applied. His examples almost invariably came from Western art. What did he think of Chinese art? He never quite said, but in a talk to an art students' club at Peking University, Cai urged the students to draw from nature more, which he attributed to the Western tradition, and urged them to copy masterworks, a core element of the Chinese tradition, less. At least, Cai told them, in an age of cultural interchange, as Westerners had learned something of the Chinese tradition, Chinese should be free to adopt Western techniques. "Zai Beijing daxue huafa yanjiuhui shang de yanshuoci" 在北京大學畫法研究會上的演說詞 (1918), in *Cai Yuanpei wenji, meiyu*, 85–87. Cai also criticized the lack of beautiful things in China, especially in public, and he even dismissed the core art of calligraphy, largely based on

imitating ancients, as a somewhat decadent practice of little signifance to most people. "Wenhua yundong buyao wangle meiyu," in *Cai Yuanpei wenji, meiyu*, 92. At the same time, Cai was not shy, as we have seen, in citing classical sources, and he may have owed much to the traditional Confucian "six arts"—see Chen Pingyuan, *Touches of History*, 205. Arts, in this view, were part of a culture that offered the potential of civilizational transformation.

133. Chaohua Wang, "Cai Yuanpei," 230–43; quote from 241.

134. Kang Liu usefully highlights that, for Cai, "[f]irst, the aesthetic was conceived as a preeminent discourse of enlightenment and cultural revolution, against China's stagnant tradition; second, it provided a humanistic and utopian dimension to Chinese modernity, influenced primarily by Western scientific reason. As a utopian discourse, it promised new formations of universalism and cultural syncretism. Underlying his assumptions of the aesthetic is a distinctly urban and cosmopolitan vision. Although his aesthetic idea was extremely influential, Cai was primarily an educator rather than a literary theorist or an aesthetician. His aesthetics, then, is best grasped as a key constituent of his overall project of enlightenment and education." *Aesthetics and Marxism: Chinese Aesthetic Marxists and Their Western Contemporaries* (Durham: Duke University Press, 2000), 27. This seems to me a precise statement of Cai's place in Chinese aesthetics theory, though I doubt that Cai was much influenced by "scientific reason" as we understand the term today. Liu goes on to point out that Cai regarded science as inseparable from philosophy, and that science and metaphysics were interconnected and reciprocal (28–29), though I suspect Cai in fact privileged metaphysics. A greater problem is that Liu fails to emphasize the transcendental nature of Cai's aesthetics.

Chapter 4

1. Sooyoung Kim, "Individualism and Nationalism in the Thought of Chen Duxiu, 1904–1919," in *Radicalism, Revolution, and Reform in Modern China: Essays in Honor of Maurice Meisner*, ed. Catherine Lynch et al. (Lanham, MD: Lexington Books, 2011), 11–28; Yü-sheng Lin, *The Crisis of Chinese Consciousness: Radical Antitraditionalism in the May Fourth Era* (Madison: University of Wisconsin Press, 1979), 56–81. The standard English-language biography is Lee Feigon, *Chen Duxiu: Founder of the Chinese Communist Party* (Princeton: Princeton University Press, 1983); a relatively recent and balanced Chinese account is Hu Ming 胡明, *Zhengwu jiaozhi Chen Duxiu: sixiang de quanshi yu wenhua de pipan* 正误交织陈独秀: 思想的诠释与文化的批判 (Beijing: Renmin wenxue chubanshe, 2004).

2. Chen Duxiu, "Shian zizhuan" 實庵自傳, in *Chen Duxiu zhuzuo xuan* 陳獨秀著作選, ed. Ren Jianshu 任建樹 et al. (Shanghai: Shanghai renmin chubanshe 1993), 3: 413.

3. Gregor Benton, *China's Urban Revolutionaries: Explorations in the History of Chinese Trotskyism, 1921–1952* (Atlantic Highlands, NJ: Humanities Press International, 1996), 72.

4. Therefore, I do not accept the narratives of Chen's political life either as a march toward Marxism or as a cycle of liberal-Marxist-liberal. According to the latter view, Chen's life culminates in a "return" to liberalism toward the end of his life. Chen's contemporaries as well as later historians have different understandings of these narratives, and I will return to them in the conclusion of this chapter.

5. For Chen's concept of "civilization" see Joseph Ciaudo, "Replacer Chen Duxiu dans son vocabulaire: La Nouvelle Jeunesse et le problème de la culture chinoise," *Oriens Extremus* no. 54 (2015): 23–57.

6. "Falanxiren yu jinshi wenming" 法蘭西人與近世文明, in Chen Duxiu, *Duxiu wencun* 獨秀文存 (Shanghai: Yadong tushuguan, 1927), 1: 11–12. Chen's particular interest in French contributions to modern civilization, a major point of the essay, need not concern us here.

7. That is, that the French Revolution of 1789 would be eventually (soon) "completed" in a sense by the institutionalization of socialism, whether through government action or through further violent revolution. Chen was not overly concerned with the specific issue of revolution at this point. *Duxiu wencun*, 1: 13–14.

8. Chen Duxiu, "Jinggao qingnian" 敬告青年, *Duxiu wencun*, 1: 3.

9. See inter alia "Wuren zuihou zhi juewu" 吾人最後之覺悟, in *Duxiu wencun*, 1: 55–56; and "Xianfa yu Kongjiao" 憲法與孔教 (1916), in *Duxiu wencun*, 1: 103–12; "Fubi yu zun-Kong" 復辟與尊孔 (1917), *Duxiu wencun*, 1: 161–68; and "Zai zhiwen *Dongfang zazhi* jizhe" 再質問東方雜誌記者, *Duxiu wencun*, 2: 315–42.

10. That is, that in spite of the 1911 Revolution, they had not absorbed the principles of republicanism. Even after the defeat of Yuan's monarchism—precisely because of the failure of the republican revolutionaries to achieve power in the wake of Yuan's defeat—Chen's tone in 1917 became apocalyptic. See "Jiu sixiang yu guoti wenti" 舊思想與國體問題, *Duxiu wencun*, 1: 147–51; and "Jindai Xiyang jiaoyu" 近代西洋教育, *Duxiu wencun*, 1: 153–59.

11. Chen Duxiu "Jinri zhi jiaoyu fangzhen" 今日之教育方針, *Duxiu wencun*, 1: 23.

12. Chen Duxiu, "Wuren zuihou zhi juewu," *Duxiu wencun*, 1: 49–56.

13. Ibid., 54.

14. Chen Duxiu, "Jinri Zhongguo zhi zhengzhi wenti" 今日中國之政治問題, *Duxiu wencun*, 1: 221–25.

15. For Dewey in China, see Barry Keenan, *The Dewey Experiment in China: Educational Reform and Political Power in the Early Republic* (Cambridge: CEAS, Harvard University Press, 1977); Jessica Ching-Sze Wang, *John Dewey in China: To Teach and to Learn* (Albany: State University of New York Press,

2008); Barbara Schulte, "The Chinese Dewey: Friend, Fiend, and Flagship," in *The Global Reception of John Dewey's Thought: Multiple Refractions Through Time and Space*, ed. Rosa Bruno-Jofré and Jürgen Schriewer (New York: Routledge, 2012), 83–115; Tse-tsung Chow, *The May Fourth Movement: Intellectual Revolution in Modern China* (Stanford: Stanford University Press 1967), pp. 228–32 and passim. For the occasions of Dewey's lectures and events in China, see Gu Hongliang 顾红亮, *Duwei zai-Hua xuepu* 杜威在华学谱 (Shanghai: Huadong shifan daxue chubanshe, 2019).

16. Chen Duxiu, "Shixing minzhi de jichu" 實行民治的基礎, *Duxiu wencun*, 2: 373–89. While Chen's acceptance of the social reformism of the Deweyan presentation of democracy may have been temporary, his democratic utopianism lingered. For the role of democracy in Chen's conceptualization of politics, see Thomas Fröhlich, "The Concept of Politics in the May Fourth Era: Hu Shi, Chen Duxiu, and Their Struggle with 'Politics,'" *Sixiangshi* 思想史 no. 9 (Dec. 2019): 365–415. I disagree with the skeptical view of Chen's commitment to liberal democracy taken by earlier scholars—see Benjamin I. Schwartz, *Chinese Communism and the Rise of Mao* (Cambridge: Harvard University Press, 1951), 21–23; and Lee Feigon, *Chen Duxiu*, 144–46.

17. Commenting on Chinese neglect of "the social question" (economic problems), Chen noted that attention to political questions was to be expected due to the failure of the Republic to keep its promises. "Shixing minzhi de jichu," *Duxiu wencun*, 2: 2: 376.

18. Duwei [John Dewey], "Meiguo zhi minzhi de fazhang" ("The Development of Democracy in the United States") 美國之民治的發展, published in Chen's own *Meizhou pinglun* 每週評論 no. 26, 1–5 (15 June 1919) and widely republished, e,g., in *Juewu* 覺悟, 21 June 1919, sec. 8. Dewey spoke in English with Chinese interpretation provided, often by Hu Shi, as in this case. Dewey usually made some notes available to the translators and recorders; Chinese publication then followed, though the original plan to publish in English as well was never carried out.

My limited knowledge of Dewey, an intimidating thinker to the uninitiated (and one who has inspired a vast commentariat), is largely derived from Robert B. Westbrook, *John Dewey and American Democracy* (Ithaca: Cornell University Press, 1991); Alan Ryan, *John Dewey and the High Tide of American Liberalism* (New York: W. W. Norton, 1995); Thomas M. Alexander, *John Dewey's Theory of Art, Experience, and Nature: The Horizons of Feeling* (Albany: State University of New York Press, 1987); Robert Westbrook, "The Making of a Democratic Philosopher: The Intellectual Development of John Dewey," in *The Cambridge Companion to Dewey*, ed. Molly Cochran (Cambridge: Cambridge University Press, 2010), 13–33; and Richard J. Bernstein, "Dewey's Vision of Radical Democracy," in ibid., 288–308. To be clear: I am not attempting to give anything like a complete account of Deweyan democracy (a topic, in any case, which Alan Ryan has tartly noted to be "an elusive thing to describe in positive terms"—*John Dewey and the High Tide of American Liberalism*, 217), but simply to note certain themes in Dewey's writings up to the 1920s of interest to Chinese audiences. I discuss certain aspects of Dewey's thought somewhat more fully in the next chapter.

19. *Duwei wu da jiangyan* 杜威五大講演 (Beijing: Chenbaoshe, 1920); translated as *Lectures in China, 1919–1920*, ed. and trans. Robert W. Clopton and Tsuin-chen Ou (Honolulu: East-West Center, University Press of Hawaii, 1973), 45–180. The essays in this volume were back-translated from the Chinese, the compilers being unable to find the original English versions.

20. John Dewey, "Philosophy and Democracy." In *The Middle Years, 1899–1924*, vol. 11 (Carbondale: Southern Illinois University Press, 1982), 41–53.

21. Ibid., 52.

22. John Dewey, "The Ethics of Democracy" (1888), *The Early Works, 1882–1898*, vol. 1 (Carbondale: Southern Illinois University Press, 1969), 227–49; quotes from 248, 232, 243–44.

23. Richard J. Bernstein, "Dewey's Vision of Radical Democracy," 291. In his later thought, Dewey consistently criticized metaphysical idealism.

24. John Dewey, *Reconstruction in Philosophy*. In *The Middle Works, 1899–1924*, vol. 12, 77–201.

25. Ibid., 103–104.

26. Ibid., 188–89.

27. Ibid., 196.

28. Ibid.

29. Ibid., 199–200.

30. *Duwei wu da jiangyan*, 34; cf. John Dewey, *Lectures in China*, 90. Dewey criticized institutions such as the caste system and the patriarchal family as well as dictatorial government.

31. *Duwei wu da jiangyan*, 65–66; John Dewey, *Lectures*, 123–24.

32. It is noteworthy that Dewey admired (without being a true believer) Edward Bellamy's *Looking Backward* as well as Henry George's *Progress and Poverty*—see Robert Westbrook, *John Dewey and American Democracy*, 24; and Alan Ryan, *John Dewey and the High Tide of American Liberalism*, 113–16. Consistently, Dewey was sharply critical of laissez-faire and many aspects of Spencerian individualism; he regarded any "rights of property" as ultimately subordinate to democratic morality: on the one hand, the egalitarianism necessary to his vision of the organic community, and on the other, every individual's right to develop their capacities to the extent possible.

33. Chen Duxiu, "Shixing minzhi de jichu," *Duxiu wencun*, 2: 375–76.

34. Chen Duxiu, "Shixing minzhi de jichu," *Duxiu wencun*, 2: 378. Contrary to Tse-tsung Chow (*May Fourth Movement*, 231), I doubt Chen was thinking primarily of such specific institutions as initiative, referendum, and recall (as

advocated by Sun Yat-sen), but rather in more general terms of truly direct, if necessarily local, participatory democracy. If so, he was simply following Dewey's description of Rousseau's notion of the general will—*Duwei wu da jiangyan*, 89–90; John Dewey, *Lectures*, 144.

35. Chen's citations were a little forced. In fact, the egalitarianism of Xu Xing (fl. 4th–3rd c. BCE) was thoroughly refuted in the *Mencius* (3A4); and, deliberately or not, Chen was distorting Confucius (*Analects*, 16:1:10), where the phrase in modern Chinese "all without poverty" (*jun wupin*) refers to maintenance of a hierarchical social order. But no matter.

36. Chen Duxiu, "Shixing minzhi de jichu," *Duxiu wencun*, 2: 376–77.

37. Yet Chen's position probably owed much to Dewey's respect for guild socialism and its outright advocacy by Bertrand Russell, who also gave a lecture tour in China in 1920–21.

38. Chen Duxiu, "Shixing minzhi de jichu," *Duxiu wencun*, 2: 379–82.

39. Ibid., 382–87.

40. Chen Duxiu, "Ouxiang pohuai lun" 偶像破壞論, *Duxiu wencun*, 1: 227–30.

41. Chen Duxiu, "Tan zhengzhi" 談政治, *Duxiu wencun*, 3: 541–56; and "Shandong wenti yu guomin juewu" 山東問題與國民覺悟, *Duxiu wencun*, 3: 643–47.

42. Of a number of excellent studies of the first Chinese communists, of greatest relevance are Arif Dirlik, *The Origins of Chinese Communism* (New York: Oxford University Press, 1989); Hung-Yok Ip, "The Origins of Chinese Communism: A New Interpretation," *Modern China* 20, no. 1 (Jan. 1994): 34–63. See also Hung-Yok Ip, *Intellectuals in Revolutionary China, 1921–1949: Leaders, Heroes and Sophisticates* (London: RoutledgeCurzon, 2005).

43. Feng Chongyi 馮崇義, *Zhonggong dangnei de ziyou zhuyi: cong Chen Duxiu dao Li Shenzhi* 中共黨內的自由主義——從陳獨秀到李慎之 (Carle Place, NY: Mingjing chubanshe, 2009), 113–21.

44. Hung-Yok Ip, "The Origins of Chinese Communism"; and for the "utopian pulse of populistic democracy beating in the minds of May Fourth intellectuals" among May Fourth intellectuals, see Edward X. Gu, "Who Was Mr Democracy? The May Fourth Discourse of Populist Democracy and the Radicalization of Chinese Intellectuals (1915–1922)," *Modern Asian Studies* 35, no. 3 (July 2001): 589–621 (quote from 613).

45. Cai Yuanpei had firmly put intellectuals in the category of labor. Chen Duxiu began excluding them but retained a fairly heterogeneous sense of the "laboring classes" (*laogong jieji*), only in July 1921 using the reified formula of "proletariat" (*wuchan jieji*)—Edward X. Gu, "Who Was Mr Democracy?" 616–17.

46. Chen Duxiu, "Shehuizhuyi piping" 社會主義批評, *Xin qingnian* 9, no. 3 (July 1921): 1–13. Chen attributed the scientific nature of Marxist socialism to

its grasp of historical materialism—"Makesi xueshuo" 馬克思學說, *Xin qingnian* 9, no. 3 (July 1922): 5–6.

47. Chen Duxiu, "Shehuizhuyi piping," 11.

48. Ibid., 12.

49. Chen Duxiu, "Makesi xueshuo," 5–8.

50. Ibid., 8–9.

51. Chen Duxiu, "Wuchanjieji zhuanzheng" 無產階級專政, *Xin qingnian* 9, no. 3 (July 1922): 90–91.

52. Arif Dirlik, *The Origins of Chinese Communism* (New York: Oxford University Press, 1989), ch. 10; see also Arif Dirlik, *Anarchism and the Chinese Revolution* (Berkeley: University of California Press, 1991), 204–19. For a comprehensive study of first generation of communists, see Ishikawa Yoshihiro, trans. Joshua A. Fogel, *The Formation of the Chinese Communist Party* (New York: Columbia University Press, 2013).

53. Chen Duxiu, "Tan zhengzhi," *Duxiu wencun*, 3: 541–56.

54. Chen Duxiu, "Suiganlu 101: Minzhudang yu gongchandang" 隨感錄: (101) 民主黨與共產黨, *Xin qingnian* 8, no. 4 (Dec. 1920): n.p.

55. The classic account is Harold R. Isaacs, *The Tragedy of the Chinese Revolution* (New York: Atheneum, 1966).

56. Wang Fan-hsi, *Chinese Revolutionary: Memoirs 1919–1949*, trans and ed. Gregor Benton (Oxford: Oxford University Press, 1980), 121–26; Zheng Chaolin, *An Oppositionist for Life: Memoirs of the Chinese Revolutionary Zheng Chaolin*, trans. and ed. Gregor Benton (Atlantic Highlands, NJ: Humanities Press, 1997), 229. The most thorough account is Zheng Chaolin, "Chen Duxiu and the Trotskyists," in Gregor Benton, *China's Urban Revolutionaries*, 124–202; and see Gregor Benton, *China's Urban Revolutionaries*, esp. ch. 6; Gregor Benton, "Editor's Introduction," in Chen Duxiu, *Chen Duxiu's Last Articles and Letters, 1937–1942*, trans. and ed. Gregor Benton (Honolulu: University of Hawai'i Press, 1998), 11–30; Peter Kuhfus, "Chen Duxiu and Leon Trotsky: New Light on Their Relationship," *China Quarterly* 102 (June 1985): 253–76; Lee Feigon, *Chen Duxiu*, 196–204.

57. According to Gregor Benton, a key step in Chen's progress toward becoming a Trotskyist in 1929 was his final acceptance of the notion of "proletarian dictatorship as an immediate goal of the revolution" (*China's Urban Revolutionaries*, 32), but on the whole, in the early 1930s, as we will see, Chen was more enthusiastic about the notion of promoting a national assembly.

58. In the early 1930s, self-identified Chinese Trotskyists regarded themselves as China's true communists, as opposed to the party that had been taken over by Stalinists. Although from the CCP's official point of view, "Trotskyist" was bad enough, given Chen's prestige it was also necessary to attack him with being an "opportunist" (going back to 1928) and then with the utterly ridiculous charge that he was a traitor to China.

59. "Zhongguo gongchandang zuopai fanduipai gangling" 中國共產黨左派反對派綱領, in *Chen Duxiu wannian zhuzuoxuan* 陳獨秀晚年著作選, ed. Lin Zhiliang 林致良 et al. (hereafter CDXWZ; Hong Kong: Tiandi tushu youxian gongsi, 2012), 109–11.

60. Ibid., 111–16.

61. Chen Duxiu, "Guomindang yu Zhongguo tongyi—tongyi shi Zhongguo jinbu de biyao tiaojian" 國民黨與中國統一——統一是中國進步的必要條件, CDXWZ, 288.

62. Gregor Benton, *China's Urban Revolutionaries*, ch. 9.

63. Trotsky considered that Marxism *had* predicted the Russian Revolution as a bourgeois revolution. Leon Trotsky, *The Permanent Revolution and Results and Prospects* (New York: Merit Publishers, 1969), 180. *Results and Prospects*, first published in 1906, did not use the term *permanent revolution*, which became widespread in the 1920s. In his 1919 preface to a new edition of *Results and Prospects*, Trotsky introduced the term in his discussion of the 1905 Revolution: "The Revolution, having begun as a bourgeois revolution as regards its first tasks, will soon call forth powerful class conflicts and will gain final victory only by transferring power to the only class capable of standing at the head of the oppressed masses, namely, to the proletariat. Once in power, the proletariat not only will not want, but will not be able to limit itself to a bourgeois democratic programme. It will be able to carry through the Revolution to the end only in the event of the Russian Revolution being converted into a Revolution of the European proletariat. The bourgeois-democratic programme of the Revolution will then be superseded, together with its national limitations, and the temporary political domination of the Russian working class will develop into a prolonged Socialist dictatorship. But should Europe remain inert, the bourgeois counter-revolution will not tolerate the government of the toiling masses in Russia and will throw the country backwards—far back from a democratic workers' and peasants' republic. Therefore, once having won power, the proletariat cannot keep within the limits of bourgeois democracy. It must adopt the tactics of *permanent revolution*, i.e., must destroy the barriers between the minimum and maximum programme of Social Democracy, go over to more and more radical social reforms and seek direct and immediate support in revolution in Western Europe" (30–31).

64. Leon Trotsky, *The Permanent Revolution*, 69–74.

65. Ibid., 276, 278; italics in original.

66. Ibid., 131.

67. Ibid., 129. I have switched the order of the second and third aspects of permanent revolution as listed by Trotsky.

68. Ibid., 132.

69. Ibid., 64.

70. For Trotsky's evolving views, see Leon Trotsky, *Problems of the Chinese Revolution*, trans. Max Shachtman (Ann Arbor: University of Michigan Press,

1967); *Leon Trotsky on China*, ed. Les Evans and Russell Block (New York: Monad Press, 1976).

71. Leon Trotsky, "The Chinese Revolution and the Theses of Comrade Stalin," in *Leon Trotsky on China*, 160–61; my italics.

72. Leon Trotsky, "Class Relations in China," in *Leon Trotsky on China*, 142.

73. Trotsky used both terms. "Democratic Slogans in China," in *Leon Trotsky on China*, 342–44; "The Slogan of a National Assembly in China," in *Leon Trotsky on China*, 433. Gregor Benton points out that the original term *constituent assembly* (*lixian huiyi*) had acquired negative connotations in Chinese due to the sorry succession of meaningless constitutions promulgated since 1912 (in Zheng Chaolin, *An Oppositionist for Life*, 306–307 n. 338).

74. Leon Trotsky "The Chinese Question after the Sixth Congress," in *Leon Trotsky on China*, 367, 377, 380; romanization modified.

75. Leon Trotsky "China and the Constituent Assembly," in ibid., 399.

76. Zheng Chaolin, *An Oppositionist for Life*, 233–39; Wang Fan-Hsi, *Chinese Revolutionary*, 88.

77. Chen Duxiu, "Women zai xian jieduan zhengzhi douzheng de celue wenti" 我們在現階段政治鬥爭的策略問題, CDXWZ, 32–39. See Lee Feigon, *Chen Duxiu*, 199–216.

78. Chen Duxiu, "Women zai xianjieduan zhengzhi douzheng de celue wenti," 40–41.

79. Ibid., 44–47.

80. Chen Duxiu, "Liangge luxian—da Minjie ji xiao-Chen liang tongzhi" 兩個路線——答民傑及小陳兩同志, CDXWZ, 160–66.

81. Chen Duxiu, "Lun guomin huiyi kouhao" 論國民會議口號, CDXWZ, 250.

82. Chen Duxiu, "Wo de genben yijian" 我的根本意見, CDXWZ, 437; translated as "My Basic Views" in *Chen Duxiu's Last Articles and Letters*, 71. See also Chen Duxiu, "Gei Xiliu deng de xin" 給西流等的信, CDXWZ, 477; "Letter to Xiliu" in *Chen Duxiu's Last Articles and Letters*, 65.

83. Chen Duxiu, "Women yao zeyang de minzhu zhengzhi?" 我們要怎樣的民主政治? CDXWZ, 370–71.

84. Ibid., 371–72.

85. Ibid., 373–75.

86. Chen Duxiu, "Women zai xian jieduan zhengzhi douzheng de celue wenti," CDXWZ, 43.

87. Chen Duxiu, "Women yao zeyang de minzhu zhengzhi?" CDXWZ, 376. Here, Chen cited Lenin's *State and Revolution* (1918): "Democracy is of enormous importance to the working class in its struggle against the capitalists for its emancipation. But democracy is by no means a boundary not to be over-stepped; it is only one of the stages on the road from feudalism to capitalism, and from capitalism to communism." As Chen certainly knew, Lenin went on to distinguish between the formal equality of bourgeois democracy and the "actual

equality" that would stem from the abolition of classes, the political form of which, however, can scarcely be guessed at. V. I. Lenin, *The State and Revolution* (Peking: Foreign Languages Press, 1973), 118.

88. Chen Duxiu, "Women wei zeyang de guomin huiyi douzheng" 我們為怎樣的國民會議鬥爭, CDXWZ, 88–91 (quote from 91).

89. Ibid., 88–91.

90. Chen Duxiu, "Shiyue geming yu buduan geming" 十月革命與不斷革命, CDXWZ, 72–75. Chen quoted Chinese Karl Marx and Frederick Engels, "Address of the Central Committee to the Communist League," London, March 1850. See also Chen Duxiu, "Guoji luxian yu Zhongguodang" 國際路線與中國黨, CDXWZ, 81–88.

91. Chen Duxiu, "Liangge luxian," 163–64.

92. Chen Duxiu, "Zhongguo minzhong yinggai zeyang jiuguo ji zijiu" 中國民眾應該怎樣救國即自救, CDXWZ, 150.

93. The rhetoric of "lost country" and comparison to India harkened back to the late Qing nationalist discourse of Chen's youth.

94. Chen Duxiu, "Women zhenglun zhi zhongxindian," 我們爭論之中心點 CDXWZ, 322.

95. Chen Duxiu, "You fan-Ri dao fan-Guomindang" 由反日到反國民黨, CDXWZ, 152–57.

96. Chen Duxiu, "Guomindang yu Zhongguo tongyi," 國民黨與中國統一 CDXWZ, 288; "You fan-Ri dao fan-Guomindang," CDXWZ, 154–55.

97. Chen Duxiu, "Zhengzhi jueyi an (changweihui tongguo)—muqian de jushi yu women de renwu" 政治決議案 (常委會通過)——目前的局勢與我們的任務, CDXWZ, 206–209.

98. Leon Trotsky, "For a Strategy of Action, Not Speculation: A Letter to Friends in Peking," in *Leon Trotsky on China*, 532–40.

99. Chen Duxiu, "Wuchan jieji yu minzhu zhuyi" 無產階級與民主主義, CDXWZ, 410–15 (quote from 410). See also Chen Duxiu, "Guanyu minzhu zhuyi de jidian genben sixiang" 關於民主主義的幾點根本思想, CDXWZ, 416–19.

100. Chen Duxiu, "Wuchan jieji yu minzhu zhuyi" 無產階級與民主主義, 411.

101. Ibid., 412.

102. Ibid., 414. Chen cited Lenin's *State and Revolution* on the importance of using democracy to eliminate bureaucratism, that enemy of democracy that Stalin represents (414–15).

103. Though Chen did from time to time note fascism in the Guomindang's opposition to even formal bourgeois democracy. Chen Duxiu, "Lun guomin huiyi kouhao," CDXWZ, 251; "Qianjin yu houtui," 291; "Wuchan jieji yu minzhu zhuyi," 411.

104. Chen Duxiu, "Guanyu minzhu zhuyi de jidian genben sixiang" 416.

105. Ibid., 416–17.

106. Chen Duxiu, "Wo de genben yijian," 437; "My Basic Views," 71. See also "Gei Xiliu de xin," 477; "Letter to Xiliu," 64.

107. Chen Duxiu, "Gei Lian'gen de xin" 給連根的信, CDXWZ, 472–74; "Letter to Liangen," in *Chen Duxiu's Last Articles and Letters*, 59–61.

108. Chen Duxiu, "Wo de genben yijian," 437; "My Basic Views," 71–72.

109. Chen Duxiu, "Gei Xiliu de xin," 475–81; "Letter to Xiuliu," 62–69.

110. Chen Duxiu, "Guanyu minzhu zhiyi de jidian genben sixiang," CDXWZ, 419.

111. Chen Duxiu, "Women zai shijuzhong de renwu" 我們在時局中的任務, CDXWZ, 432.

112. Chen Duxiu, "Gei Xiliu deng de xin," 470–71; "Letter to Xiliu," 56–58.

113. Chen Duxiu, "Gei Lian'gen de xin," 472–73; "Letter to Liangen," 60.

114. Leon Trotsky, "Japan and China," in *Leon Trotsky on China*, 568.

115. Leon Trotsky, "On the Sino-Japanese War," in *Leon Trotsky on China*, 547–48.

116. Chen Duxiu, "Zhanhou shijie dashi zhi lunguo" 戰後世界大勢之輪廓, CDXWZ, 441–48; "A Sketch of the Post-War World," in *Chen Duxiu's Last Articles and Letters*, 78–87.

117. Chen Duxiu, "Zhanhou shijie dashi zhi lunguo," CDXWZ, 447.

118. Chen Duxiu, "Zailun shijie dashi" 再論世界大勢, CDXWZ, 449–54; "Once Again on the World Situation," in *Chen Duxiu's Last Articles and Letters*, 88–94.

119. Chen Duxiu, "Zhanhou shijie dashi zhi lunguo," CDXWZ, 447.

120. Chen Duxiu, "Bei yapo minhu zhi qiantu" 被壓迫民族之前途, CDXWZ, 455–59; "The Future of Oppressed Nations," in *Chen Duxiu's Last Articles and Letters*," 95–101.

121. Chen Duxiu, "Bei yapo minzu zhi qiantu," 456.

122. Zheng Chaolin, *An Oppositionist for Life*, 175. Trotsky is said to have held this view of Chen as well. Zheng's views of Chen were in fact more nuanced. Zheng claimed that Chen was the only Communist who, in the wake of the great defeat of 1927–28 "ever did any thinking" (177). Zheng also commented, "But that doesn't mean that he [Chen] was in no sense a theoretician. . . . [H]e advanced original theories and wrote theoretical essays. . . . [H]is acute vision enabled him to grasp the main elements in the objective situation and to propose policies for dealing with it." Zheng Chaolin, "Chen Duxiu and the Trotskyists," 186.

123. Gregor Benton suggests that Chen was moved by the mid-1930s to rethink his views of democracy by the Moscow show trials and the Stalin-Hitler alliance—*China's Urban Revolutionaries*, 75. Of course, it was the debacle of 1927–28 that first jerked Chen out of Stalinist complacency.

124. Chen Duxiu, "Gei Xiliu deng de xin," 478; "Letter to Xiliu," 66.

125. Falanxiren yu jinshi wenming," *Duxiu wencun*, 1: 10–13.

126. Lee Feigon, *Chen Duxiu*, 225; Jerome B. Grieder, *Hu Shih and the Chinese Renaissance: Liberalism in the Chinese Revolution, 1917–1937* (Cambridge: Harvard University Press, 1970), 187, n. 29. Chen was expelled from the CCP in 1929. Feng Chongyi states that Chen returned to liberalism the day he left the party, but this neglects the evolution of Chen's late thought and its continued basis in Marxist historical materialism. Feng Chongyi, *Zhonggong dangnei de ziyou zhuyi*, 133, 140.

127. "Interviews with Wang Fanxi on Tang Baolin's *History of Chinese Trotskyism*," in Gregor Benton, *China's Urban Revolutionaries*, 207.

128. See Jin Huanling 金焕玲, *Chen Duxiu: lunli sixiang yanjiu* 陈独秀: 伦理思想研究 (Beijing: Zhongguo shehui chubanshe, 2009), 123–41.

Chapter 5

1. Hao Chang considers Hu a utopian and indeed Promethean thinker, but if this is so, utopianism still only constituted a part of Hu's political thought, which was equally marked by the skepticism inherent in his commitment to pragmatism. Zhang Hao, "Zhuanxing shidai Zhongguo wutuobang zhuyi," 16–20.

2. Hu Shi, "Wenti yu zhuyi" 問題與主義 in *Hu Shi quanji* 胡適全集 (hereafter "HSQJ"; Hefei: Anhui jiaoyu chubanshe, 2003), ed. Ji Xianlin 季羡林, 1: 324–59; "Shiyan zhuyi" 實驗主義 ("Pragmatism" or, better, "Experimentalism"), HSQJ 1: 276–23; discussed below.

3. D. W. Y. Kwok, *Scientism in Chinese Thought, 1900–1950* (New Haven: Yale University Press, 1965), ch. 4.

4. Hu Shi himself admitted at times his tendency to emphasize America's strong points and ignore its real weaknesses and problems. See "Meiguo de funü: zai Beijing nüzi shifan xuexiao yanjiang" 美國的婦女: 在北京女子師範學校演講, HSQJ 1: 618–32. In this 1918 lecture Hu insisted that he did despise Westerners looking down on the Chinese and said that when he was in the United States he emphasized good points of Chinese culture. Nonetheless, he did not think the Chinese were in a position to criticize others, and when in China he wanted to raise the strong points of other civilizations for the Chinese to learn from.

5. Hu Shi, "Women duiyu xiyang jindai wenming de taidu" 我們對於西洋近代文明的態度, HSQJ 3: 1–14.

6. In the English version of this essay, Hu snapped that Europeans had no reason to be so depressed in the postwar period; their condemnation of Western materialism and praise of Eastern spiritual qualities were "gratifying the vanity of Oriental apologists and thereby strengthening the hand of reaction in the East." "The Civilizations of the East and the West," in *Whither Mankind: A Panorama of Modern Civilization*, ed. Charles A. Beard (New York: Longmans, Green, 1928), 25–41 (quote from 25). A Japanese version also appeared in 1926:

"Kindai seiyō bunmei ni taisuru gojin no taido" 近代西洋文明に對する吾人の態度, *Kaizō* 改造, 5-1926, 4–17.

7. Hu Shi, "Women duiyu xiyang jindai wenming de taidu," HSQJ 3: 2.

8. Ibid., 3. The "we" here is an editorial we as Hu claims to be speaking for Chinese youth in general.

9. Ibid., 4.

10. A clear discussion is Stephen Angle, *Human Rights and Chinese Thought: A Cross Cultural Inquiry* (Cambridge: Cambridge University Press, 2002), 75–98.

11. Hu Shi, "Women duiyu xiyang jindai wenming de taidu," HSQJ 3: 4–5.

12. Hu Shi, "Manyou de ganxiang" 漫遊的感想, HSQJ 3: 37–38.

13. Hu Shi, "Qing dajia lai zhaozhao jingzi" 請大家來照照鏡子, HSQJ 3: 29.

14. Ibid., 28–29.

15. Charles Babbage, *On the Economy of Machinery and Manufacturers* (London: Charles Knight, 1832), 6. This book was essentially a technical introduction to the principles of mechanics but written for the layman.

16. The *Oxford English Dictionary* gives first use of "industrialization" as 1892, though "industrialize" is older, and "industry" can be traced back to the fifteenth century.

17. For technology as civilizing mission, see Michael Adas, *Dominance by Design: Technological Imperatives and America's Civilizing Mission* (Cambridge, MA: Belknap Press, 2006).

18. Hu Shi, "Women duiyu xiyang jindai wenming de taidu," HSQJ 3: 5; my emphasis.

19. Duwei, "Shehui zhexue yu zhengzhi zhexue," *Duwei wu da jiangyan*, 46; cf. John Dewey, *Lectures*, 102–103.

20. See above, chapter 4 for Dewey's trip to China. My purpose here is not to give a comprehensive overview of Dewey's China lectures but to highlight particular themes relevant to the utopian impulse found in Hu Shi's thought. Dewey's topic of "social and political philosophy" for a series of lectures was chosen based on Hu Shi's suggestion and represented a new area for Dewey, though he had taught a course at Columbia University (that Hu had taken) on moral, social, and political philosophy. Barry C. Keenan, *The Dewey Experiment in China*, 129–30. My general sources on Dewey are cited above in chapter 4, n. 18. I am especially grateful to Thomas Alexander for his comments on an earlier draft of this chapter.

21. Duwei, "Shehui zhexue yu zhengzhi zhexue," *Duwei wu da jiangyan*, 111; John Dewey, *Lectures*, 164.

22. Barry Keenan, *The Dewey Experiment in China*, 39–42.

23. Duwei, "Jiaoyu zhexue" 教育哲學, *Duwei wuda jiangyan*, 61–62; John Dewey, *Lectures*, 237–38.

24. Duwei, "Jiaoyu zhexue," *Duwei wu da jiangyan*, 63; John Dewey, *Lectures*, 238; for the influence of the scientific method on the move in people's minds

of the golden age from the past to the future, see Duwei, "Jiaoyu zhexue," 76; John Dewey, *Lectures*, 249.

25. Although Dewey never reworked his China lectures into an English book, and his lecture notes were not found among his papers, partial typescripts that seem to be his original notes for some of his lectures were discovered in the Hu Shi Archives in Beijing by Yung-chen Chiang. See Yung-chen Chiang, "Appropriating Dewey: Hu Shi and His Translation of Dewey's 'Social and Political Philosophy' Lecture Series in China," *European Journal of Pragmatism and American Philosophy* 7, no. 2 (2015): 71–97. Dewey's typescripts are slightly revised and published in that same journal issue, 7–44. I have used the typescript copies held in the archives of the Hu Shih Memorial Hall 胡適紀念館, Institute of Modern History, Academia Sinica 中央研究院 近代史研究所.

Chiang believes that Hu Shi "appropriated" Dewey's ideas for his own "cultural and political agenda"—that is, distorted what Dewey said. However, while the typescripts differ in many particulars from the published version of Dewey's lectures, I find no significant distortions. Hu Shi and Dewey had their disagreements, and Hu Shi did "appropriate" Dewey's ideas selectivity for his own purposes—naturally enough—but the typescripts, though mostly written in complete sentences, also functioned as notes. Therefore, differences between the typescripts and the published lectures might be due to several factors: Dewey's interpreters might have misunderstood or modified his spoken remarks; Dewey might have expanded and changed them in his actual lectures; and Dewey or others might have edited his lecture transcripts before they were finally translated and published in Chinese. Chiang doubts that Dewey's spoken remarks would have differed much from his typed notes, but the typescripts are often pithy, even gnomic, and obviously a first draft, and it seems to me likely that Dewey would at least have expanded on them. The additional material found in the published version supports this notion; as well, there are materials that appear in one lecture in the typescript version that emerge in an entirely different lecture in the published version, which raises the possiblity that Dewey was editing himself through his spoken lectures.

In the citations that follow I have modified the typescripts by using standard spellings.

26. "Social Pol Phil Lecture I," 2.

27. Ibid., 8.

28. "SPP II," 3. Dewey also argued that the social sciences could never be as "pure" or objective as they hoped, since they always involved human participation and interest in addition to observation.

29. Duwei, "Jiaoyu zhexue," *Duwei wu da jiangyan*, 68–69; John Dewey, *Lectures*, 242–43.

30. The issue is explored in David Hollinger, "The Problem of Pragmatism in American History," *Journal of American History* 67, no. 1 (June 1980): 88–107;

Peter T. Manicas, "Pragmatic Philosophy of Science and the Charge of Scientism," *Transactions of the Charles S. Peirce Society* 24, no. 2 (Spring 1988): 179–22.

31. Duwei, "Xiandai de sange zhexuejia" 現代的三個哲學家, in *Duwei wuda jiangyan*, 1–19; *John Dewey: The Middle Works, 1899–1924*, vol. 12, 205–20.

32. Duwei, "Jiaoyu zhexue," 71; John Dewey, *Lectures*, 246. "Shiyan" was how Hu Shi generally spoke of Pragmatism.

33. Duwei, "Jiaoyu zhexue," *Duwei wu da jiangyan*, 76–77; John Dewey, *Lectures*, 249–50.

34. Duwei, "Jiaoyu zhexue," *Duwei wu da jiangyan*, 72; John Dewey, *Lectures*, 247. This point echoed the famous formulation of Wang Yangming (1472–1526) on the "unity of knowledge and action" and would have been familiar to Dewey's audience, though Wang was trying to talk about morality, not science.

35. John Dewey, "Some Stages of Logical Thought," *Middle Works, 1899–1924*, vol. 1, 151–74; *Studies in Logical Theory*, ibid., vol. 2, 295–375; and *How We Think*, ibid., vol. 6, 177–356.

36. Joachim Kurtz, *The Discovery of Chinese Logic* (Leiden: Brill, 2011), 346–50.

37. David Hildebrand, "Dewey's Pragmatism: Instrumentalism and Meliorism," in *The Cambridge Companion to Pragmatism*, ed. Alan Malachowski (Cambridge: Cambridge University Press, 2013), 55–80, quote from 59.

38. John Dewey, "Some Stages of Logical Thought," *Middle Works*, vol. 1, 156–57.

39. Ibid., 158.

40. Ibid., 162–64.

41. Ibid., 171–72.

42. John Dewey, *How We Think*, ibid., vol. 6, 242–44.

43. Ibid., 293–301.

44. Ibid., 236–41.

45. Alan Ryan, *John Dewey*, 144–46.

46. Hu Shi, "Duwei xiansheng yu Zhongguo" 杜威先生與中國, HSQJ 1: 360–62.

47. Hu Shi, "Shiyan zhuyi," HSQJ 1: 278–80.

48. Hu Shi, "Women duiyu xiyang jindai wenming de taidu," HSQJ 3: 5. By way of contrast, according to Hu, the "old civilization of the East" not only failed to pursue knowledge, but generally suppressed it. A search for enlightenment through meditation merely represented a commitment to ignorance (ibid., 5). Hu could be a scold; at one point he accused Chinese culture of fostering corruption though its inability to distinguish private from public, though this was not entirely a new genre of cultural self-critique ("Qing dajia lai zhaozhao jingzi," HSQJ 3: 29–31). Nonetheless, the dichotomizing of old-East versus modern-West that Hu occasionally indulged in, with its self-Orientalizing rhetoric, was not typical of his thought as a whole, though he consistently despised Buddhism.

49. Hu Shi, "Women duiyu xiyang jindai wenming de taidu," HSQJ 3: 13–14; in Hu's English version: "[T]hat civilization which makes the fullest possible use of human ingenuity and intelligence in search of truth in order to control nature and transform matter for the service of mankind, to liberate the human spirit from ignorance, superstition, and slavery to the forces of nature, and to reform social and political institution for the benefit of the greatest number—such a civilization is highly idealistic and spiritual. This civilization will continue to grow and improve itself" ("The Civilizations of the East and the West," 41).

50. Hu Shi, "Women duiyu xiyang jindai wenming de taidu," HSQJ 3: 7–9.

51. Ibid., 9–10.

52. Ibid., 11.

53. Ibid., 12.

54. Ibid., 7–8.

55. As Hu put it in the English version, "The change has come because in the last two centuries men have hit upon a few key inventions out of which a vast number of tools and machines have been constructed for the control of the resources and powers in nature. By means of these machines men have been able to save labor and reduce distance, to fly in the air, tunnel the mountains and sail underneath the deep seas, to enslave lightning to pull our carriages and employ 'ether' to deliver our messages throughout the world . . . and man's confidence in his own powers has greatly increased. *Man has become the master of himself and of his own destiny.*" "The Civilizations of the East and the West," 31; my italics.

56. Hu Shi, "Women duiyu xiyang jindai wenming de taidu," HSQJ 3: 8–9.

57. Ibid., 6.

58. As Hu put it in the English version, "But the most spiritual phase of the modern civilization of the West is its new religion which, in the absence of a better name, I shall term the religion of Democracy. . . . The religion of Democracy, which not only guarantees one's own liberty, nor merely limits one's liberty by respective of the liberty of other people, but endeavors to make it possible for every man and every woman to live a free life; which not only succeeds through science and machinery in creating enhancing the happiness and comfort of the individual, but also seeks through organization and legislation to extend the good of life to the greatest number—this is the greatest spiritual heritage of Western civilization"—"The Civilizations of the East and the West," 37, 40.

59. Hu Shi, "Women duiyu xiyang jindai wenming de taidu," HSQJ 3: 11.

60. F. C. S. Schiller, *Studies in Humanism* (London: MacMillan, 1907). Schiller (1864–1937), a lively writer who evidently enjoyed a good fight, spent most of his career at Oxford University, regarded by many as the leading proponent of pragmatism in Europe.

61. Ibid., 462.

62. Ibid., 12.

63. Ibid., 14. See also F. C. S. Schiller, *Humanism: Philosophical Essays* (London: MacMillan, 1903), xvi–xvii, for the concept of a "re-humanized universe."

64. Hu Shi, "Bu xiu: wo de zongjiao" 不朽: 我的宗教, HSQJ 1: 659–68 [originally published in 1919].

65. Hu Shi, "Ibusheng zhuyi" 易卜生主義, HSQJ 1: 599–617.

66. Hu Shi, "*Kexue yu renshengguan* xu《科學與人生觀》序, HSQJ 2: 195–230. For the debate, see Tse-Tsung Chow, *The May Fourth Movement*, 333–37; Jerome B. Grieder, *Hu Shi and the Chinese Renaissance*, 150–59; D. W. Y. Kwok, *Scientism in Chinese Thought*, 85–108. The debate was instigated by Zhang Junmai and Liang Qichao who, shocked and disillusioned by the destruction of the war, argued that science had its destructive side and—even more basically—demanded that supporters of science acknowledge that science could not answer all of humanity's questions. The Chinese defenders of science considered their opponents to be Bergsonian obscurantists and accused them of claiming that science was completely harmful. For his part, Hu did indeed hold the position that science was "omnipotent."

67. Hu Shi, "*Kexue yu renshengguan* xu," HSQJ 2: 199.

68. Ibid., 211–12.

69. John Dewey, "A Common Faith," *John Dewey: The Later Works, 1925–1953*, vol. 9, ed. Jo Ann Boydston (Carbondale: Southern Illinois University Press, 1986), 1–58 (quote from 36). I am grateful to Gu Hongliang for pointing me to this essay.

70. Ibid., 23.

71. Ibid., 8–9.

72. Ibid., 23.

73. Ibid., 12–14.

74. Thomas M. Alexander, "John Dewey's Uncommon Faith: Understanding 'Religious Experience,'" *The American Catholic Philosophical Quarterly* 87, no. 2 (2013): 347–62 (quote from 351).

75. John Dewey, "A Common Faith," 29–30.

76. Ibid., 34; italics in the original.

77. Ibid., 52.

78. Ibid., 36.

79. Of course, it may have been almost unimaginable for Dewey to envision humanity living without any kind of religiosity: his concern was how to encourage the transition from the religions of the day, all based on some version of the supernatural, to the religious attitude appropriate to the scientific understanding of nature. As well, he may have assumed the bulk of the audience that he hoped to sway consisted of liberal Christians (as well as some atheists) worried that, without religion, moral norms would collapse. Dewey concluded by making a much stronger case against even liberal Christian versions of the

supernatural (ibid., 40–58) than his case for why the religious attitude is still important. Thomas Alexander suggests a source for Dewey's religiosity in the broad sense of the term: "The sense of human nature connected with a larger whole gives rise to awe and reverence. Thus faith, in Dewey's sense, must not only involve an inclusive, integrating self-in-world ideal, but in transcending the self it marks that connection with a pervasive sense of reverent awe. This is 'natural piety' and it opposes hubris" ("John Dewey's Uncommon Faith," 361).

80. John Dewey, "A Common Faith," 52.

81. Pan Guangzhe 潘光哲, "Qingnian Hu Shi de 'minzhu jingyan'" 青年胡適的「民主經驗」, in *Pupian yu teshu de bianzheng: zhengzhi sixiang de tanjue* 普遍與特殊的辯證: 政治思想的探掘, ed. Qian Yongxiang 錢永祥 (Taibei: Zhongyang yanjiuyuan renwen shehui kexue yanjiu zhongxin, 2012), 151–94.

82. Hu Shi, "*Zhengzhi gailun* xu" 《政治概論》序, HSQJ 2: 415–20.

83. Ibid., 416–17.

84. Ibid., 418.

85. Ibid., 419.

86. See Sor-hoon Tan, "China's Pragmatist Experiment in Democracy: Hu Shih's Pragmatism and Dewey's Influence in China," in *The Challenge of Pragmatism and the Limits of Philosophy*, ed. Richard Shusterman (Malden, MA: Blackwell, 2004), esp. 51–59; see also Tan, "How Can a Chinese Democracy be Pragmatic?" *Transactions of the Charles S. Peirce Society* 47, no. 2 (2011): 196–225.

87. Duwei, *Duwei wuda jiangyan*, 113; John Dewey, *Lectures*, 167.

88. Duwei, *Duwei wuda jiangyan*, 113–16; John Dewey, *Lectures*, 166–69.

89. Sor-hoon Tan, "China's Pragmatist Experiment," 45–46.

90. John Dewey, "Philosophies of Freedom," *Later Works*, vol. 3, 92–114. In a series of essays written for the *New Republic* in 1929 and 1930, Dewey was deeply concerned with the growth of "corporativeness" in the United States and the powerful conformity it imposed. Without romanticizing the premodern, Dewey noted the alienation entailed in the new system of mass production, mass consumption, and mass culture. To foster a new kind of individualism, then, Dewey faced a different problem than overcoming the atomistic and entrepreneurial individualism of classical liberalism. See John Dewey, *Individualism Old and New*, in *Later Works*, vol. 5, 43–123.

Dewey did not call for a "new individualism" during his sojourn in China, which came, after all, ten years before he wrote these essays. But if, instead of contrasting collectivist China to individualist America, we were to draw a loose analogy between the supposed traditional lack of individualism in China and the new threats to individualism of corporativeness in the United States, Dewey's remarks on the inaptness of classical individualism might seem to apply. On the other hand, Dewey's acute worries over the culture that industrialization had made perhaps meant little to contemporary Chinese who wished to go through a phase of liberal individualism, at least in its social if not economic form.

91. See John J. Stuhr, "Old Ideas Crumble: War, Pragmatist Intellectuals, and the Limits of Philosophy," in *The Challenge of Pragmatism and the Limits of Philosophy*, ed. Richard Shusterman (Malden, MA: Blackwell, 2004), 86–89.

92. John Dewey, *Democracy and Education: An Introduction to the Philosophy of Education* (New York: MacMillan, 1916), 96.

93. See David T. Hansen, ed., *John Dewey and Our Educational Prospect: A Critical Engagement with Dewey's* Democracy and Education (Albany: State University of New York Press, 2006); and Leonard J. Waks and Andrea R. English, eds., *John Dewey's* Democracy and Education: A Centennial Handbook (Cambridge: Cambridge University Press, 2017).

94. John Dewey, *Democracy and Education*, 101.

95. Ibid., 102.

96. Ibid., 109–15.

97. Ibid., 142, 300.

98. Ibid., 357.

99. Ibid., 369–70.

100. Duwei, *Duwei wuda jiangyan*, 14–27; John Dewey, *Lectures*, 64–81.

101. "SPP III," 3.

102. Ibid., 12.

103. "SPP IV," 12–13; emphasis in the original.

104. Duwei, *Duwei wuda jiangyan*, 32–33; John Dewey, *Lectures*, 87–88.

105. Duwei, *Duwei wuda jiangyan*, 34; John Dewey, *Lectures*, 90.

106. "SPP 12," 9.

107. "SPP 16," 6; my emphasis.

108. Duwei, *Duwei wuda jiangyan*, 37, 41; John Dewey, *Lectures*, 94, 98.

109. Duwei, *Duwei wuda jiangyan*, 101–103; John Dewey, *Lectures*, 154–55.

110. Duwei, *Duwei wuda jiangyan*, 111–12; John Dewey, *Lectures*, 165.

111. Duwei, *Duwei wuda jiangyan*, 126–27; John Dewey. *Lectures*, 180.

112. Duwei, *Duwei wuda jiangyan*, 93; John Dewey, *Lectures*, 147.

113. Duwei, *Duwei wuda jiangyan*, 151; John Dewey, *Lectures*, 98–99.

114. John Dewey, "Creative Democracy—The Task Before Us," *Later Works* 14, 224–30.

115. Ibid., 226–27.

116. Ibid., 229.

117. See Jerome Grieder, *Hu Shi and the Chinese Renaissance*, 169.

118. Hu Shi, "Qing dajia lai zhaozhao jingzi," 31–32.

119. Ibid., 32–33.

120. Hu Shi, "Woman zou natiao lu" 我們走那條路, HSQJ 4: 455–70.

121. Ibid., 468; my italics.

122. Hu Shi, "Du Liang Shuming xiansheng de *Dong Xi wenhua jiqi zhexue*" 讀梁漱溟先生的《東西文化及其哲學》, HSQJ 1: 235–55.

123. Ibid., 237–38.

124. Ibid., 254; my italics.

125. Hu Shi, "Manyou de ganxiang," HSQJ 3: 39.

126. Hu Shi, "Ou you daozhong jishu" 歐游道中寄書 (letter to Xu Zhimo 徐志摩, Oct. 1926), HSQJ 3: 54–60.

127. Ibid., 51.

128. Ibid., 49–50.

129. Ibid., 57.

130. Hu Shi, "Ou you daozhong jishu," 52–53. Xu Zhimo (1897–1931) was a romantic poet and translator who wrote in the vernacular, a literary movement that Hu Shi had championed.

131. John Dewey, *How We Think, Middle Works*, vol. 6, 232; italics in original.

132. John Dewey, *Democracy and Education*, 401.

133. Jerome Grieder, *Hu Shih*, 47, 111–21.

134. Ibid., 93, 338.

135. Barry Keenan, *The Dewey Experiment in China*, 5, 147–54, 159–61; for a more nuanced view, see Jerome Grieder, *Hu Shi and the Chinese Renaissance*, 322–48, and for the conservatism inherent in the experimental method, 118–21.

136. Shen Songqiao 沈松僑, "Yidai zongshi de suzao: Hu Shi de minchu wenhua, shehui" 一代的宗師的塑造: 胡適的民初文化、社會, in Zhou Cezong 周策縱 et al., *Hu Shi yu jindai Zhongguo* 胡適與近代中國 (Taibei: Shibao wenhua, 1991), 132.

137. As Sor-Hoon Tan remarks in "China's Pragmatist Experiment," 60.

138. Jessica Ching-Sze Wang, *John Dewey in China: To Teach and to Learn* (Albany: State University of New York Press, 2007), 31–36.

139. Sor-Hoon Tan, "China's Pragmatist Experiment," 54–55.

140. Jerome Grieder, *Hu Shi and the Chinese Renaissance*, 117.

141. Gu Hongliang 顾红亮, *Shiyong zhuyi de wudu: Duwei zhexue dui Zhongguo xiandai zhexue de yingxiang* 实用主义的误读: 杜威哲学对中国现代哲学的影响 (Guilin: Guangxi shifan daxue chubanshe, 2015), 2, 6.

Conclusion

1. "Utopophobia, we may say, is the unreasonable fear of the sin of utopianism, and it can lead to the marginalization of inquires and insights without demonstrating any defect in them." David Estlund, *Utopophobia: On the Limits (If Any) of Political Philosophy* (Princeton: Princeton University Press, 2020), 6. Estlund accepts a negative definition of "utopian" wherein "a social proposal has the vice of being utopian if, roughly, there is no evident basis for believing that efforts to achieve it would have any significant tendency to succeed" (11). But this does not condemn us only to perform nonideal or realistic theory: it

is still worthwhile to consider theories of justice, for example, that may not be realizable, or at least that this enterprise cannot be proved worthless.

2. Wang Hui, "From Empire to State: Kang Youwei, Confucian Universalism, and Unity," trans. Ban Wang, in *Chinese Visions of World Order: Tianxia, Culture, and World Politics*, ed. Ban Wang (Durham: Duke University Press, 2017), 61.

3. Emma Jinhua Teng, "Eurasian Hybridity in Chinese Utopian Visions: From 'One World' to 'A Society Based on Beauty' and Beyond," *positions* 14, no. 1 (2006): 131–63.

4. It is also possible to understand Cai as a revolutionary nationalist intrigued by anarchism who later was more comfortable promoting a kind of establishmentarian liberalism. In other words, a standard example of youthful leftism evolving in a moderate, even right-wing direction. One problem with this story line as it applies to Cai, however, is that he was not so youthful when he turned to revolution in his thirties, nor did his idealism simply disappear even as he told students to go back to class.

5. Carol Pateman, "Participatory Democracy Revisited," *Perspectives on Politics* 10, no. 1 (March 2012): 7–19. See also, inter alia: Caroline Patsias, Anne Latendresse, and Laurence Bherer, "Participatory Democracy, Decentralization and Local Governance: The Montreal Participatory Budget in the Light of 'Empowered Participatory Governance,'" *International Journal of Urban and Regional Research* 37, no. 6 (Nov. 2013): 2214–30; Yves Sintomer, "From Deliberative to Radical Democracy? Sortition and Politics in the Twenty-First Century," *Politics & Society* 46, no. 3 (2018): 337–57; and Scott David Parker, "The Truth is Revolutionary: Mills and Turner as Theoreticians of Participatory Democracy," *South African Historical Journal* 69, no. 2 (April 2017): 288–303.

6. In calling Maoism "utopian," unlike many scholars who make this judgment I am not condemning Maoism as irrational or criminally irresponsible. Of numerous studies of Maoism, highly suggestive in this regard remain Maurice J. Meisner, *Marxism, Maoism, and Utopianism: Eight Essays* (Madison: University of Wisconsin Press, 1982); and Frederic Wakeman Jr., *History and Will: Philosophical Perspectives of Mao Tse-tung's Thought* (Berkeley: University of California Press, 1973).

7. Jiwei Ci, *Dialectic of the Chinese Revolution*. I am not offering a summary of this pathbreaking work, much less exploring the relationships Ci draws among utopianism, hedonism, and nihilism.

8. Ibid., 77.

9. Ibid., 161–62.

10. Ibid., 207–208.

11. A more precise analysis might cite two moments of enthusiasm for capitalism: the late 1980s, when it was clear that the Dengist reforms were not going to be rescinded and a large segment of youth, workers, and intellectuals

joined the democracy movement, promoting both economic and political liberalism; and again in the early 1990s, in the wake of the Tiananmen Square massacre, when Deng Xiaoping doubled down on economic reforms, leading to the "get rich quick" fever. These were brief moments, however.

12. Alexander Cook, *The Cultural Revolution on Trial: Mao and the Gang of Four* (Cambridge: Cambridge University Press, 2016).

13. Chun Lin, *The Transformation of Chinese Socialism* (Durham: Duke University Press, 2006); *China and Global Capitalism 2013: Reflections on Marxism, History, and Contemporary Politics* (Basingstoke: Palgrave MacMillan, 2013). Lin eloquently argues that socialism in China might be revitalized. However, while such a future is of course possible, I doubt it is any more likely in China than elsewhere.

14. This is not to deny that Chinese capitalism since the 1980s—perhaps best termed "state capitalism"—was built on the foundations of the Maoist political and economic order. Ironically, the Maoist period was relatively successful in terms of the standards established by modernization theory: building up an infrastructure of physical projects, education, and health care; stabilizing the rural sphere; and jump-starting industrialization. However, it failed to build a socialist economy.

Nor is this to deny the possibility of a distinct "Chinese model" of development. However, it is to dismiss the hopes of socialists who, like liberal economists, doubt whether China is a capitalist society, but on the grounds that a weakened but still living strand of Maoism may shape a more socialist and democratic future. In fact, except for a somewhat larger platform, Chinese leftists are roughly in the same marginalized position as leftists in other countries.

15. Ian Johnson, *The Souls of China: The Return of Religion After Mao* (New York: Pantheon Books, 2017).

16. If utopianism is defined as a textual genre, to the best of my knowledge there were no utopias written between late Qing fiction (and of course Kang Youwei's *Datongshu*) and perhaps the emergence of science fiction at the end of the century. Again, as a study of the utopian impulse in modern political thought, though he does not use this term, Zhang Hao's "Zhuanxing shidai Zhongguo wutuobang zhuyi de xingqi" stands out.

17. That the utopian impulse informs virtually any and all thinking about the future is a notion that has been applied to Western cultures. See Ernst Bloch, *The Principle of Hope*; also Bloch, *The Spirit of Utopia*, trans. Anthony A. Nassar (Stanford: Stanford University Press, 2000).

18. Thomas A. Metzger, *A Cloud across the Pacific: Essays on the Clash between Chinese and Western Political Theories Today* (Hong Kong: Chinese University Press, 2005), esp. ch. 1.

19. Ibid., 29; see also 91–95.

20. Ibid., 383–84.

21. Jiwei Ci, *Moral China in the Age of Reform* (Cambridge: Cambridge University Press, 2015), 66–68.

22. Ibid., 73–76.

23. See also Jiwei Ci, *Moral China*, 78–79. There are two further problems with Metzger's analysis. First, from a methodological point of view, it seems useless to categorize all Chinese thinkers as utopians: the category does not lead to any analytical insight (in itself, this does not contradict Metzger's truth claims). In Metzger's case the point is to contrast modern China to the modern West, where, he says, Chinese-style utopianism did not exist. Rather, Western utopias were advocated by social critics who did not believe they were practical (but presumably thought they were simply social critiques), while Chinese utopias represented a "radical determination" that they be implemented (*Cloud across the Pacific*, 700–701). So, second, Metzger utilizes binary contrasts that are grossly reductionist. From Fourier to Marx to Bellamy and beyond, Western utopian thinkers have radically sought to implement their goals. Whereas even if many Chinese thinkers displayed a utopian impulse, utopianism was not the real key to their thought (Liang Qichao, Hu Shi, and as Metzger mentions, Yan Fu); furthermore, the greatest utopian, Kang Youwei, may or may not have believed his goals could all be implemented, but in any case he did not try to implement them.

24. According to his own account. Metzger, *Cloud across the Pacific*, xxii; and see 392.

25. Cruder versions are Jin Guantao 金觀濤, "Zhongguo wenhua de wutuobang jingshen" 中國文化的烏托邦精神, *Ershiyi shiji* no. 2 (Dec. 1990): 17–32; and Shiping Hua, *Chinese Utopianism: A Comparative Study of Reformist Thought with Japan and Russia, 1898–1997* (Stanford: Stanford University Press, 2008).

Bibliography

Adas, Michael. *Dominance by Design: Technological Imperatives and America's Civilizing Mission*. Cambridge, MA: Belknap Press, 2006.

Alexander, Thomas M. *John Dewey's Theory of Art, Experience and Nature: The Horizons of Feeling*. Albany: State University of New York Press, 1987.

————. "John Dewey's Uncommon Faith: Understanding 'Religious Experience.'" *The American Catholic Philosophical Quarterly* 87, no. 2 (2013): 347–62.

Andolfatto, Lorenzo. *Hundred Days' Literature: Chinese Utopian Fiction at the End of Empire, 1902–1910*. Leiden: Brill, 2019.

Angle, Stephen C. *Human Rights and Chinese Thought: A Cross Cultural Inquiry*. Cambridge: Cambridge University Press, 2002.

Appiah, Kwame Anthony. "Cosmopolitan Patriots." *Critical Inquiry* 23, no. 3 (April 1997): 617–39.

Babbage, Charles. *On the Economy of Machinery and Manufacturers*. London: Charles Knight, 1832.

Bauer, Wolfgang. *China and the Search for Happiness: Recurring Themes in Four Thousand Years of Cultural History*. Translated by Michael Shaw. New York: Seabury Press, 1976.

Bellamy, Edward. *Huitoukan jilue* 回頭看紀略. Translated by Timothy Richard. *Wanguo gongbao* 萬國公報. 1891–92.

————. *Looking Backward 2000–1887*. New York: Grosset and Dunlap, 1898.

Benton, Gregor. *China's Urban Revolutionaries: Explorations in the History of Chinese Trotskyism, 1921–1952*. Atlantic Highlands, NJ: Humanities Press International, 1996.

Berlin, Isaiah. *Four Essays on Liberty*. Oxford: Oxford University Press, 1969.

Bernstein, Richard J. "Dewey's Vision of Radical Democracy." In *The Cambridge Companion to Dewey*, edited by Molly Cochran, 288–308. Cambridge: Cambridge University Press, 2010.

Bloch, Ernst. *The Principle of Hope*. Translated by Neville Plaice, Stephen Plaice, and Paul Knight. Cambridge: MIT Press, 1986.

————. *The Spirit of Utopia*. Translated by Anthony A. Nassar. Stanford: Stanford University Press, 2000.

Bonner, Joey. *Wang Kuo-wei: An Intellectual Biography*. Cambridge: Harvard University Press, 1986.

Boos, Stephen. "Rethinking the Aesthetic: Kant, Schiller, and Hegel." In *Between Ethics and Aesthetics: Crossing the Boundaries*, edited by Dorota Glowacka and Stephen Boos, 15–27. Albany: State University of New York Press, 2002.

Bowman, Sylvia E. et al. *Edward Bellamy Abroad: An American Prophet's Influence*. New York: Twayne, 1962.

Brooks, Linda M. *The Menace of the Sublime to the Individual Self: Kant, Schiller, Coleridge, and the Disintegration of Romantic Identity*. Lewiston, NY: Edwin Mellen Press, 1995.

Brusadelli, Federico. "Transforming Benevolence: Classicism, Buddhism and Politics in Kang Youwei's Lecture on 'Ren' 講仁字 (1897)." *Archiv orientální* no. 85 (2017): 99–117.

Buber, Martin. *Paths in Utopia*. Translated by R. F. C. Hull. London: Routledge and Kegan Paul, 1949.

Cai Jianguo 蔡建国. *Cai Yuanpei yu jindai Zhongguo* 蔡元培与近代中国. Shanghai: Shanghai shehui kexue chubanshe, 1997.

Cai, Yuanpei 蔡元培. "Replacing Religion with Aesthetic Education." Translated by Julia F. Andrews. In *Modern Chinese Literary Thought: Writings on Literature, 1893–1945*, edited by Kirk A. Denton, 182–89. Stanford: Stanford University Press, 1996.

———. *Cai Yuanpei wenji* 蔡元培文集. Edited by Gao Pingshu 高平叔. Taibei: Jinxiu chuban, 1995.

———. *Cai Yuanpei xiansheng yiwen leichao* 先生遺文類鈔. Edited by Sun Dezhong 孫德中. Taibei: Fuxing shuju, 1966.

Chang, Hao [Zhang Hao]. *Chinese Intellectuals in Crisis: Search for Order and Meaning, 1890–1911*. Berkeley: University of California Press, 1987.

———. *Liang Ch'i-ch'ao and Intellectual Transition in China, 1890–1907*. Cambridge: Harvard University Press, 1971.

Chen Duxiu 陳獨秀. *Chen Duxiu wannian zhuzuoxuan* 陳獨秀晚年著作選. Edited by Lin Zhiliang 林致良, Wu Mengming 吳孟明, and Zhou Lüqiang 周履鏘. Hong Kong: Tiandi tushu youxian gongsi, 2012.

———. *Duxiu wencun* 獨秀文存. Shanghai: Yadong tushuguan, 1927.

———. "Makesi xueshuo" 馬克思學說. *Xin qingnian* 9, no. 3 (July 1921): n.p.

———. "Shehuizhuyi piping" 社會主義批評. *Xin qingnian* 9, no. 3 (July 1921): 1–13.

———. "Shian zizhuan" 實庵自傳. In *Chen Duxiu zhuzuo xuan* 陳獨秀著作選, edited by Ren Jianshu 任建樹, Zhang Tongmo 張統模, and Wu Xinzhong 吳信忠, vol. 3, 413–26. Shanghai: Shanghai renmin chubanshe 1993.

———. "Suiganlu (101): Minzhudang yu gongchandang" 隨感錄: (101) 民主黨與共產黨. *Xin qingnian* 8, no. 4 (December 1920): n.p.

———. "Wuchanjieji zhuanzheng" 無產階級專政. *Xin qingnian* 9, no. 3 (July 1921): n.p.

Chen, Anna Gustafsson "Dreams of the Future: Communal Experiments in May Fourth China." PhD dissertation, Lund University, 1998.

Chen, Pingyuan. *Touches of History: An Enquiry into 'May Fourth' China*. Translated by Michel Hockx et al. Leiden: Brill, 2011.

Cheng, Anne. "Nationalism, Citizenship, and the Old Text/New Text Controversy in Late Nineteenth Century China." In *Imagining the People: Chinese Intellectuals and the Concept of Citizenship, 1890–1920*, edited by Joshua A. Fogel and Peter G. Zarrow, 61–81. Armonk, NY: M. E. Sharpe, 1997.

Cheng Tingting 程婷婷 and Gao Wenqiang 高文强. "'Yi meiyu dai zhongjiao shuo' yanjiu shuping" "以美育代宗教说"研究述评, *Zhongguo meixue yanjiu* no. 6 (February 2015): 182–93.

Chiang, Yung-chen. "Appropriating Dewey: Hu Shi and His Translation of Dewey's 'Social and Political Philosophy' Lecture Series in China." *European Journal of Pragmatism and American Philosophy* 7, no. 2 (2015): 71–97.

Ching, Julia, and Willard G. Oxtoby, eds, *Discovering China: European Interpretations in the Enlightenment*. Rochester: University of Rochester Press, 1992.

Chow, Tse-tsung. *The May Fourth Movement: Intellectual Revolution in Modern China*. Stanford: Stanford University Press 1967.

Ci, Jiwei. *Dialectic of the Chinese Revolution: From Utopianism to Hedonism*. Stanford: Stanford University Press, 1994.

———. *Moral China in the Age of Reform*. Cambridge: Cambridge University Press, 2015.

Ciaudo, Joseph. "Replacer Chen Duxiu dans son vocabulaire: La Nouvelle Jeunesse et le problème de la culture chinoise." *Oriens Extremus* no. 54 (2015): 23–57.

Claeys, Gregory. "The Origins of Dystopia: Wells, Huxley and Orwell." In *The Cambridge Companion to Utopian Literature*, edited by Gregory Claeys, 107–32. Cambridge: Cambridge University Press, 2010.

Clinton, Maggie. *Revolutionary Nativism: Fascism and Culture in China, 1925–1937*. Durham: Duke University Press, 2017.

Cohen, Ted. "Why Beauty Is a Symbol of Morality." In *Essays in Kant's Aesthetics*, edited by Ted Cohen and Paul Guyer, 221–36. Chicago: University of Chicago Press, 1982.

Cook, Alexander. *The Cultural Revolution on Trial: Mao and the Gang of Four*. Cambridge: Cambridge University Press, 2016.

Cooper, Davina. *Everyday Utopias: The Conceptual Life of Promising Spaces*. Durham: Duke University Press, 2014.

Crowther, Paul. *The Kantian Sublime: From Morality to Art*. Oxford: Oxford University Press, 1989.

Dewey, John [Duwei]. *Democracy and Education: An Introduction to the Philosophy of Education*. New York: MacMillan, 1916.

———. *The Early Works, 1882–1898.* Edited by Jo Ann Boydston. Carbondale: Southern Illinois University Press, 1969.

———. *The Later Works, 1925–1953.* Edited by Jo Ann Boydston. Carbondale: Southern Illinois University Press, 1986.

———. *Lectures in China, 1919–1920.* Edited and translated by Robert W. Clopton and Tsuin-chen Ou. Honolulu: East-West Center, University Press of Hawaii, 1973.

———. *The Middle Works, 1899–1924.* Edited by Jo Ann Boydston. Carbondale: Southern Illinois University Press, 1982.

Dirlik, Arif. *Anarchism and the Chinese Revolution.* Berkeley: University of California Press, 1991.

———. *The Origins of Chinese Communism.* New York: Oxford University Press, 1989.

Donskis, Leonidas. "The End of Utopia?" *Soundings: An Interdisciplinary Journal* 79, no. 1/2 (Spring/Summer 1996): 197–219.

Du, Wei. "Aesthetic Utilitarianism: Heritage of Modern Chinese Aesthetics." *Neohelicon* 43, no. 2 (December 2016): 529–42.

Duwei 杜威 [John Dewey]. *Duwei wu da jiangyan* 杜威五大講演. Beijing: Chenbaoshe, 1920.

———. "Meiguo zhi minzhi de fazhan" 美國之民治的發展, *Meizhou pinglun* 每週評論 no. 26 (15 June 1919): 1–5.

Duiker, William J. "The Aesthetics Philosophy of Ts'ai Yuan-p'ei." *Philosophy East and West* 22, no. 4 (October 1972): 385–401.

———. *Ts'ai Yuan-p'ei: Educator of Modern China.* University Park: Pennsylvania State University Press, 1977.

Dutton, Jacquelin. "'Non-Western' Utopian Traditions." In *The Cambridge Companion to Utopian Literature*, edited by Gregory Claeys, 223–58. Cambridge: Cambridge University Press, 2010.

Eagleton, Terry. *The Ideology of the Aesthetic.* Oxford: Basil Blackwell, 1990.

Elman, Benjamin A. *Classicism, Politics, and Kingship: The Chang-chou School of New Text Confucianism in Late Imperial China.* Berkeley: University of California Press, 1990.

———, and Martin Kern, eds., *Statecraft and Classical Learning: The Rituals of Zhou in East Asian History.* Leiden: Brill, 2009.

Erjavec, Aleš, ed., *Aesthetic Revolutions and Twentieth-Century Avant-Garde Movements.* Durham: Duke University Press, 2015.

Estlund, David. *Utopophobia: On the Limits (If Any) of Political Philosophy.* Princeton: Princeton University Press, 2020.

Feigon, Lee. *Chen Duxiu: Founder of the Chinese Communist Party.* Princeton: Princeton University Press, 1983.

Feng Chongyi 馮崇義, *Zhonggong dangnei de ziyou zhuyi: cong Chen Duxiu dao Li Shenzhi* 中共黨內的自由主義——從陳獨秀到李慎之. Carle Place, NY: Mingjing chubanshe, 2009.

Fitzgerald, John. *Awakening China: Politics, Culture, and Class in the Nationalist Revolution*. Stanford: Stanford University Press, 1996.

Fokkema, Douwe. *Perfect Worlds: Utopian Fiction in the China and the West*. Amsterdam: Amsterdam University Press, 2011.

Fröhlich, Thomas. "The Concept of Politics in the May Fourth Era: Hu Shi, Chen Duxiu, and Their Struggle with 'Politics.'" *Sixiangshi* 思想史 no. 9 (December 2019): 365–415.

Gan Chunsong 干春松. *Baojiao liguo: Kang Youwei de xiandai fanglue* 保教立国: 康有为的现代方略. Beijing: Sanlian, 2015.

———. *Kang Youwei yu Ruxue de "xinshi": cong Ruxue fenqi kan Ruxue de weilai fazhan lujing* 康有为与儒学的"新世": 从儒学分期看儒学的未来发展路径. Shanghai: Huadong daxue chubanshe, 2015.

Geoghegan, Vincent. *Utopianism and Marxism*. London: Methuen, 1987.

Ginsborg, Hannah. "Kant's Aesthetics and Teleology." In *The Stanford Encyclopedia of Philosophy* (Fall 2014), edited by Edward N. Zalta. http://plato.stanford.edu/archives/fall2014/entries/kant-aesthetics/.

Gluck, Carol, and Anna Lowenhaupt Tsing, eds. *Words in Motion: Toward a Global Lexicon*. Durham: Duke University Press, 2009.

Goto-Jones, C. S. "Transcending Boundaries: Nishida Kitarō and K'ang Yu-Wei, and the Politics of Unity." *Modern Asian Studies* 39, no. 4 (October 2005): 793–816.

Grange, Joseph. *John Dewey, Confucius, and Global Philosophy*. Albany: State University of New York Press, 2004.

Grieder, Jerome B. *Hu Shih and the Chinese Renaissance: Liberalism in the Chinese Revolution, 1917–1937*. Cambridge: Harvard University Press, 1970.

Gu Hongliang 顾红亮. *Duwei zai-Hua xuepu* 杜威在华学谱. Shanghai: Huadong shifan daxue chubanshe, 2019.

———. *Shiyong zhuyi de wudu: Duwei zhexue dui Zhongguo xiandai zhexue de yingxiang* 实用主义的误读: 杜威哲学对中国现代哲学的影响. Guilin: Guangxi shifan daxue chubanshe, 2015.

Gu, Edward X. "Who Was Mr Democracy? The May Fourth Discourse of Populist Democracy and the Radicalization of Chinese Intellectuals. 1915–1922." *Modern Asian Studies* 35, no. 3 (July 2001): 589–621.

Guyer, Paul. *Kant and the Claims of Taste*. Cambridge: Harvard University Press, 1979.

———. "Kant's Ambitions in the *Third Critique*." In *The Cambridge Companion to Kant and Modern Philosophy*, edited by Paul Guyer, 538–87. Cambridge: Cambridge University Press, 2006.

Han Chenghua 韓承樺. "Sibinsai dao Zhongguo—yige fanyishi de taolun" 斯賓塞到中國——一個翻譯史的討論, *Bianyi luncong* 編譯論叢 3, no. 2 (September 2010): 33–60.

Hansen, David T., ed. *John Dewey and Our Educational Prospect: A Critical Engagement with Dewey's Democracy and Education*. Albany: State University of New York Press, 2006.

Henrich, Dieter. "Beauty and Freedom: Schiller's Struggle with Kant's Aesthetics." In *Essays in Kant's Aesthetics*, edited by Ted Cohen and Paul Guyer, 237–57. Chicago: University of Chicago Press, 1982.

Hildebrand, David. "Dewey's Pragmatism: Instrumentalism and Meliorism." In *The Cambridge Companion to Pragmatism*, edited by Alan Malachowski, 55–80. Cambridge: Cambridge University Press, 2013.

Hollinger, David. "The Problem of Pragmatism in American History." *Journal of American History* 67, no. 1 (June 1980): 88–107.

Howard, Richard C. "K'ang Yu-wei (1858–1927): His Intellectual Background and Early Thought." In *Confucian Personalities*, edited by Arthur F. Wright and Denis Twitchett, 294–16. Stanford: Stanford University Press, 1962.

Hsiao, Kung-chuan. *A Modern China and a New World: K'ang Yu-wei, Reformer and Utopian, 1858–1927*. Seattle: University of Washington Press, 1975.

Hsuan Hua. *The Vajra Prajna Paramita Sutra*. Burlingame, CA: Dharma Realm Buddhist University, 2002.

Hu Ming 胡明. *Zhengwu jiaozhi Chen Duxiu: sixiang de quanshi yu wenhua de pipan* 正误交织陈独秀——思想的诠释与文化的批判. Beijing: Renmin wenxue chubanshe, 2004.

Hu Shi 胡適. *Hu Shi quanji* 胡適全集. Edited by Ji Xianlin 季羨林. Hefei: Anhui jiaoyu chubanshe, 2003.

Hu, Shih [Hu Shi]. "The Civilizations of the East and the West." In *Whither Mankind: A Panorama of Modern Civilization*, edited by Charles A. Beard, 25–41. New York: Longmans, Green, 1928.

Hua, Shiping. *Chinese Utopianism: A Comparative Study of Reformist Thought with Japan and Russia, 1898–1997*. Washington, DC: Woodrow Wilson Center Press, 2009.

Huters, Theodore. *Bringing the World Home: Appropriating the West in Late Qing and Early Republican China*. Honolulu: University of Hawai'i Press, 2005.

Ip, Hung-Yok. *Intellectuals in Revolutionary China, 1921–1949: Leaders, Heroes, and Sophisticates*. London: RoutledgeCurzon, 2005.

———. "The Origins of Chinese Communism: A New Interpretation." *Modern China* 20, no. 1 (January 1994): 34–63.

Isaacs, Harold R. *The Tragedy of the Chinese Revolution*. New York: Atheneum, 1966.

Ishikawa Yoshihiro. *The Formation of the Chinese Communist Party*. Translated by Joshua A. Fogel. New York: Columbia University Press, 2013.

Jackisch, Barry A. "The Nature of Berlin: Green Space and Visions of a New German Capital, 1900–45." *Central European History* 47, no. 2 (June 2014): 307–33.

Jacoby, Russell. *Picture Imperfect: Utopian Thought for an Anti-Utopian Age*. New York: Columbia University Press, 2005.

Jameson, Frederic, *Archaeologies of the Future: The Desire Called Utopia and Other Science Fictions*. London: Verso, 2005.

Jenco, Leigh. "Culture as History: Envisioning Change Across and Beyond 'Eastern' and 'Western' Civilizations in the May Fourth Era." *Twentieth-Century China* 38, no. 1 (January 2013): 34–52.

———. "Histories of Thought and Comparative Political Theory: The Curious Thesis of 'Chinese Origins for Western Knowledge,' 1860–1895." *Political Theory* 42, no. 6 (December 2014): 658–81.

———. *Making the Political: Founding and Action in the Political Theory of Zhang Shizhao*. Cambridge: Cambridge University Press, 2010.

Jin Guantao 金觀濤. "Zhongguo wenhua de wutuobang jingshen" 中國文化的烏托邦精神. *Ershiyi shiji* no. 2 (December 1990): 17–32.

Jin Huanling 金焕玲. *Chen Duxiu: lunli sixiang yanjiu* 陈独秀: 伦理思想研究. Beijing: Zhongguo shehui chubanshe, 2009.

Joeres, Ruth-Ellen Boetcher. "The German Enlightenment (1720–1790)." In *The Cambridge History of German Literature*, edited by Helen Watanabe-O'Kelly, 147–201. Cambridge: Cambridge University Press, 1997.

Johnson, Ian. *The Souls of China: The Return of Religion after Mao*. New York: Pantheon Books, 2017.

Kang Youwei 康有為. *Datongshu* 大同書. Taibei: Longtian, 1979.

———. *Kang Nanhai ziding nianpu* 康南海自訂年譜. Taibei: Wenhai, 1972.

———. *Kang Youwei quanji* 康有為全集. Shanghai: Shanghai guji chubanshe, 1987.

———. *Ta T'ung Shu: The One-World Philosophy of K'ang Yu-Wei*. Translated and edited by Laurence G. Thompson. London: George Allen and Unwin, 1958.

Kant, Immanuel. *The Educational Theory of Immanual Kant*. Translated and edited by Edward Franklin Buchner. Philadelphia; J. B. Lippincott, 1904.

———. *Kant's Critique of Judgement* Translated by J. H. Bernard. London: Macmillan, 1931.

Keenan, Barry. *The Dewey Experiment in China: Educational Reform and Political Power in the Early Republic*. Cambridge: CEAS, Harvard University Press, 1977.

Kim, Sooyoung. "Individualism and Nationalism in the Thought of Chen Duxiu, 1904–1919." In *Radicalism, Revolution, and Reform in Modern China: Essays in Honor of Maurice Meisner*, edited by Catherine Lynch, Robert B. Marks, and Paul G. Pickowicz, 11–28. Lanham, MD: Lexington Books, 2011.

Ko, Dorothy. "Bodies in Utopia and Utopian Bodies in Imperial China." In *Thinking Utopia: Steps into Other Worlds*, edited by Jörn Rüsen, Michael Fehr, and Thomas W. Rieger, 89–103. New York: Berghahn Books, 2005.

Köhnke, Klaus Christian. *The Rise of Neo-Kantianism: German Academic Philosophy between Idealism and Positivism*. Translated by R. J. Hollingdale. Cambridge: Cambridge University Press, 1991.

Kooy, Michael John. *Coleridge, Schiller, and Aesthetic Education*. Houndmills: Palgrave, 2002.

Koselleck, Reinhart. *Disseminating German Tradition: The Thyssen Lectures*. Edited by Dan Diner and Moshe Zimmermann. Leipzig: Lepziger Universität, 2009.

———. *The Practice of Conceptual History: Timing History, Spacing Concepts.* Translated by Todd Presener et al. Stanford: Stanford University Press, 2002.

Kuhfus, Peter. "Chen Duxiu and Leon Trotsky: New Light on Their Relationship." *China Quarterly* no. 102 (June 1985): 253–76.

Külpe, Oswald. *Introduction to Philosophy.* Translated by W. B. Pillsbury and E. B. Titchener. London: Swan Sonnenschein, 1897.

Kumar, Krishan. "The Ends of Utopia." *New Literary History* 41, no. 3 (Summer 2010): 549–69.

———. *Utopia and Anti-Utopia in Modern Times.* Oxford: Basil Blackwell, 1987.

———. *Utopianism.* Minneapolis: University of Minnesota Press, 1991.

Kuo, Ya-pei. "The Making of the New Culture Movement: A Discursive History." *Twentieth-Century China* 42, no. 1 (2017): 52–71.

Kurtz, Joachim. " 'Cosmopolitanism in Late Qing China: Local Refractions of a Global Concept." In *Reading the Signs: Philology, History, Prognostication: Festschrift for Michael Lackner,* edited by Iwo Amelung and Joachim Kurtz, 367–88. München: Iudicium, 2018.

———. *The Discovery of Chinese Logic.* Leiden: Brill, 2011.

———. "Domesticating a Philosophical Fiction: Chinese Translations of Immanuel Kant's 'Things in Themselves.' " *Concept and Communication* 7 (2011): 165–200.

Kwok, D. W. Y. *Scientism in Chinese Thought, 1900–1950.* New Haven: Yale University Press, 1965.

Legge, James, trans. *The Four Books.* Taipei: Culture Book Co., 1981.

Lenin, V. I. *The State and Revolution.* Peking: Foreign Languages Press, 1973.

Levitas, Ruth. *The Concept of Utopia.* Oxford: Peter Lang, 2010.

———. *Utopia as Method: The Imaginary Reconstruction of Society.* London: Palgrave Macmillan, 2013.

Li, Guangyi. " 'New Year's Dream': A Chinese Anarcho-cosmopolitan Utopia." *Utopian Studies* 24, no. 1 (April 2013): 89–104.

Li, San-pao. "K'ang Yu-wei's *Shih-li kung-fa ch'üan-shu.*" *Zhongyang yanjiuyuan jindaishi yanjiusuo jikan* no. 7 (June 1978): 683–725.

Li Shuqiao 李書巧. *Lixiang zhixu de tanqiu: jindai Zhongguo wutuobang sixiang yanjiu* 理想秩序的探求: 近代中國烏托邦思想研究. Xinbeishi, Taiwan: Hua Mulan wenhua chubanshe, 2013.

Li, Zehou. *The Chinese Aesthetic Tradition.* Translated by Maija Bell Samei. Honolulu: University of Hawaii Press, 2009.

Li Zehou 李泽厚. *Zhongguo jindai sixiang shilun* 中国近代思想史论. Beijing: Renmin, 1986.

Li Zongze 李宗澤. "Cai Yuanpei sixiang zhong de Deguo ziyuan" 蔡元培思想中的德國資源. In *Jindai dong-xi sixiang jiaoliu zhong de chuanbozhe* 近代東西思想交流中的傳播者, edited by Yang Zhende 楊貞德, 199–229. Taibei: Zhongyang yanjiuyuan, Zhongguo wenzhe yanjiusuo, 2017.

Lin, Chun. *China and Global Capitalism 2013: Reflections on Marxism, History, and Contemporary Politics*. Basingstoke: Palgrave MacMillan, 2013.

———. *The Transformation of Chinese Socialism*. Durham: Duke University Press, 2006.

Lin, Yü-sheng. *The Crisis of Chinese Consciousness: Radical Antitraditionalism in the May Fourth Era*. Madison: University of Wisconsin Press, 1979.

Lin Yüsheng 林毓生. "Ershi shiji Zhongguo de fanchuantong sichao yu Zhongshi malie zhuyi ji Mao Zedong de wutuobang zhuyi" 二十世紀中國的反傳統思潮與中式馬列主義及毛澤東的烏托邦主義. *Xin shixue* 新史學 6, no. 3 (September 1995): 95–154.

Liu, Kang. *Aesthetics and Marxism: Chinese Aesthetic Marxists and Their Western Contemporaries*. Durham: Duke University Press, 2000.

Liu Shipei 劉師培. "Renlei junli shuo" 人類均力說. *Tianyi bao* 天義報 no. 3 (July 1907): 24–36.

Lo, Jung-pang, ed. *K'ang Yu-wei: A Biography and a Symposium*. Tucson: University of Arizona Press, 1967.

Lu Shanqing 卢善庆. *Zhongguo jindai meixue sixiangshi* 中国近代美学思想史. Shanghai: Huadong shifan daxue chubanshe, 1991.

Luo Zhitian 羅志田. "Lixiang yu xianshi: Qingji minchu shijie zhuyi yu minzu zhuyi de guanlian hudong" 理想與現世——清季民初世界主義與民族主義的關聯互動. In Wang Fansen et al. 王汎森 等, *Zhongguo jindai sixiang de zhuanxing shidai: Zhang Hao yuanshi qizhi zhushou lunwenji* 中國近代思想史的轉型時代: 張灝院士七秩祝壽論文集. Taipei: Lianjing Press, 2007, 271–314.

Lyons, Sara. "The Disenchantment/Re-Enchantment of the World: Aesthetics, Secularization, and the Gods of Greece from Friedrich Schiller to Water Pater." *The Modern Language Review* 109, no. 4 (October 2014): 873–95.

Manicas, Peter T. "Pragmatic Philosophy of Science and the Charge of Scientism." *Transactions of the Charles S. Peirce Society* 24, no. 2 (Spring 1988): 179–222.

Mannheim, Karl. *Ideology and Utopia*. Translated by Louis Wirth and Edward Shils. New York: Harcourt, Brace and World, 1936.

Manuel, Frank, and Fritzie Manuel. *Utopian Thought in the Western World*. Cambridge: Harvard University Press, 1979.

Meisner, Maurice J. *Marxism, Maoism, and Utopianism: Eight Essays*. Madison: University of Wisconsin Press, 1982.

Mengzi 孟子. *Mencius*. Translated by W. A. C. H. Dobson. Toronto: University of Toronto Press, 1969.

Metzger, Thomas A. *A Cloud across the Pacific: Essays on the Clash between Chinese and Western Political Theories Today*. Hong Kong: Chinese University Press, 2005.

Moggach, Douglas. "Aesthetics and Politics." In *The Cambridge History of Nineteenth-Century Political Thought*, edited by Gareth Stedman Jones and Gregory Claeys, 479–520. Cambridge: Cambridge University Press, 2011.

Moyn, Samuel, and Andrew Sartori, eds. *Global Intellectual History*. New York: Columbia University Press, 2015.

Muller, A. Charles, comp. and trans. *The Sutra of Perfect Enlightenment: Korean Buddhism's Guide to Meditation*. Albany: State University of New York Press, 1999.

Mungello, David E. *Leibniz and Confucianism: The Search for Accord*. Honolulu: University of Hawaii Press, 1977.

Ng, K. K. "Ending as Beginning: Chinese Translations of Edward Bellamy's Utopian Novel *Looking Backward*. *Frontiers of Literary Studies in China* 10, no. 1 (June 2016): 9–35.

Nylan, Michael. *The Five "Confucian" Classics*. New Haven: Yale University Press, 2014.

Ouyang Zhesheng 歐陽哲生. *Tanxun Hu Shi de jingshen shijie* 探尋胡適的精神世界. Taibei: Xiuwei zixun keji gongsi, 2011.

Pan Guangzhe 潘光哲. "Qingnian Hu Shi de 'minzhu jingyan'" 青年胡適的「民主經驗」. In *Pupian yu teshu de bianzheng: zhengzhi sixiang de tanjue* 普遍與特殊的辯證: 政治思想的探掘, edited by Qian Yongxiang 錢永祥, 151–94. Taibei: Zhongyang yanjiuyuan renwen shehui kexue yanjiu zhongxin, 2012.

Parker, Scott David. "The Truth Is Revolutionary: Mills and Turner as Theoreticians of Participatory Democracy." *South African Historical Journal* 69, no. 2 (April 2017): 288–303.

Pateman, Carol. "Participatory Democracy Revisited." *Perspectives on Politics* 10, no. 1 (March 2012): 7–19.

Patsias, Caroline, Anne Latendresse, and Laurence Bherer. "Participatory Democracy, Decentralization and Local Governance: The Montreal Participatory Budget in the Light of 'Empowered Participatory Governance.'" *International Journal of Urban and Regional Research* 37, no. 6 (November 2013): 2214–30.

Paulsen, Friedrich. *A System of Ethics*. Edited and translated by Frank Thilly. New York: Charles Scribner's Sons, 1899.

Price, Don C. *Russia and the Roots of the Chinese Revolution, 1896–1911*. Cambridge: Harvard University Press, 1974.

Qian Mu 錢穆. *Zhongguo jinsanbainian xueshushi* 中國近三百年學術史. Shanghai: Shangwu, 1937.

Qian Zhixiu 錢智修. "Xianjin liang da zhexuejia xueshuo gailun" 現今兩大哲學家學說概論. *Dongfang zazhi* 10, no. 1 (1913).

Rahav, Shakhar. "How Shall We Live? Chinese Communal Experiments after the Great War in Global Context." *Journal of World History* 27, no. 3 (September 2016): 521–48.

———. *The Rise of Political Intellectuals in Modern China: May Fourth Societies and the Roots of Mass Politics*. Oxford, Oxford University Press, 2015.

———. "Scale of Change: The Small Group in Chinese Politics, 1919–1921." *Asian Studies Review* 43, no. 4 (2019): 674–90.

Ricoeur, Paul. *Lectures on Ideology and Utopia*. New York: Columbia University Press, 1986.

Rubinson, Claude James. "The Production of Style: Aesthetic and Ideological Diversity in the Arts and Crafts Movement, 1875–1914." PhD dissertation, University of Arizona, 2010.

Ryan, Alan. *John Dewey and the High Tide of American Liberalism*. New York: W. W. Norton, 1995.

Sargent, Lyman Tower. "A Note on the Other Side of Human Nature in the Utopian Novel." *Political Theory* 3, no. 1 (February 1975): 88–97.

———. "The Three Faces of Utopianism Revisited." *Utopian Studies* 5, no. 1 (January 1994): 1–37.

Schaper, Eva. "Taste, Sublimity, and Genius: The Aesthetics of Nature and Art." In *The Cambridge Companion to Kant*, edited by Paul Guyer, 367–93. Cambridge: Cambridge University Press, 1992.

Schiller, F. C. S. *Studies in Humanism*. London: MacMillan, 1907.

Schiller, Friedrich. "Letters on the Aesthetical Education of Man." In *The Aesthetical Essays*. Project Gutenberg EBook: George Bell and Sons, 1879.

Schneider, Axel. "Nation, History and Ethics: The Choices of Post-Imperial Chinese Historiography." In *Transforming History: The Making of a Modern Academic Discipline in Twentieth-Century China*, edited by Brian Moloughney and Peter Zarrow, 271–302. Hong Kong: Chinese University Press, 2012.

Schulte, Barbara. "The Chinese Dewey: Friend, Fiend, and Flagship." In *The Global Reception of John Dewey's Thought: Multiple Refractions Through Time and Space*, edited by Rosa Bruno-Jofré and Jürgen Schriewer, 83–115. New York: Routledge, 2012.

Schwartz, Benjamin I. *Chinese Communism and the Rise of Mao*. Cambridge: Harvard University Press, 1951.

———. *In Search of Wealth and Power: Yen Fu and the West*. Cambridge: Belknap Press, Harvard University Press, 1964.

Shen Songqiao 沈松僑. "Yidai zongshi de suzao: Hu Shi de minchu wenhua, shehui" 一代的宗師的塑造: 胡適的民初文化、社會. In Zhou Cezong 周策縱 et al., *Hu Shi yu jindai Zhongguo* 胡適與近代中國. Taibei: Shibao wenhua, 1991, 131–86.

Sintomer, Yves. "From Deliberative to Radical Democracy? Sortition and Politics in the Twenty-First Century." *Politics & Society* 46, no. 3 (2018): 337–57.

Snow, Edgar. *Red Star over China*. New York: Grove Press, 1961.

Song Rongpei 松榮培. "Kang Youwei 'ren' de zhexue yu datong wutuobang" 康有為「仁」的哲學與大同烏托邦 *Ehu yuekan* 鵝湖月刊 38, no. 1 (July 2012): 13–21.

Song, Mingwei. *Young China: National Rejuvenation and the Bildungsroman, 1900–1959*. Cambridge: HUAC, Harvard University Press, 2015.

Spencer, Herbert. *Essays: Scientific, Political, and Speculative*. New York: D. Appleton, 1916.

Stuhr, John J. "Old Ideas Crumble: War, Pragmatist Intellectuals, and the Limits of Philosophy." In *The Challenge of Pragmatism and the Limits of Philosophy*, edited by Richard Shusterman, 80–95. Malden, MA: Blackwell, 2004.

Tan, Sor-hoon. "China's Pragmatist Experiment in Democracy: Hu Shih's Pragmatism and Dewey's Influence in China." In *The Challenge of Pragmatism and the Limits of Philosophy* edited by Richard Shusterman, 43–62. Malden, MA: Blackwell, 2004.

———. "How Can a Chinese Democracy be Pragmatic?" *Transactions of the Charles S. Peirce Society* 47, no. 2 (2011): 196–225.

Tan Sitong. *An Exposition of Benevolence: The Jen-hsüeh of T'an Ssu-t'ung*. Edited and translated by Sin-wai Chan. Hong Kong: The Chinese University Press, 1984.

Tang, Xiaobing *Chinese Modern: The Heroic and the Quotidian*. Durham: Duke University Press, 2000.

Tang Zhijun 汤志钧. *Kang Youwei yu wuxu bianfa* 康有为与戊戌变法. Beijing: Zhonghua shuju, 1984.

Teng, Emma Jinhua. "Eurasian Hybridity in Chinese Utopian Visions: From 'One World' to 'A Society Based on Beauty' and Beyond." *positions* 14, no. 1 (Spring 2006): 131–63.

Trotsky, Leon. *Leon Trotsky on China*. Edited by Les Evans and Russell Block. New York: Monad Press, 1976.

———. *The Permanent Revolution and Results and Prospects*. New York: Merit Publishers, 1969.

———. *Problems of the Chinese Revolution*. Translated by Max Shachtman. Ann Arbor: University of Michigan Press, 1967.

Tsui, Brian *China's Conservative Revolution: The Quest for a New Order, 1927–1949*. Cambridge: Cambridge University Press, 2018.

Wagner, Rudolf G. "A Classic Paving the Way to Modernity: The *Ritual of Zhou* in the Chinese Reform Debate Since the Taiping Civil War." In *Modernity's Classics*, edited by Sarah C. Humphreys and Rudolf G. Wagner, 77–99. Berlin: Springer-Verlag, 2013.

———. "The Free Flow of Communication between High and Low: The *Shenbao* as Platform for Yangwu Discussions on Political Reform 1872–1895." *T'oung Pao* 104, no. 1–3 (2018): 116–88.

———. "The *Zhouli* as the Late Qing Path to the Future." In *Statecraft and Classical Learning: The Rituals of Zhou in East Asian History*, edited by Benjamin A. Elman and Martin Kern, 359–87. Leiden: Brill, 2010.

Wakeman, Frederic Jr. *History and Will: Philosophical Perspectives of Mao Tse-tung's Thought*. Berkeley: University of California Press, 1973.

Waks, Leonard J., and Andrea R. English, eds. *John Dewey's Democracy and Education: A Centennial Handbook.* Cambridge: Cambridge University Press, 2017.

Waley, Arthur, trans. *The Analects of Confucius.* New York: Vintage Books, 1938.

Wang, Ban. "The Moral Vision in Kang Youwei's *Book of the Great Community.* In *Chinese Visions of World Order: Tianxia, Culture, and World Politics,* edited by Ban Wang, 87–105. Durham: Duke University Press, 2017.

Wang, Chaohua. "Cai Yuanpei and the Origins of the May Fourth Movement: Modern Chinese Intellectual Transformations, 1890–1920." PhD dissertation, University of California-Los Angeles, 2008.

Wang, David Der-wei. *Fin-de-siècle Splendor: Repressed Modernities of Late Qing Fiction, 1849–1911.* Stanford: Stanford University Press, 1977.

———. "Panglossian Dream and Dark Consciousness: Modern Chinese Literature and Utopia." In *Utopia and Utopianism in the Contemporary Chinese Context.* Hong Kong: Hong Kong University Press.

"Utopian Dream and Dark Consciousness: Chinese Literature at the Millennial Turn." *Prism* 16, no. 1 (2019): 136–56.

Wang, Fan-hsi, *Chinese Revolutionary: Memoirs 1919–1949.* Translated and edited by Gregor Benton. Oxford: Oxford University Press, 1980.

Wang Fansen 王汎森. *Gushibian yundong de xingqi* 古史辨運動的興起. Taibei: Yunchen wenhua gongsi, 1987.

Wang Hui 汪晖. *Xiandai Zhongguo de sixiang de xingqi* 现代中国思想的兴起. Beijing: Sanlian, 2015.

———. "From Empire to State: Kang Youwei, Confucian Universalism, and Unity." Translated by Ban Wang. In *Chinese Visions of World Order: Tianxia, Culture, and World Politics,* edited by Ban Wang, 49–64. Durham: Duke University Press, 2017.

Wang, Jessica Ching-Sze. *John Dewey in China: To Teach and to Learn.* Albany: State University of New York Press, 2008.

Westbrook, Robert B. *John Dewey and American Democracy.* Ithaca: Cornell University Press, 1991.

———. "The Making of a Democratic Philosopher: The Intellectual Development of John Dewey." In *The Cambridge Companion to Dewey,* edited by Molly Cochran, 13–33. Cambridge: Cambridge University Press, 2010.

Weston, Timothy. *The Power of Position: Beijing University, Intellectuals, and Chinese Political Culture, 1898–1929.* Berkeley: University of California Press, 2004.

Willey, Thomas E. *Back to Kant: The Revival of Kantianism in German Social and Historical Thought, 1860–1914.* Detroit: Wayne State University Press, 1978.

Windelband, W. *A History of Philosophy: With Special Reference to the Formation and Development of Its Problems and Conceptions.* Translated by James H. Tufts. Taibei: Zhuangyuan chubanshe, 1969.

Winter, Jay. *Dreams of Peace and Freedom: Utopian Moments in the Twentieth Century*. New Haven: Yale University Press, 2006.

Wong, Young-tsu. "The Search for Material Civilization: Kang Youwei's Journey to the West." *Taiwan Journal of East Asian Studies* 5, no. 1 (June 2008): 39–59.

Wooldbridge, Chuck. *City of Virtues: Nanjing in an Age of Utopian Visions*. Seattle: University of Washington Press, 2015.

Wu Xianwu 吳先伍. *Xiandai xing zhuiqiu yu piping: Bogesen yu Zhongguo jindai zhexue* 現代性追求與批評: 柏格森與中國近代哲學. Hefei: Anhui renmin chubanshe, 2005.

Wundt, Wilhelm. *Elements of Folk Psychology: Outlines of a Psychological History of the Development of Mankind*. London: George Allen and Unwin, 1928 [1916].

Xu, Jilin. "Social Darwinism in Modern China." *Journal of Modern Chinese History* 6, no. 2 (December 2012): 182–97.

Yan Fu 嚴復. *Yan Fu heji* 嚴復合集. Edited by Wang Qingcheng 王慶成, Ye Wenxin 葉文心, and Lin Zaijue 林載爵. Taibei: Gu Gongliang wenjiao jijinhui, 1998.

Yan Jianfu 顏健富. *Cong "shenti" dao "shijie": wan-Qing xiaoshuo xingainian ditu* 從「身體」到「世界」: 晚清小說新概念地圖. Taibei: Taiwan daxue chuban zhongxin, 2014.

Yeh, Catherine Vance. *The Chinese Political Novel: Migration of a World Genre*. Cambridge: HUAC, Harvard University Press, 2015.

Yu, Wen "The Search for a Chinese Way in the Modern World: From the Rise of Evidential Learning to the Birth of Chinese Cultural Identity." PhD dissertation, Harvard University, 2018.

Zanasi, Margherita. "Western Utopias, Missionary Economics, and the Chinese Village." *Journal of World History* 24, no. 2 (June 2013): 359–87.

Zarrow, Peter. "Adventures of 'Utopia' (烏托邦) in Republican China: Setting the Stage for May Fourth Idealism." *Sixiangshi* 思想史 (Taipei) no. 9 (December 2019); 265–312.

———. *Anarchism and Chinese Political Culture*. New York: Columbia University Press, 1990.

———. "The Reform Movement, the Monarchy, and Political Modernity." In *Rethinking the 1898 Reform Period: Political and Cultural Change in Late Qing China*, edited by Rebecca E. Karl and Peter Zarrow, 17–47. Cambridge: HUAC, Harvard University Press, 2002.

Zhang, Longxi. "The Utopian Vision, East and West." *Utopian Studies* 13, no. 1 (Winter 2002): 1–21.

Zhang Binglin 章炳麟. "Wuwulun" 五無論. *Minbao* no. 16 (25 September 1907): 1–22.

Zhang Hao 張灝 [Hao Chang]. "Zhuanxing shidai Zhongguo wutuobang zhuyi de xingqi" 轉型時代中國烏托邦主義的興起. *Xinshixue* 新史學 46, no. 2 (June 2003): 1–42.

Zhang Xiaowei 张晓唯. *Cai Yuanpei pingzhuan* 蔡元培评传. Nanchang: Baihuazhou wenyi chubanshe, 1993.

Zhang Zai 張載. "Ximing" 西銘. Translated by B. W. Norden. https://www.google.com/search?q=zhang+zai+western+inscription&ie=utf-8&oe=utf-8; accessed April 20, 2017.

Zheng, Chaolin, *An Oppositionist for Life: Memoirs of the Chinese Revolutionary Zheng Chaolin.* Translated and edited by Gregor Benton. Atlantic Highlands, NJ: Humanities Press, 1997.

Zhongguo kexueyuan zhexue yanjiusuo Zhongguo zhexueshizu 中國科學院哲學研究所中國哲學史組, ed. *Zhongguo datong sixiang ziliao* 中國大同思想資料. Beijing: Zhonghua shuju, 1959.

Zhou Ning 周宁. *Xiangxiang Zhongguo: cong "kongjiao wutuobang" dao "hongse shengdi"* 想像中国: 从"孔教乌托邦"到"红色圣地." Beijing: Zhonghua shuju, 2004.

Index